How to Do Everything
Adobe® Illustrator® CS4

About the Author

Sue Jenkins is an illustrator, web and graphic designer, photographer, teacher, and writer, and the owner and creative director of Luckychair (www.luckychair.com), a full-service design studio serving businesses across the United States since 1997. When not designing, this Adobe Certified Expert/Adobe Certified Instructor teaches three-day courses in Illustrator, Dreamweaver, and Photoshop at Noble Desktop in New York City. In addition to this Illustrator book, Sue is the author of *Dreamweaver All-in-One Desk Reference For Dummies* (Wiley), *Web Design: The L Line, The Express Line to Learning* (Wiley), and *Web Design All-in-One Desk Reference For Dummies* (Wiley). Sue is also the software instructor in three of ClassOnDemand's award-winning Adobe training DVDs, namely *Dreamweaver for Designers* (winner of a 2008 Bronze Telly Award), *Designer's Guide to Photoshop*, and *Designer's Guide to Illustrator*. Sue lives with her husband and son in Pennsylvania.

About the Technical Editor

Mara Zebest is a graphic artist who uses her knowledge and skills in both volunteer and commercial work. Mara has taught classes on Adobe and Microsoft programs for a local school district, and has also been a guest instructor at a nearby community college. She has experience working in a graphic marketing department, which has also afforded her printing production experience. Mara has been a contributing author and technical editor for numerous books covering a multitude of Adobe and Microsoft products. Mostly she hates talking about herself in the third person so she'll stop now.

How to Do Everything
Adobe® Illustrator® CS4

Sue Jenkins

New York   Chicago   San Francisco   Lisbon
London   Madrid   Mexico City   Milan   New Delhi
San Juan   Seoul   Singapore   Sydney   Toronto

The McGraw·Hill Companies

Library of Congress Cataloging-in-Publication Data

Jenkins, Sue, 1966-
  How to do everything : Adobe Illustrator CS4 / Sue Jenkins.
    p. cm.
  ISBN 978-0-07-160310-2 (alk. paper)
  1. Computer graphics. 2. Adobe Illustrator (Computer file) I. Title.
  T385.J445 2009
  006.6'86—dc22

                                                    2009002389

How to Do Everything: Adobe® Illustrator® CS4

ISBN   978-0-07-160310-2
MHID   0-07-160310-7

Sponsoring Editor	Roger Stewart
Editorial Supervisor	Jody McKenzie
Project Manager	Vastavikta Sharma, International Typesetting and Composition
Acquisitions Coordinator	Carly Stapleton
Technical Editor	Mara Zebest
Copy Editor	Mike McGee
Proofreader	Julie Searls
Indexer	WordCo Indexing Services, Inc.
Production Supervisor	James Kussow
Composition	International Typesetting and Composition
Illustration	International Typesetting and Composition
Cover Designer	Jeff Weeks

To my mom, Marilyn May, for her love and support,
and for encouraging me to be an artist.

—Sue Jenkins

Contents at a Glance

Contents

Acknowledgments

A warm and heartfelt thank you goes to my agent, Matt Wagner, for getting me this wonderful and creative project; to Roger Stewart, Sponsoring Editor, for his kindness and down-to-earth professionalism and his suggested five obstructions; to Carly Stapleton, my Acquisition Coordinator, for keeping everything organized and on track; to Mara Zebest, my Technical Editor, for carefully reading through every word and offering great suggestions to improve this book throughout all of the iterations of the beta software; to Jody McKenzie, David Zielonka, Mike McGee, Julie Searls, Jim Kussow, Jeff Weeks, Vastavikta Sharma, and everyone else in Editorial/Production at McGraw-Hill and ITC for working to make this book look good; and to illustrators Barbara Zuckerman, Chris Reed, Heidi Udvardy, Susan Hunt Yule, and Janet Allinger who contributed to the gallery—great work everyone! Thank you to all my dear friends in New York City and to Scott Carson, Megan Hefflin, and the other teachers and staff at Noble Desktop, each of you help to make every trip to Manhattan a special one. Thank you to all my family and friends around this great country of ours, you know who you are. Most importantly, I'd like to thank my sweet husband, Phil, and our delicious son, Kyle, for their love, support, and patience while I spent most of our lazy, hazy, crazy days of summer write, write, writing.

Introduction

Welcome to *How to Do Everything: Adobe Illustrator CS4*! Adobe Illustrator is the number-one vector graphics program being used today by professionals. This program is the essential tool for graphic artists, video production artists, web and interactive designers, and professionals in other industries who use graphics to communicate ideas visually in print, on the Web, in motion graphics, and via mobile devices. Adobe Illustrator CS4 is superior in design features to prior versions of the program. It has better integration with other Adobe applications and a new and improved workspace layout, plus several new and enhanced drawing tools and controls.

Who this Book Is For

This book is written for illustrators, artists, designers, hobbyists, scrapbookers, craftspeople, and anyone else who wants to take their illustrations, drawings, sketches, page layouts, web designs, patterns, craft projects, and artwork into the computerized vector-art world of Illustrator. Whether you're new to Illustrator or upgrading from an earlier version, you will discover in these pages how to master the most important features of Illustrator CS4.

You don't need any prior experience with Illustrator to read this book, but you should already know how to use a computer and a mouse, know the difference between a click and a double-click, and understand the basic workings of a software program in order to do things like access commands from the main menu, use keyboard shortcuts and the context menu, and open and close windows and dialog boxes.

The Structure of this Book

How to Do Everything: Adobe Illustrator CS4 introduces and explains all facets of the Illustrator workspace with full-color graphic examples and screenshots to illustrate key concepts and tasks. The book takes you step by step through the process of creating various types of illustrations, and demonstrates professional techniques, shortcuts, and solutions. Each chapter begins with a "How To" listing outlining the essential skills you will be taught.

Here you will learn how to use all the program's tools and settings to draw just about anything you can imagine. Even if you have never used any illustration or graphics programs before, you will be able to jump in and learn by example in each chapter. Later in the book you'll even discover how to create logos, editorial illustrations, page layouts, book jackets, magazine ads, and business graphs for business, not to mention all the essential techniques and tools you need for creating graphics for web sites, blogs, and MySpace and Facebook pages, as well as integrating Illustrator artwork into Adobe Flash to create motion graphics.

This book is divided into four parts with a bonus gallery profiling professional illustrators at the end.

Part I - Illustrator Basics   The first part of this book teaches you the basics of Illustrator, including getting a workspace orientation, learning how to set up and create new documents, and finding out how to use all the general drawing, painting, selection, and arrangement tools.

Part II - The Basics and Beyond   The second part goes into more advanced basic training about working with colors and swatches, using type effectively, transforming and reshaping your objects, exploring the world of patterns and gradients, working with symbols and integrating artwork with Flash, and designing custom business graphs.

Part III - Special Tools and Techniques   In this next part, you'll learn how to use some of the more advanced special tools and techniques that Illustrator CS4 has to offer, including how to work with blends, clipping paths, and masks; how to use transparency and blending modes; how to apply special effects and use third-party plug-ins; how to create and edit custom graphic styles through the Appearance and Graphic Styles panels; and how to create artwork using the Live Paint and Live Trace tools.

Part IV - Real World   In the previous parts, you learned how to get around the workspace and use Illustrator's tools and commands. In this part, you'll discover what it takes to create professional projects in the worlds of print, graphic, and web design. Learn about creating logos, editorial illustration, print layouts, T-shirt designs, book jackets, and crafts. Web topics include web layouts, buttons and image maps, and slicing and optimizing web graphics. The last chapter delves into printing topics so you can learn how to best prepare your work for print.

Appendix - Real World Illustrators   In the bonus section, you'll meet five professional working artists who use Illustrator as part of their everyday professional design kit. Learn about their personal backgrounds and interests, and their favorite keyboard shortcuts. Each profile includes a short bio and samples of their artwork created in Illustrator.

How to Make Best Use of this Book

This book can be read from front to back or as a general Illustrator reference guide. I would strongly urge new users read the book from beginning to end in a linear fashion since the chapters teach skills that successively build on one another. The time it takes to read through the book will be well worth the investment, because you'll come away with knowledge equivalent to that from an 18-hour $1000 training seminar with a professional Adobe Certified Instructor.

For more experienced Illustrator users, feel free to skip around from chapter to chapter to discover new information as you need it. Each chapter is written to teach you how to best use the workspace, tools, and commands in Illustrator to quickly comprehend new information and start performing new tasks.

Whether you are a new Illustrator user looking to ramp up your skills quickly or are already familiar with the program and have selected this book to enhance your proficiency and learn about CS4's new features, this is the book for you.

PART I

Illustrator Basics

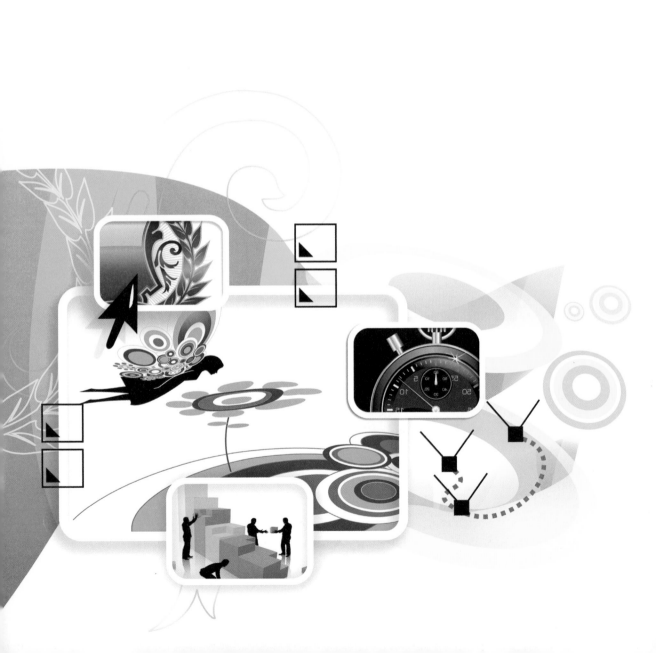

1

Workspace Orientation

How to...

- Use the Welcome Screen
- Use and organize panels
- Use the Tools panel
- Use the Control panel and Status bar
- Set up your artboard
- Create custom workspaces
- Edit Preferences
- Create and use keyboard shortcuts
- Learn about undoing, reverting, and automation

Illustrator is the number one drawing program, and with the help of this book you'll soon understand why. With a little know-how and a few clicks of your mouse, you can learn to draw nearly anything your mind can imagine! While it's true this application has many different tools, panels, customizable options, and special features that you will need to understand to get the most out of it, Adobe does a great job of creating tools and panels that have repeating functionality, making it easy for you to learn the program quickly and intuitively. This chapter will introduce you to the workspace, tools, and panels.

The Illustrator Workspace

When you first launch Illustrator, you'll see a workspace that includes a welcome screen in the center, an application bar at the top with the application frame below it, the Tools panel to the left, and the collapsed default panels docked to the right.

The Welcome Screen

The Welcome Screen, shown in Figure 1-1, is persistent and appears when you first open Illustrator and remains visible even if no documents are open in the workspace. In it, you'll see a list of quick links to open the nine most recently opened files, links to create blank documents for different project types, and links to visit Adobe's web site for tips, tricks, tutorials, and support. Click a link and the corresponding file or web site opens.

Tip   To hide the Welcome Screen, click the Don't Show Again checkbox on the bottom left and then close the Welcome Screen window. To show the Welcome Screen, select Help | Welcome Screen.

The Workspace

With the exception of a few minor platform-specific interface differences and keyboard commands, Illustrator looks and

FIGURE **1-1** The Illustrator Welcome Screen

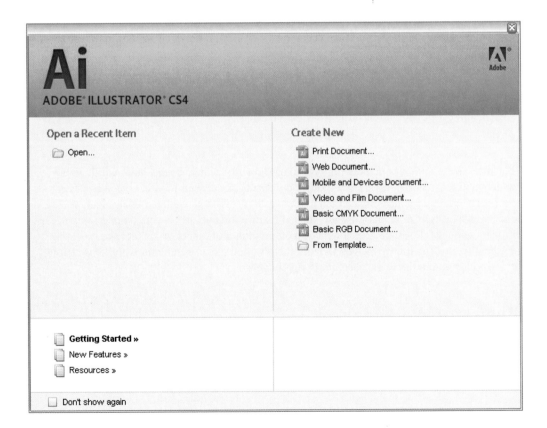

works essentially the same on Windows as it does on the Mac, as seen in Figure 1-2. This book includes keyboard commands for both Windows and Mac, such as the following keyboard shortcuts:

Windows Shortcuts	Mac Shortcuts
ALT	OPTION
CTRL (CONTROL)	CMD (COMMAND)
BACKSPACE	DELETE
Right-click (to open context menus with a two-button mouse)	CTRL+click (to open context menus without a two-button mouse)

Inside the workspace, the gray bar at the top of the screen is called the Application bar. This bar is comprised of two parts: the Menu bar on top and the Control panel below.

The Menu Bar

The Menu bar (refer to Figure 1-2) contains links to all of Illustrator's features, tools, and commands, as well as a button to open the Bridge, a menu to select a Layout Widget, and a shortcut menu to select different workspace configurations.

The Control Panel

The Control panel is a context-specific tool-support panel that changes its contents to match the currently selected tool and/ or the object(s) selected in the workspace. Figure 1-3 shows an example of the Control panel in support of the Selection tool. Use the various features inside the Control panel to customize your tools and edit your work as you create it.

The Status Bar

The status bar is located at the bottom left edge of the artboard. When visible, this area displays three special features: the current magnification of the artboard (or zoom level), artboard navigation buttons, and an information display area, as seen in Figure 1-4.

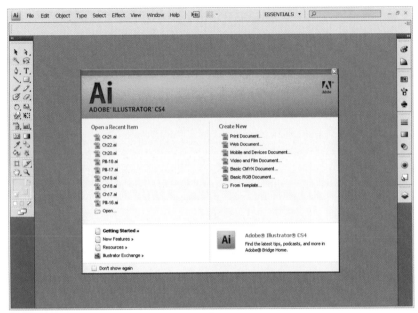

A

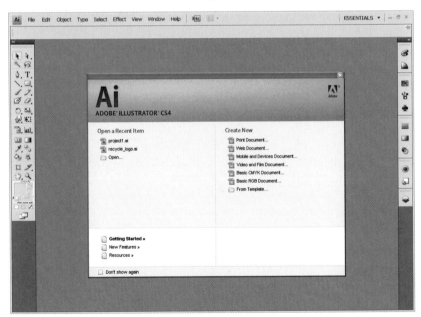

B

FIGURE 1-2 The Illustrator interface (A) in Windows and (B) on the Mac

FIGURE 1-3 The Control panel displays tool-specific options

Magnification

The magnification area displays the document's magnification, which can be any number between 3.13% and 6400%. Use the dropdown menu button to adjust the zoom setting.

Artboard Navigation

When more than one artboard is detected, the first, previous, next, and last buttons become active, allowing you to quickly jump to or select the desired artboard in the workspace.

FIGURE 1-4 The Status bar

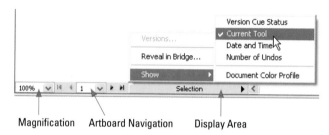

Magnification   Artboard Navigation   Display Area

Display Area

This area can be customized through the menu's Show submenu to display the current tool, date and time, number of undos and redos, the document's color profile, or the status of the managed file. You can also use this area to access Version Cue commands or see the current file in Adobe Bridge by selecting Reveal In Bridge.

The Artboard

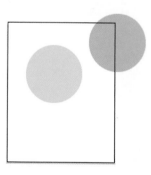

The artboard is the active rectangular area in your workspace that defines what will be printed, as shown in the example in Figure 1-5. Objects can be positioned right up to the edge (to create a "bleed") or even outside of the artboard bounds, but only the objects inside the artboard will print. You'll set the size and quantity of artboards each time you create a new file.

Customizing the Workspace

Different projects can often require different configurations of panels and tools within the workspace. In Illustrator, you can create and save your own custom layouts and reuse them at any time. To save your own custom workspace, first set up the

FIGURE 1-5 The artboard

workspace the way you want it to be, and then follow these steps:

1. Select Window | Workspace | Save Workspace.

2. In the Save Workspace dialog box that opens, type in a name for this new workspace and click the OK button.

3. To use the new workspace, select its name from the Window | Workspace menu.

Panels

Use Illustrator's panels, located in the "dock" along the right side of your screen, to edit your work, customize tool settings, accomplish particular tasks, and improve your workflow. By default, the dock is collapsed. To expand it, click the tiny left-facing double arrows once at the top of the dock. Panels are grouped into families of similar tools. For example, the Swatches panel is grouped with the Brushes and Symbols, as shown in Figure 1-6.

Most panels share certain features, such as a button bar at the bottom, a flyout options menu, and the ability to expand, collapse, and be docked to the right edge of the workspace. Here's a brief overview of each panel:

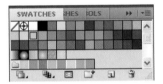

Figure 1-6 A group of panels

- **Actions**   Use this panel to record and play a series of steps or operations.

- **Align**   This panel allows you to align objects.

- **Appearance**   This panel lets you view, build, and apply attributes to objects such as multiple fills, multiple strokes, transparency, and effects.

- **Attributes**   Use this panel to view overprinting information and any web URLs associated with a selected object.

- **Brushes**   This panel lets you select a brush type.

- **Color**   Use this panel to select and apply color to your work.

- **Color Guide**   This panel gives you access to the Live Color guide.

- **Control**   This is the Control panel, where you can customize individual tool settings.

Document Info   Use this panel to view file information such as artboard size, color mode, font details, and ruler units.

Flattener Preview   This panel lets you see flattened artwork and adjust flattener settings.

Gradient   This panel lets you apply and adjust gradients.

Graphic Styles   Use this panel to view, create, and apply custom graphic styles.

Info   This panel displays information about selected objects, such as X/Y coordinates, width and height, and color values for the stroke and fill.

Layers   Use this panel to organize your work on different layers.

Links   This panel shows a listing of all placed objects that are linked to the active document.

Magic Wand   Use this panel to adjust the Magic Wand tool settings.

Navigator   Use this panel to view and adjust the magnification of a document.

Pathfinder   This panel allows you to apply transformations to add, subtract, trim, intersect, exclude, and merge objects.

Separations Preview   This panel gives you a separations overprint preview of your document.

Stroke   Use this panel to adjust stroke settings such as weight, miter limit, alignment, dashed line, and cap and join shape.

SVG Interactivity   This panel allows you to link JavaScript functions to vector graphics from external JavaScript files.

Swatches   This panel displays preset color, gradient, and pattern swatches, custom swatches, and swatch libraries.

Symbols   This panel displays preset vector symbols and symbol libraries. It also lets you define and work with new custom symbols.

Tools   This is your Tools panel, where you can access and use each of the program's tools to create and manipulate the paths and shapes on your artboard.

Work with Panels

With panels you can do any of the following:

- To open a panel, select the panel by its name from the Window menu (or use the keyboard shortcut listed next to the panel name in the Window menu). When a panel is opened, a checkmark will appear next to the panel name in the Window menu.

- To close a panel, click the tiny X on the top right corner of the panel, or right-click (Win) or CTRL+click (Mac) in the gray area of the panel's tab to show the context menu and then choose Close Panel or Close Group.

- To dock and undock panels, click and drag a panel by its tab to the new desired location, which can be inside the existing panel group, into another panel group, into the dock as its own panel group, or outside the dock.

- To adjust the height of some of the panels within the dock, place your cursor above the dark gray divider line between any two panel groups, then click and drag when you see the vertical double-sided arrow.

- To reset the panel locations to their default layout positions, press the new Workspace button on the Control panel (or select Window | Workspace) and choose the Basic or Essentials layout from the submenu, as seen in Figure 1-7.

- **Transform**   Use this panel to apply transformations, such as scaling, rotating, and shearing, to selected artwork.

- **Transparency**   This panel lets you adjust the opacity of selected objects, apply blending modes, and apply special opacity settings to grouped objects.

- **Type**   Use this panel to access text-related panels, including Character, Character Styles, Flash Text, Glyphs, OpenType, Paragraph, Paragraph Styles, and Tabs.

- **Variables**   Use this panel to set database options when creating data-driven graphics.

Organizing Panels

While you'll likely grow to love the organized layout of the docked panels along the right edge of your workspace, there

FIGURE 1-7 Reset panels with the new Workspace button

may be times when you really need a panel to be closer to your work area. Not only can you undock any panel or panel group from the docking area and put them back again, you can also completely close and reopen panels as needed, adjust the width, height, and appearance of any panel both inside and outside the dock, and drag on the tabs within a panel group to change the order of their display within the group.

Despite their individual differences, most panels have a lot of the same features, including the panel name tab, a hide/show panel features button, an options menu, and various buttons, sliders, menus, and input fields, as shown in the Stroke panel in Figure 1-8.

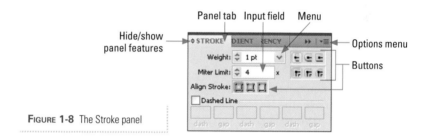

FIGURE 1-8 The Stroke panel

The Tools Panel

The Tools panel, seen in Figure 1-9, can be expanded, collapsed, hidden, visible, docked, and undocked for free-floating placement in your workspace. To see a tooltip displaying the name and keyboard shortcut of a tool (such as P for the Pen Tool), hover your mouse over any of the tool icons. You can also do any of the following:

- To hide or show the Tools panel, select Window | Tools.

- To use a tool, click its icon to select it.

- To undock and move the Tools panel into the workspace, click and drag it from its top tab.

- To toggle between single column and double column display, click the double arrow in the tab bar at the top of the Tools panel.

- To open a tool's options dialog box, double-click the tool's icon.

Flyout Menus

Each of the tools that has a tiny black triangle next to it has a flyout menu beneath it containing a family of similar tools. To see the flyout menu, like the one shown in Figure 1-10, click and hold your mouse on that tool. When the flyout menu appears, select any of the other tools by releasing your mouse when your cursor is floating above the desired tool.

- To cycle through the tools that are hidden without opening the flyout menu, hold down the ALT (Win) or OPTION (Mac) key while clicking the desired tool.

- With the flyout menu showing, drag your pointer over the tiny black arrow at the right edge of the tearoff menu to detach the flyout menu onto your artboard.

- To close a detached flyout menu panel, click the close button in the panel's title bar.

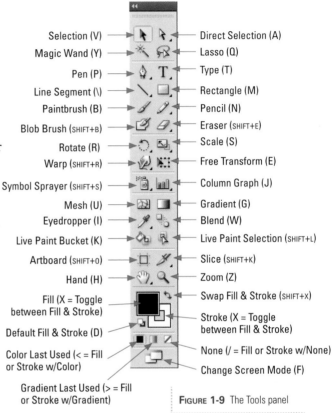

FIGURE 1-9   The Tools panel

Selection (V) → ← Direct Selection (A)
Magic Wand (Y) → ← Lasso (Q)
Pen (P) → ← Type (T)
Line Segment (\) → ← Rectangle (M)
Paintbrush (B) → ← Pencil (N)
Blob Brush (SHIFT+B) → ← Eraser (SHIFT+E)
Rotate (R) → ← Scale (S)
Warp (SHIFT+R) → ← Free Transform (E)
Symbol Sprayer (SHIFT+S) → ← Column Graph (J)
Mesh (U) → ← Gradient (G)
Eyedropper (I) → ← Blend (W)
Live Paint Bucket (K) → ← Live Paint Selection (SHIFT+L)
Artboard (SHIFT+O) → ← Slice (SHIFT+K)
Hand (H) → ← Zoom (Z)
Fill (X = Toggle between Fill & Stroke) → ← Swap Fill & Stroke (SHIFT+X)
Default Fill & Stroke (D) → ← Stroke (X = Toggle between Fill & Stroke)
Color Last Used (< = Fill or Stroke w/Color) → ← None (/ = Fill or Stroke w/None)
Gradient Last Used (> = Fill or Stroke w/Gradient) → ← Change Screen Mode (F)

Tearoff Menus

A copy of the flyout menu can be "torn off" from the main Tools panel and moved anywhere on the artboard without permanently removing the same tools from the Tools panel. To tearoff any of the flyout menus, drag your mouse to the tearoff bar on the right edge of the flyout menu, as shown in Figure 1-11. After you release your mouse, the tearoff menu will appear as its own moveable and closeable mini Tools panel.

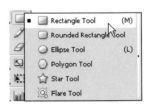

FIGURE 1-10   A flyout menu

Tools and Tool Options

This section will give you a quick overview of the Tools panel. Figure 1-12 shows you a complete listing of all the available tools on the Tools panel including all of the tools hidden in each of the flyout menus.

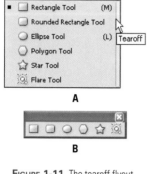

A

B

FIGURE 1-11 The tearoff flyout menu (A) before and (B) after tearoff

Selection Tools

Selection   The default tool used to select and move objects. See Chapter 4.

Direct Selection   Used to select specific lines or segments of an object. See Chapter 4.

Magic Wand   Used to make selections based on object fill and stroke color, stroke weight, object opacity, and blending mode. See Chapter 4.

Lasso   Used to make selections by dragging around desired objects. See Chapter 4.

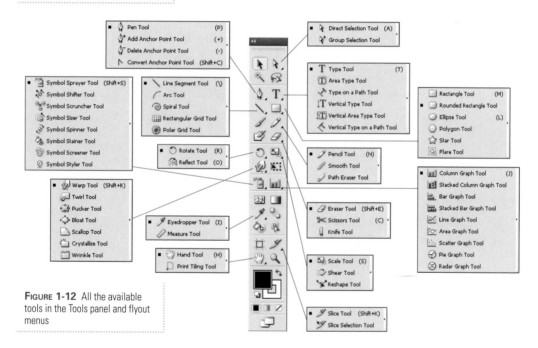

FIGURE 1-12 All the available tools in the Tools panel and flyout menus

Drawing, Painting, and Type Tools

Pen   Used to draw straight line segments and Bézier curves. See Chapter 3.

Type   Used to add text to the artboard. See Chapter 10.

Line Segment   Used to make line segments, spirals, and grids. See Chapter 3.

Rectangle   Used to draw primitive shapes such as rectangles, rounded rectangles, ellipses, polygons, stars, and flares. See Chapter 3.

- **Paintbrush**   Used to paint lines and shapes. See Chapter 5.
- **Pencil**   Used to draw freehand lines and shapes. See Chapter 5.
- **Blob Brush**   Used to paint lines with compound paths. See Chapter 5.
- **Eraser**   Used to erase strokes and fills from objects. See Chapter 5.

Reshaping, Symbol, and Graphs Tools

- **Rotate**   Used to rotate a selected object. See Chapter 11.
- **Scale**   Used to scale a selected object. See Chapter 11.
- **Warp**   Used to warp transform a selected object. See Chapter 11.
- **Free Transform**   Used to transform a selected object. See Chapter 11.
- **Symbol Sprayer**   Used to create master symbols and instances. See Chapter 13.
- **Column Graph**   Used to generate data-driven business graphs and charts. See Chapter 14.

Special Painting and Blending Type Tools

- **Mesh**   Used to apply mesh gradients to selected objects. See Chapter 12.
- **Gradient**   Used to apply gradients to selected objects. See Chapter 12.
- **Eyedropper**   Used to select objects by appearance attributes. See Chapter 4.
- **Blend**   Used to create shape and color blends between selected objects. See Chapter 15.
- **Live Paint Bucket**   Used to apply Live Paint to a Live Paint group. See Chapter 20.
- **Live Paint Selection**   Used to select specified areas within a Live Paint group. See Chapter 20.

Slicing, Artboard, Moving, and Zoom Tools

Artboard   Used to draw single and multiple artboard layouts. See Chapter 2.

Slice   Used to cut selected artwork into slices prior to optimizing graphics for the Web. See Chapters 3 and 22.

Hand   Used to reposition the view of the artboard within the workspace. See Chapter 2.

Zoom   Used to zoom in and out of the artwork. See Chapter 2.

Stroke and Fill Tools

Used to specify the stroke and fill color for any selected object or path. You can toggle the active status of the Fill and Stroke icons by pressing the x key on your keyboard.

Fill   To specify the fill color of a selected object, click the square Fill icon to activate the fill and change the color using the Swatches or Colors panel.

Stroke   To specify the stroke color of a selected object, click the Stroke icon to activate the stroke and change the color using the Swatches or Colors panel.

 To remove the color completely from an object's stroke and/or fill, select the object and click the None icon (the white square with the red diagonal slash) below the stroke and fill icons on the Tools panel. You can also apply the None color attribute to the active stroke or fill by pressing the (/) key on your keyboard.

Screen Mode Tools

Click here (or press the F key on your keyboard) to toggle between three different screen modes for the workspace:

Normal Screen Mode   Shows full screen with application bar, document groups bar, artboard, rulers, Tools panel, and panels.

Full Screen Mode with Menu Bar   Shows full screen with application bar, artboard, Tools panel, and panels.

Full Screen Mode   Shows expanded artboard with rulers. All other workspace features are hidden. To get out of this mode, press the F key on your keyboard.

Keyboard Shortcuts

The more you access the tools and menu options, the more
you'll start to notice Illustrator's many keyboard shortcuts. Use
these shortcuts at any time to access tools and features without
using your mouse.

 To download a *free* comprehensive PDF listing of Illustrator's keyboard shortcuts for both
Windows and Mac platforms, visit Noble Desktop's Keyboard Shortcut Guides web page at
www.nobledesktop.com/shortcuts.html.

Custom Shortcuts

If there's a tool or action you use repeatedly that doesn't have a
keyboard shortcut assigned to it already, make your own!

To create a custom keyboard shortcut, perform the
following steps:

1. Select Edit | Keyboard Shortcuts to open the keyboard
   shortcut dialog box.

2. Click the Save button to create a duplicate copy of the
   Illustrator Defaults keyboard shortcuts with your own
   name in order to preserve the original and keep your
   shortcuts separate.

3. In the Save Keyset File dialog box, enter a name (for
   example, MyShortcuts) for the new shortcuts file and
   click the OK button. You will now see this new name
   displaying the Set menu at the top of the dialog box.

4. Select Tools or Menu Commands from the dropdown
   menu below the Set menu to see a listing of the existing
   tool or menu command keyboard shortcuts at the bottom
   of the dialog box.

5. Scroll down to the tool or menu command you'd like to
   create a custom shortcut for.

6. Click your cursor in the blank Shortcut field next to the
   command line you'd like to customize, and then enter
   the desired keyboard shortcut. If the shortcut is already
   taken by another tool or menu command, an alert
   message will display in the bottom of the dialog box.
   If this occurs, try a different keyboard shortcut. If the
   shortcut is available, the field will accept your input.

7. Repeat steps 4 through 6 to create additional custom shortcuts.

8. Click the OK button to close the window and begin using the new shortcuts.

Preferences and Presets

Use Illustrator's Preferences dialog box to customize some of the program's settings, such as ruler units, display and tool settings, and file export information, among other things.

In addition to these, Illustrator allows you to either work with existing presets for creating transparencies, tracings, prints, PDFs, and SWFs, or create your own custom presets for each of these, which can then be loaded into the application when working on specific projects.

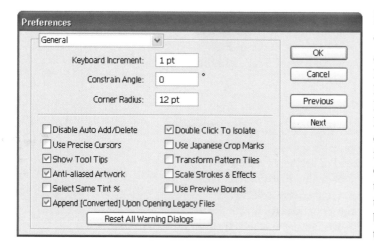

Preferences

To access the Preferences dialog box, seen in Figure 1-13, select Edit | Preferences (Win) or Illustrator | General Preferences (Mac) and then choose one of the options from the flyout menu. Once open, you can scroll through the different screens using the Previous and Next buttons to make adjustments to the different settings.

FIGURE 1-13 The Preferences dialog box

Presets

The Edit menu contains a list of preset options that refer to the default settings Illustrator will use when creating flattened transparencies, making image tracings, printing, creating PDFs, and exporting SWF files. Each of these options has a corresponding "preset" file that contains all the settings that determine how these things are handled by the application.

Transparency Flattener Presets

When a document contains transparency, you can specify and
automate how the file is flattened when saving and exporting
the file for print and PDFs, as well as when exporting files to
different formats that don't support transparency. By default,
three resolutions are available: High, Medium, and Low. Use
High for all your press outputs and high-quality proofs; Medium
for onscreen proofs and files printing to PostScript color
printers; and Low for publishing web files, exporting to SVG,
or files to be output on black-and-white desktop printers.

 When using the Live Trace tool to trace placed artwork, the tracing presets can be selected to
determine how different types of artwork should be traced. You can modify these presets and
create your own through the Tracing Presets dialog box.

Print Presets

When printing, you can create on-the-fly printing output
settings through the File | Print dialog box, or you can create
and use custom Print Presets, or output settings, to match jobs to
specific printers. Illustrator comes with two print preset files: a
Default and a Default Web/Video/Mobile preset. Edit these files
through the Print Presets dialog box.

Adobe PDF Presets

When creating a PDF from your artwork, there are several
settings you can modify to determine the quality and file size
of the PDF. These settings are stored in the Adobe PDF Presets
file. To prevent loss of data when reopening PDFs in Illustrator,
choose the Illustrator Default preset. Otherwise, select High
Quality Print or one of the other preset options for creating
PDFs of high quality. Adjust these settings and create your own
presets through the Adobe PDF Presets dialog box.

SWF Presets

SWF is the Adobe Flash file format used when exporting
artwork for inclusion in a Flash animation. Preset options
include Flash Player Version, type of export, curve quality,
frame rate, and more. To modify the SWF presets or create your
own, access the SWF Presets dialog box.

Undoing and Automation

One of the greatest things about Illustrator is the ability to undo and redo steps in your work. Illustrator supports *unlimited* undos, giving you the flexibility you need to try things out, change your mind, and make corrections as you go! You can also revert your file completely to its starting point and automate repetitive tasks using the Actions panel.

Undo and Redo

To undo or redo any operation, select Edit | Undo or Edit | Redo. Repeat the Undo action as many times as needed to revert your work to the desired state. Alternatively, the shortcut keys can be very useful for Undo: CTRL+Z (Win) and CMD+Z (Mac). Add SHIFT to these shortcut commands to Redo the action.

Revert

To revert a file you've been working on to the last saved version—which could be the version it was in when you first opened the file, or the version when you last saved the file (while still open and working on it)—select File | Revert. Keep in mind, once you save and close a file, the Undo, Redo, and Revert "memory" gets erased. Likewise, when you open a file, you start with a clean slate.

The Actions Panel

To help speed up the process of repetitious work, Illustrator comes with a whole library of prerecorded actions inside the Actions panel. Simply put, an action is a series of prerecorded steps or operations—such as selecting a tool, selecting an object, transforming that object, and optimizing the file as a web graphic—that can be played back at the push of a button.

You can use the Actions panel to play existing actions, as well as record, play, edit, and delete your own actions. Actions can include stops, where you can perform specific tasks (like drawing with the pencil tool), as well as modal controls for entering specific values into a dialog box during playback.

To view the Actions panel, select Window | Actions. The panel, shown in Figure 1-14, contains 22 prerecorded actions inside the Default Actions folder. A folder in this panel is called a Set. You can create your own Sets and fill them with your own custom actions.

Playing Actions

To play an action, select the object(s) on your artboard that you'd like to apply the action to, click the desired action in the Actions panel to select it, and click the Play button at the bottom of the panel to run the action. Actions displaying a dialog icon next to it in the Dialog column of the panel will automatically open dialog boxes requiring user input. This option can be toggled on or off in this column.

Creating an Action

To create a custom action, perform the following sample steps:

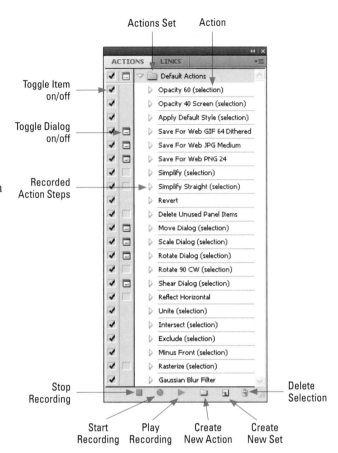

FIGURE 1-14 The Actions panel

1. Click the Create New Set button to create a new folder for all your custom actions.

2. In the New Set dialog box, give your new folder a name, such as My Actions, and click the OK button.

3. With the new Set folder selected, click the Create New Action button.

4. In the New Action dialog box, enter a name for your action, and if desired, assign a function key and highlight color. Actions should be named according to their function so they're easy to recognize, such as Rotate 45 degrees. Then, click Record.

5. Select the object(s) on your artboard and perform the action(s).

6. When finished, click the Stop button to stop the recording.

Adobe Labs "knowhow"

If you haven't heard about Adobe Labs yet, it's a division of Adobe where you can experience and evaluate new products and software enhancements. Adobe Labs is essentially an online, collaborative environment where Adobe provides free "beta" tools and prerelease applications to visitors, and then welcomes user feedback during the development process of that tool or application. This allows Adobe to get real-world feedback while you get a sneak peek—for *free*—of what's new at Adobe.

One of the latest creations from the Labs is the "knowhow" panel, which offers Adobe Creative Suite software users interactive Flash-based screen hints and links to online help. In fact, one of the things that makes this tool so powerful is that it pulls its online help files from community-generated del.icio.us accounts, so anyone can contribute!

To open the panel, select Window | Adobe Labs | knowhow. The panel, shown in Figure 1-15, lets you get quick access to online information about a selected tool or search term. (Note: You must have a live Internet connection for this feature to work.) For more information about knowhow and other Adobe Labs projects, visit http://labs.adobe.com.

FIGURE 1-15 The knowhow panel

Deleting an Action

To delete an entire action, a step within an action, or even an entire Set (folder), drag and drop the action, step, or Set into the Delete Selection trash icon at the bottom of the panel.

2

Creating Documents

How to...

- Create new documents
- Work with templates
- Place artwork
- Create multiple artboards
- Move around the workspace
- Use the Navigator panel
- Work in Preview and Outline mode
- Save and export your work
- Browse files with the Bridge

At the start of every project, the first thing you need to do is create a new document. It can either be a blank file set up for a print, mobile, video, or web project, or you can start with one of the many free Illustrator template files provided by Adobe. Setting up the file properly before you begin will help you avoid some common output mistakes. In this chapter, you'll learn important skills such as how to create documents, work with templates, and save your projects.

New Documents

To create a new Illustrator document, select File | New from the main menu, press CTRL+N (Win) or CMD+N (Mac), or click any of the Create New Document quick links on the Welcome Screen.

The New Document Dialog Box

In the New Document dialog box, seen here in Figure 2-1, set up the type of document you need by choosing one of Illustrator's preset document profiles or by creating your own custom profile. To change the document settings after you start working, select File | Document Setup.

FIGURE 2-1 The New Document dialog box

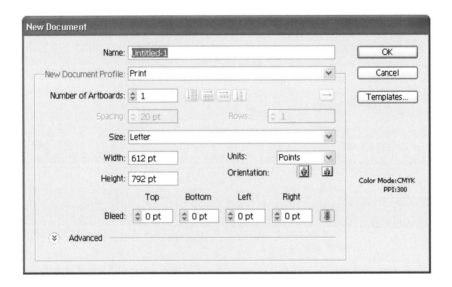

Set up your document using the New Document dialog box options:

- **Name**   Enter a name for your document here. If you plan to share your files across the Internet, get into the habit of naming your files using all lowercase letters, no spaces, and no odd characters, though hyphens and underscores are okay, as in "luckychair-logo" and "gymkids_tshirt."

- **Document Profile**   This dropdown menu includes customized profiles for documents intended for Print, Web, Mobile and Devices, Video and Film, Basic CMYK, and Basic RGB. Use each profile as is, or as a starting point for creating a custom document profile. Choose the Browse option to select and use your own custom and third-party profiles.

Number of Artboards   Create files with multiple artboards by entering a number other than 1 in the Number Of Artboards field. Spacing and Rows fields will then become active, as well as the buttons to specify grid flow and layout orientation.

Size   Choose a default document size, such as Letter, Legal, Tabloid, or A4, A3, B5, or B4 envelopes.

Width/Height   Enter the custom width and height of the document here, including the abbreviation for the desired unit of measure such as px, pt, or in.

Units   Choose a unit of measure for your file and the document rulers. Options include points, picas, inches, centimeters, millimeters, or pixels.

Orientation   Select a portrait (vertical) or landscape (horizontal) document layout.

Bleed   The default Bleed options are typically set to zero, which is fine for most situations. However, when designing a print project that requires color to extend or "bleed" to the edge of the paper (as you often see with a full-color magazine), set a bleed here. The typical setting is a minimum of 0.25 inches. Projects with bleeds are printed on oversized paper and then trimmed down. When set, bleed guidelines appear outside the edges of the artboard as an aid during layout.

Advanced   Click the double down-facing arrow icon to see advanced settings:

Color Mode   This determines the document's output color space. Choose CMYK for all your Print projects and RGB for any Web, Mobile and Devices, and Video and Film projects.

Raster Effects   Raster Effects are special bitmap effects (like a drop shadow) that are drawn with pixels instead of vectors. Select High (300 ppi) for all your Print projects, Medium (150 ppi) for your onscreen projects, and Low (72 ppi) for your Web, Mobile and Devices, and Video and Film projects.

Transparency Grid   This option appears when the Video and Film profile is selected so you can create work on a transparent background. Turn the grid on or off here, or select an option to modify the transparency grid's opacity or color.

■ **Preview Mode**   This setting determines how artwork appears in the workspace. You may access these options through the View menu. Choose Default to see your work as vectors in full color. Select Pixel to see your work as it would appear if the art was converted from vector to rasterized (pixelated art). Select Overprint to preview your work onscreen to see roughly how transparency, blending, and overprinting will look in color-separated output.

■ **Enable Oversized Canvas**   Click this checkbox to turn on the oversized canvas feature, which allows for a canvas that is 29 percent larger than normal (larger than 14400 × 14400 pts). This feature is not compatible with PDFs.

■ **Device Central Button**   This button appears when you select a profile for Mobile and Devices. Click it to launch Device Central to preview your file in a variety of simulated mobile devices.

Working with Templates

A template is a special file (with the *.ait file extension) that allows you to create an unlimited number of duplicate files that share the same features, such as the size of the artboard(s), color mode, raster effects, and even the placement of guides, text, and graphics. The template itself remains intact no matter how many times you open instances of it.

Illustrator's Sample Templates

Illustrator comes with several free template files that include royalty-free layouts and graphics, giving you the flexibility to quickly and easily create your own business cards, letterhead, brochures, CD sleeves and disc labels, invitations, newsletters, and more.

To start working with any of Illustrator's templates, launch the New From Template dialog box by either selecting File | New From Template, pressing the keyboard shortcut SHIFT+CTRL+N (Win) or SHIFT+CMD+N (Mac), or clicking the From Template folder icon on the Welcome Screen.

Inside the New From Template dialog box, you'll find templates grouped by theme inside individual folders, such as Artistic, Blank, Basic, and Restaurant. To open and begin using a template, open one of the themed folders, select the desired file from the listing, and click the New button. Once the file is open, be sure to save the file using the File | Save command.

Creating Custom Templates

It's easy to create and use your own templates. All you have to do is set up a file the way you like it—including customized settings such as swatches, brushes, rulers, grids, guides, and magnification level—and then save it as a template by selecting File | Save As Template. When you're ready to use it, select File | New From Template from the main menu, select your custom template file, and start working!

Multiple Artboards

In this section, you'll learn how to create multiple artboards, edit them, and print files that contain multiple artboards.

Creating Multiple Artboards

Creating documents with multiple artboards is easiest if you specify the number of boards you want while you're creating your file in the New Document dialog box. However, you can still modify the number of artboards in your file after the file is already open.

When creating multiple artboards by hand, as described in the following, keep in mind that as you create each new artboard, an artboard order number is automatically assigned to it. This number determines the order in which the artboards will print, and it cannot be changed once it's created. The number displays in the top left corner of the artboards when the Artboard tool is selected. Figure 2-2 shows an example of a file with three artboards when the Artboard tool is selected.

To set up or change the number of artboards in your open document, follow these steps:

1. Select the Artboard tool at the bottom of the Tools panel. Once the tool is selected, the main artboard in your file becomes active.

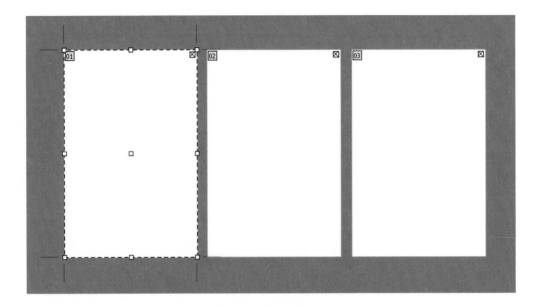

2. Adjust the size of the active artboard by hovering your mouse over any of the active artboard's edges. When the cursor turns into a double-sided arrow, click and drag to adjust the size.

3. To add another artboard, click and drag in the workspace to draw a new artboard shape.

4. To reposition an artboard in the workspace after it's been drawn, click and drag the artboard to move it to the desired new location.

5. Repeat steps 3 and 4 to add new artboards and reposition artboards in your layout.

6. To delete an artboard, select it with the Artboard tool and either click the Delete Artboard button on the Control panel or press the DELETE key on your keyboard. You may also delete an artboard, whether selected or not, by clicking its close box.

7. Click any other tool in the Tools panel to release the Artboard tool and "set" the new multiple artboard layout in your workspace.

Editing Artboards

Follow these steps to adjust the width, height, layout orientation, X/Y coordinates, and other attributes of your individual artboards:

1. Select the Artboard tool from the Tools panel.

2. Click the artboard in your workspace that you'd like to modify to make it active.

3. Use the Artboard tools and settings on the Control panel, seen in Figure 2-3, to adjust the attributes of the selected artboard:

- **Presets**   Select a preset size for your artboard from this dropdown menu.

- **Portrait/Landscape**   Click these buttons to flip the layout orientation of the artboard to either portrait or landscape, using the artboard's current dimensions.

- **New Artboard**   Click this button to add a new artboard to the center of your layout. You can then click and drag the new artboard to another location.

- **Delete Artboard**   Click this button to delete the actively selected artboard.

- **Display Options Menu**   Each artboard can have the following features turned on or off with these toggle buttons. The icon of the last selected menu item will display to the left of the menu.

  - **Show Center Mark**   Click here to add a green center mark guide to the selected artboard.

  - **Show Cross Hairs**   Click here to add green cross hair guides representing the horizontal and vertical center of the artboard.

  - **Show Video Safe Areas**   For Film and Video projects, click here to add a set of "video safe area" guides to the selected artboard.

FIGURE 2-3 The Artboard tool settings on the Control panel

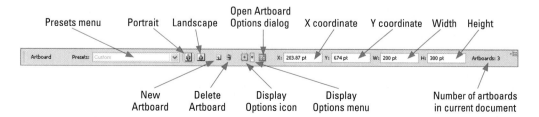

Print Multiple Artboards

With multiple artboard files, the artboards will print as separate pages in the order they were created (regardless of their placement on the artboard) unless you specify that some of the artboards print while others do not. To select which of the artboards in your document will print, choose Range in your printer's Print dialog box and type in the artboard number(s) you want to print, such as 1, 4–5, which would omit artboards 2 and 3 of a five-artboard file.

The video safe area, also sometimes called the *action safe* or *title safe area*, is a safety zone that helps you avoid video overscan, a process that cuts off part of the TV picture's outer edges to improve the middle of the image on the screen. Since the size of the overscan varies from TV to TV, use a video safe area as a guide for content placement to ensure your text and graphics will fall within the action safe area of the TV screen.

- **Open Artboard Options dialog** Click here to open the Artboard Options dialog box. You can also launch it by double-clicking the Artboard tool in the Tools panel.
- **X/Y Coordinates** Adjust the X (horizontal) and Y (vertical) coordinates here.
- **Width/Height** Set the desired width and height for the selected artboard here.
- **Artboard count** This area shows the open document's number of artboards.

Saving and Exporting Files

When you're ready to save your work, use one of these Save commands:

- **File | Save** This opens the Save As dialog box, inside which you can choose a location for the saved file, type in a File name, select a file type from the Save As Type dropdown menu, and save your file. If the file has already been saved, the Save command will update the existing file with any recent changes.

File | Save As   Similar to File | Save in that you will be confronted with a Save As dialog box, but your original file is closed and the Save As file becomes the opened active document in the Illustrator workspace.

File | Save A Copy   This option saves a copy of the open file in your desired location with your desired file name, while leaving the original file opened.

File | Save For Microsoft Office   Select this option to save a copy of your work in your desired location on your computer in the Microsoft PNG file format.

Native File Formats

You should typically consider four file formats when saving your files. These file types are called *native formats* because they preserve all of Illustrator's special features and data for future editing:

AI (*.AI)   Illustrator's native file format for creating and saving vector-based illustrations. Also supported by some desktop publishing and drawing applications.

PDF (*.PDF)   Portable Document Format. These files support documents containing bitmap and vector graphics, text, and fonts. To preserve editability, be sure to enable the Preserve Illustrator Editing Capabilities option in the Save Adobe PDF dialog box.

EPS (*.EPS)   The Encapsulated PostScript (EPS) format preserves most of the graphic elements created by Illustrator and can include both bitmap and vector art. The EPS format is a generic vector format and the option of choice if you plan to place the file into non-Adobe programs such as Microsoft Office programs or QuarkXPress.

SVG (*.SVG)   Use this high-quality vector format when creating web graphics and art for interactive web files, such as Flash animations.

After saving in one of these formats, you can safely export or create a copy of the file in any of the supported *non-native* file formats, as described next.

File Versions

While saving your files, you'll have the option of picking which Illustrator version (CS4 or earlier) your file will be saved with, along with other options related to fonts, creating PDFs, and transparency. All this is done through the Illustrator Options dialog box, shown in Figure 2-4, which opens immediately after you save your file with a filename and an AI file type. Use the dropdown menu to choose a different CS format (CS, CS2, CS3, CS4) or an older "legacy format" (Illustrator 10, 9, 8, 3, or Japanese Illustrator 3) version, which may not support all the features available in the most recent version, resulting in some loss of data.

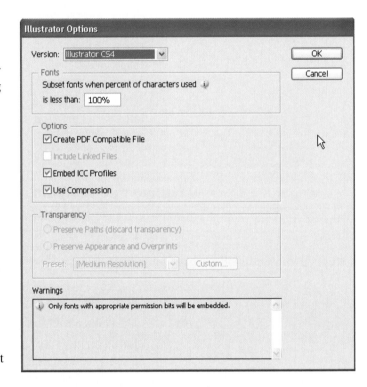

FIGURE 2-4 The Illustrator Options dialog box

Exporting Files

When you need a copy of a native Illustrator file in a *non-native* format, use the File | Export command. The dropdown menu in the Export dialog box lists all the supported file types.

For detailed descriptions on supported native and non-native file formats, visit Adobe's online Help Resource Center for Illustrator CS4 at http://livedocs.adobe.com/en_US/Illustrator/13.0/help.html?content=WS714a382cdf7d304e7e07d0100196cbc5f-6561.html and/or watch the Adobe video on saving files at www.adobe.com/designcenter/video_workshop/?id=vid0062.

Opening Files

Illustrator lets you open existing Illustrator files as well as files created with other programs. You can open a file in four different ways:

- Select File | Open, or press CTRL+O (Win) or CMD+O (Mac) on your keyboard.

- For recently opened files, click the filename link in the Open A Recent Item listing area of the Illustrator Welcome Screen.

- Select File | Open Recent Files and choose a recently opened file from the list.

- Select File | Browse In Bridge to launch the Bridge, and from within the Bridge, select a file and choose File | Open With | Adobe Illustrator CS4.

Placing Artwork

Placing (importing) artwork from another file into an open Illustrator document is different from pasting copied artwork into a file. Illustrator supports the placement of many different file types, which are visible in the Files Of Type dropdown menu in the Place dialog box. Using the File | Place command, the placed artwork becomes "linked" to or "embedded" in your document:

- **Linked art**   This gives you a low-resolution view of the linked artwork and maintains a connection with the original file. When you print the file, the linked artwork will print in full-resolution.

- **Embedded art**   This embeds a full-resolution copy of the original art into your file, which could result in a higher file size.

The Links Panel

FIGURE 2-5 The Links panel

Placed files, whether linked or embedded, are easily identified in the Control panel (when the object is selected) and in the Links panel, which can be opened by selecting Window | Links. Use the Links panel to view a list of all linked and embedded files and to select, update, embed, and access source artwork. Figure 2-5 shows an example of both linked and embedded art. Other icons that may appear in the panel include an exclamation, indicating the linked file needs to be updated (due to changes in the original artwork), and a question mark, which indicates the linked file is either missing or has been moved and the path location to the file needs updating.

Moving Around the Workspace

The following tools and panels will help you change the
magnification of your page; reposition your view of the artwork
when zoomed in or out; adjust the page orientation and units of
measure on rulers; use grids, guides, and smart guides; and look
at your work in the different preview modes.

The Zoom Tool

Use the Zoom tool, which looks like a magnifying glass, to zoom
in and out of your workspace. To zoom in, click anywhere on the
artboard or press the keyboard shortcut, CTRL++ (Win) or CMD++
(Mac). To zoom out, hold the ALT (Win) or OPTION (Mac) key
and click or press the keyboard shortcut, CTRL+- (Win) or CMD+-
(Mac). To return the zoom to 100% magnification, double-click
the Zoom tool on the Tools panel.

You can also zoom into a particular area of your work by
clicking and dragging your Zoom tool in a rectangle around
the spot you'd like to zoom into. The area will zoom into view,
filling the entire screen at the new magnification, as shown in
Figure 2-6.

Zoom magnification goes as high as 6400% and as low as
3.13%. The zoom number displays in several places, including
the Status bar, Document Title tab, and in the Info and Navigator
panels.

The Hand Tool

Use the Hand tool to reposition your view of the artboard by
dragging the view up, down, left, or right. As you drag, the
artboard within the work area shifts and will stay in the new
position when you release your mouse.

 To access the Hand tool quickly without having to select the Hand tool from the Tools panel,
press the SPACEBAR on your keyboard. When you release your mouse, the cursor returns to the
previous tool you were using.

The Navigator Panel

The Navigator panel, shown in Figure 2-7, allows you to quickly
view a thumbnail of your work and adjust the magnification

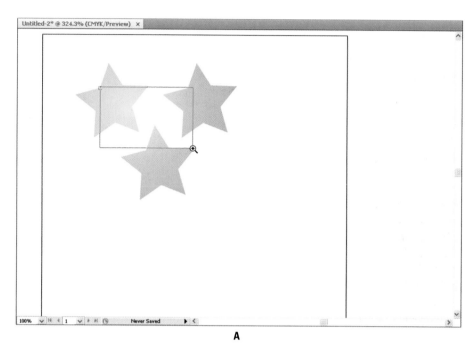

A

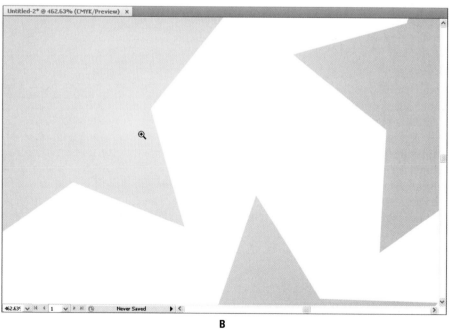

B

FIGURE 2-6 Zoom into a selected area. (A) Make a selection; (B) the selection is zoomed.

of your artboard(s) in the workspace. A colored box in the thumbnail view shows your location on the image. The panel also has a zoom slider, zoom buttons, and the current zoom magnification.

Location in image

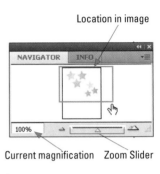

Current magnification   Zoom Slider

FIGURE 2-7 The Navigator panel

The Info Panel

The Info panel displays information about selected objects as well as any area in the workspace directly below the position of the pointer. When an object is selected, the panel will show that object's x and y coordinates, width (W) and height (H), and color (CMYK or RGB and Hexadecimal) for strokes and fills. The panel also displays additional information when using the following tools: Pen, Type, Gradient, Zoom, Reflect, Rotate, Scale, Shear, and Paintbrush.

Rulers, Grids, Guides, and Smart Guides

When opening a new document, the document rulers, guides, and grids are hidden from view. These visual aids are a must when creating art that requires precision alignment. Each can be easily turned on and off, and customized to meet your every need.

Rulers

Turn your rulers on and off by selecting View | Show Rulers or by pressing the keyboard shortcut CTRL+R (Win) or CMD+R (Mac) to toggle the rulers on or off. The rulers will automatically display the unit of measure selected when you created the document (points, picas, inches, millimeters, centimeters, or pixels). Change the unit of measure by right-clicking (Win) or CTRL+clicking (Mac) on the ruler itself, along the top or left edge of your open document, as seen in Figure 2-8.

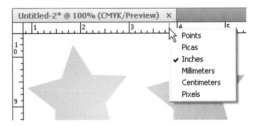

FIGURE 2-8 Change ruler units with the Context menu

Tip   To see special artboard rulers directly above and along the left edge of your artboard, select View | Show Artboard Rulers. You may also hide and show them with the keyboard shortcuts ALT+CTRL+R (Win) or OPTION+CMD+R (Mac).

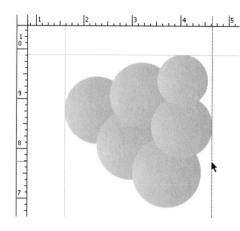

FIGURE 2-9 Adding guides to your page

Guides

Once your rulers are displayed, you can easily drag nonprinting vertical and horizontal guides into the page to assist you with the alignment and placement of objects and text.

To create a guide, click the inside of the top or left ruler and drag your mouse into the workspace. As you drag, you'll notice a guide indicator appear beneath your mouse. Drag the guide indicator into the desired position on your artboard and then release. Upon release you'll see a thin blue guide line appear across the workspace. Repeat this process to bring additional guides into the workspace as needed. Figure 2-9 shows a document with two guides in place and a third in the process of being placed.

Tip   Guides can display as either lines or dots and in any color. To edit guide attributes, select Edit | Preferences | Guides & Grid (Win) or Illustrator | Preferences | Guides & Grid (Mac).

How to. . .   Work with Guides

When using guides, you can also do any of the following:

- To lock and unlock guides, select View | Guides | Lock.
- To delete a guide, unlock the guides, select a guide with the Selection tool and press the DELETE key on your keyboard.
- To hide and show guides, select View | Guides | Hide Guides or View | Guides | Show Guides, or use the keyboard shortcuts CTRL+; (Win) or CMD+; (Mac).
- To create guides from objects, create an object and select View | Guides | Make Guides.
- To clear guides from the workspace, whether visible or hidden, select View | Guides | Clear Guides.

Grids

Turn the grids on and off by selecting View I Show Grid, or using the keyboard shortcut, CTRL+" (Win) or CMD+" (Mac) to toggle the grid on or off. By default, the grid will display as nonprinting gray lines every 72 points with eight subdivisions (the equivalent of 1 inch with lines at every 1/8-inch increment), like the example shown here in Figure 2-10. To edit the grid size, select Edit I Preferences I Guides & Grid (Win) or Illustrator I Preferences I Guides & Grid (Mac).

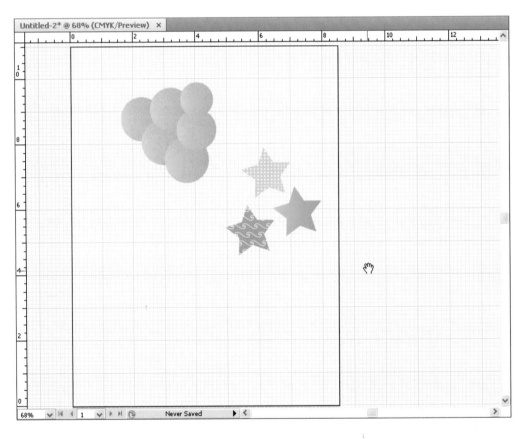

FIGURE 2-10 Working with grids

Snap to Grid   When grids are visible, you can specify that Illustrator snaps objects to the gridlines when repositioning objects in the workspace. To toggle this feature on or off, select View I Snap To Grid or press SHIFT+CTRL+" (Win) or SHIFT+CMD+" (Mac).

The grid need not be horizontal! To change the angle of the grid, open the Preferences dialog box with the keyboard shortcut CTRL+K (Win) or CMD+K (Mac), and in the General area, change the Constrain Angle field from 0° to the angle you'd like the grid to follow. Once you click OK to close the dialog box, the grid will display at the new angle. So awesome! When finished, reset the angle to zero to go back to the horizontal/vertical grid alignment.

Smart Guides

Smart Guides are visual aids that assist you with the creation, placement, alignment, transformation, and editing of objects. Toggle them on and off as needed by selecting View | Smart Guides, or by pressing CTRL+U (Win) or CMD+U (Mac).

When Snap To Grid is also enabled, the Snap To Grid feature takes precedence and the Smart Guides will become temporarily disabled.

Snap to Point

To have objects snap to anchor points or guides in the workspace, select View | Snap To Point. You can then drag objects to the desired position in the workspace and have them snap into place when the mouse pointer moving the object gets within 2 pixels of the anchor point. You can actually feel the snapping occur with your mouse!

Preview and Outline Mode

The default full-color view of your page is called Preview mode. You can change this view to Outline mode so you see only the outlines, or paths, of your work without any color, gradients, or patterns applied to the fill or stroke. In Outline mode, which is especially helpful for selecting objects hiding behind other objects or finding stray paths and points, the objects are represented as outlined shapes and text is displayed in black with an X and the bottom left edge of the first letter's baseline. To switch from Preview to Outline mode, select View | Outline. To return to Preview mode, select View | Preview. You may also use the keyboard shortcut CTRL+Y (Win) or CMD+Y (Mac) to toggle between Preview and Outline mode. Figure 2-11 shows an object in both Preview and Outline mode.

FIGURE 2-11 Objects in Preview mode and Outline mode

Print Tiling Tool

The Print Tiling tool, located in the flyout menu under the hand tool on the Tools panel, lets you adjust the printable area of your artboard, which by default matches the size of the artboard(s) minus any margins as specified by your chosen printer. To adjust the printable area, select the Print Tiling tool and click the artboard. Immediately you'll see the printable area guides, which can be repositioned in the workspace by dragging with your mouse. Any work that falls outside these printable area guides will not be printed. With multiple artboards, each artboard has its own page tiling (printable) area that can be adjusted with the Print Tiling tool.

Using Adobe Bridge

Adobe's Bridge software, included in the Adobe CS bundle, helps you to browse, preview, find, open, and organize files for all your web, print, video, film, mobile, special devices, and audio projects. The Bridge can be launched from any Adobe CS software application and supports both native (Adobe) and non-native file formats.

To launch the Bridge in Illustrator, either select File | Browse In Bridge, click the Launch Bridge button on the main Menu bar, or select Reveal In Bridge from the Status Bar popup menu. When the Bridge opens, use the Folders panel on the left side of the application to browse for and find folders and files on your computer. The Content panel in the center of the Bridge will display thumbnail views of your files inside the selected directory.

This is a wonderfully powerful program that can streamline your work process and perform tasks such as batch renaming files, let you apply star label ratings to your files, preview files in a Slide Show format, and much more.

For further information visit the Adobe Bridge CS4 Help Center at http://help.adobe.com/en_US/ Bridge/3.0/. When the page opens in your browser, click the Adobe Bridge link on the left to expand the navigation menu. Then click the Working With Adobe Bridge link to begin learning more about this useful tool.

3

Drawing and Editing Lines and Shapes

How to...

- Draw rectangles, ellipses, and other shapes
- Create lines, arcs, spirals, and grids
- Change an object's color
- Edit strokes
- Create dotted and dashed lines
- Use the Scissors and Knife tools

In this chapter, you'll learn how to work with Illustrator's "primitive shape" tools to create rectangles, rounded rectangles, ellipses, polygons, and stars. You'll also see how to create paths with the various Line Segment tools, learn to edit an object's color fill and stroke, and use the Scissors and Knife tools to modify the shapes of your objects.

The Shape Tools

Making shapes in Illustrator is incredibly easy to do! In fact, all of the shape tools work in a similar fashion, so once you learn how to use one, you can apply those same skills to the rest. The shape tools are all located in the flyout menu under the Rectangle tool. The shape tools include the Rectangle, Rounded Rectangle, Ellipse, Polygon, and Star. There's also a special Flare tool, which you'll learn about at the end of this section.

Because Illustrator is a vector-based program, all the shapes are drawn mathematically, which means you can alter the size of them as often as you like without any loss of resolution. You can even do things like enter the size of the shape in one unit of measure, such as inches, and have Illustrator automatically convert those units into another unit of measure, such as pixels. Once shapes are created, you can modify their strokes and fills and further transform them with the other tools. Figure 3-1 shows a star can be transformed into something new.

FIGURE 3-1 A star shape before and after transformation

For best results, use the following guidelines when working with the shape tools:

- **Drawing shapes** To create a shape with any of the shape tools, you'll be clicking and dragging your mouse on the artboard. The place you click before dragging is called the shape's *point of origin*. Once the origin is set, drag in any direction to create the desired shape. For instance, drag up or down to create a tall shape, drag to the side to create a wide shape, or drag diagonally to create a more proportioned shape.

- **Drawing from the center** To set the point of origin at the center of the shape (instead of at an edge, as described earlier), hold down the ALT (Win) or OPTION (Mac) key while dragging out the shape. For best results, release the ALT (Win) or OPTION (Mac) key *after* you release your mouse.

- **Constraining shapes** To create a perfectly proportioned square, a square with rounded corners, or a circle, select the Rectangle, Rounded Rectangle, or Ellipse tool, hold down the SHIFT key while dragging the shape, and then release the SHIFT key *after* you release your mouse. The SHIFT key also constrains the paths and objects created by the other shape, pen, and line tools by aligning them to the artboard as you drag, or by ensuring the objects conform to 90- or 45-degree angles.

Tip To draw a perfectly constrained shape with the point of origin in the center of the shape, hold down the SHIFT+ALT (Win) or SHIFT+OPTION (Mac) keys while dragging. Release the keys *after* you've released the mouse.

▓ **Creating shapes with exact measurements**   To create shapes with precise dimensions, select the desired shape tool on the Tools panel and click once on the artboard *without* dragging. This opens the tool's dialog box, inside which you may enter the desired dimensions and unit of measure, such as 2.75 in or 315 px.

▓ **Moving shapes as you draw**   To reposition a shape on the artboard *as you're drawing*, hold down the SPACEBAR as you drag. When you release the SPACEBAR, you can either continue dragging or release your mouse to add the object to the artboard.

▓ **Paths and points**   Each shape—whether straight-edged, circular, or some combination of the two—is created with a series of line segments (called paths) connected by anchor points. You can see these anchor points and paths as blue lines and blue dots around the edges of any selected object, like the example in Figure 3-2. Later, in Chapters 4, 5, and 6, you'll learn how to edit your shapes using these points and paths.

▓ **Bounding Box**   If the Bounding Box is enabled (View | Show Bounding Box), selected objects will also display a rectangular blue outline around the object's outer edge, as shown in Figure 3-3. The hollow blue boxes on the corners and midpoints of the bounding box are like "handles" that you can drag to make quick object transformations, like scaling and rotating.

▓ **Deleting shapes**   To delete a shape from the workspace, select it with the Selection tool and either press the DELETE key on your keyboard or choose Edit | Clear.

FIGURE 3-2 Objects are created with paths and points

FIGURE 3-3 Selected object with Bounding Box

The Rectangle Tool

Use the Rectangle tool to draw rectangular and square shapes with hard-edged corners. Once you understand how to draw this shape, you can apply the same techniques for drawing shapes with the other tools. Here's how to create a rectangle:

1. Select the Rectangle tool on the Tools panel.

2. Click and drag your cursor diagonally on the artboard to create the desired shape.

3. Release your mouse to add the shape to the artboard.

Your shapes will take on whatever stroke and fill colors are displaying at the bottom of the Tools panel. In new, blank documents, the Stroke and Fill colors are set to a default white fill with a black 1-pt stroke.

When you need to create a rectangle or square using exact width and height measurements, select the Rectangle tool and click once on the artboard, without dragging, in the spot where you want the upper left corner (the point of origin) of your rectangle to be. This opens the tool's options dialog box, inside which the measurements of the last created rectangle will auto-populate the Width and Height fields. Enter the new desired Width and Height along with the desired unit of measure abbreviation, such as 3.12 in, 450 px, or 72 pt. Click the OK button. The new shape will be added to the artboard with the same stroke and fill attributes displaying in the Fill and Stroke boxes at the bottom of the Tools panel.

 Tip   To set the point of origin at the center of the shape while opening the tool's dialog box, hold down the ALT key on your keyboard as you click the artboard.

The Rounded Rectangle Tool

The Rounded Rectangle tool creates rectangular shapes with rounded corners. You can adjust the angle of the corner shape, called the corner radius, by manually adjusting the corner as you drag and draw a shape, by entering a corner radius number into the Rounded Rectangle's dialog box, or by adjusting the default Corner Radius for rounded rectangles (which, by default, is set to 12 pt) in the General Preferences.

To create a rounded rectangle, select the Rounded Rectangle tool on the Tools panel and click and drag your cursor diagonally on the artboard to create the desired shape. Before you release your mouse, adjust the corner radius of your shape, if desired, by pressing the arrow keys on your keyboard: UP increases the corner radius, DOWN decreases the corner radius, LEFT removes the corner radius to create square corners, and RIGHT adds the maximum amount of curviness to create super-rounded corners. Release your mouse to add the shape to the artboard. Figure 3-4 shows examples of some rounded rectangles with different corner radius sizes.

To create a rounded rectangle with a precisely sized corner radius, select the Rounded Rectangle tool and click the artboard

FIGURE 3-4 Create rounded rectangles with any sized corner radius

without dragging to launch the Rounded Rectangle dialog box. Enter the desired Width and Height with the abbreviated unit of measure, such as 1 in, and then enter the desired Corner Radius size with unit of measure, such as 12 pt or 0.25 in. Click the OK button to add the new shape to your artboard.

Once you create a shape, though you can edit it with other tools, there is no way to re-open the rounded rectangle radius dialog box to make precise adjustments to the corner radius. Instead, your options include either creating a new shape with the desired dimensions and corner radius (and deleting the old shape), or using a Convert To Shape effect, which can modify any shape into a rectangle, rounded rectangle, or ellipse.

To modify a shape using the Convert To Shape effect, select the object to be modified and open the Shape Options dialog box by choosing Effect | Convert To Shape and then selecting a shape (such as Rounded Rectangle) from the submenu. When the dialog box opens, select Absolute to precisely resize the shape, or choose Relative to modify the size of the shape by adding extra width and height. When applicable, enter the desired Corner Radius. To preview the shape effect, check the Preview checkbox. To accept the transformation, click the OK button. To reject it, click Cancel. Effects like this, which you'll learn more about in Chapter 18, are considered non-destructive, meaning the effect can be re-edited or deleted without altering the original object.

The Ellipse Tool

When you need to draw a circle or oval shape, select the Ellipse tool and click and drag on the artboard to create the desired shape. Then, release the mouse to add the shape to the artboard.

To create circles and ellipses with exact measurements, select the Ellipse tool and click without dragging on the artboard to open the Ellipse dialog box. Enter the desired measurements in the Width and Height fields, along with the unit of measure. For perfect circles, input the same unit, such as 1 in, in both the Width and Height fields. Click OK to add the shape to your artboard.

The Polygon Tool

To draw polygons with three or more sides, select the Polygon tool and then click and drag on the artboard to create the desired shape. Before you release your mouse, you can add or subtract sides from the polygon by pressing the UP and DOWN ARROWS on your keyboard. When the shape meets your needs, release your mouse to add the polygon to your artboard.

To create polygons with exact measurements, including the desired number of sides, select the Polygon tool and then click, without dragging, on the artboard to open the Polygon dialog box. Enter a radius with the desired unit of measure, such as 2 in, enter the number of sides for your polygon in the Sides field, and click OK to add the polygon to your artboard.

The Star Tool

With the Star tool you can draw stars with three or more sides and with any length inner and outer radius for the points. To create a star, select the Star tool, and then click and drag on the artboard to create a star shape. Before you release your mouse, use the following keyboard shortcuts to add or subtract points as well as increase or decrease the length of the points and center of the star:

- **To add or subtract points**   Press the UP or DOWN ARROW.
- **To increase the inner radius of the star**   Press and hold the ALT (Win) or OPT (Mac) key on your keyboard as you drag, then release *after* you release your mouse.
- **To increase the outer radius of the star**   Press and hold the CTRL (Win) or CMD (Mac) key as you drag, then release *after* you release your mouse.

When the star has the shape you want, release your mouse to add the shape to your artboard.

To draw a star that is perfectly sized with an exact number of points, select the Star tool and click without dragging on the artboard to open the Star dialog box. Enter the desired units and the unit of measure in the Radius 1 (inner radius), Radius 2 (outer radius), and Points (number of points) fields. Then, click OK to add the star to your artboard. Figure 3-5 shows a sample of the variety of shapes you can create with the Star tool.

FIGURE 3-5 Star shapes made with the Star tool

The Flare Tool

The Flare tool creates the illusion of a lens flare. When the flare object is placed on top of another object, the flare takes on some of the underlying object's properties. To use the Flare

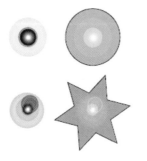

FIGURE 3-6 Flares

tool, select it from the Tools panel, and then click and drag on the artboard. You'll see an outline of the flare shape on the artboard as you drag. Release the mouse to add the shape to your artboard.

With the Selection tool you can move the flare object into position on top of another object to see how the flare's properties change. For example, Figure 3-6 shows how different flares look by themselves and on top of other objects.

To customize the properties of the flare shape, select the Flare tool and click without dragging on the artboard to open the Flare Tool Options dialog box. Enter the desired settings to the Center, Halo, Rays, and Rings fields. For best results, enable the Preview checkbox to see the adjustments before you apply them. When satisfied, click the OK button to add the flare to your artboard, and then reposition the object as needed using the Selection tool.

The Line Segment Tools

Drawing line segments with a vector tool is much simpler than trying to draw them by hand. These tools, located in the Line Segment tool's flyout menu, include the Line Segment, Arc, Spiral, Rectangular Grid, and Polar Grid. All of the tools' dialog boxes can be accessed by selecting the tool and clicking the artboard, which sets the point of origin for the line segment or grid shape and brings up the dialog box.

The Line Segment Tool

To create a horizontal, vertical, or diagonal straight line, select the Line Segment tool, click and drag on the artboard, and release the mouse to add the line segment to your artboard. To draw a line with precise dimensions, select the Line Segment tool and click the artboard to set the point of origin for the line and launch the Line Segment Tool Options dialog box. Enter the desired length and angle for the line. If no stroke color is specified in the Tools panel but a fill color is, click the Fill Line checkbox to fill the line with the current fill color. Leave it unchecked to fill the line with the color specified for the stroke. Click OK to add the line segment to your artboard.

The Arc Tool

Use the Arc tool to draw curved line segments. To draw an arc, select the Arc tool from the Tools panel, click the artboard, and drag to the desired length. Before you release your mouse, you can control the angle and direction of the arc by pressing the UP and DOWN ARROWS on your keyboard. After you release your mouse, the arc will be added to the artboard.

To create an arc with greater precision, select the Arc tool and click without dragging on the artboard to launch the tool's dialog box. Enter the desired arc attributes:

- **Length X-Axis**   Enter a number to set the arc width.
- **Length Y-Axis**   Enter a number to set the arc height.
- **Reference Point**   Click a corner square in the reference point locator to set the point of origin for the arc.
- **Type**   Select Open or Closed to create an open arc or a closed arc shape.
- **Base Along**   Set the arc's direction along the horizontal (x) or vertical (y) axis.
- **Slope**   Set the arc's slope by adjusting the slider for a convex or concave arc.
- **Fill Arc**   Fill the arc (whether Opened or Closed) with the current fill color.

FIGURE 3-7 An open arc, an open arc with fill, and a closed arc with fill

When satisfied, click OK to add the arc to the artboard. Figure 3-7 shows examples of an open arc, an open arc with fill, and a closed arc with fill.

The Spiral Tool

To create spirals quickly and easily, select the Spiral tool and do one of the following:

- Click and drag on the artboard to draw and rotate the spiral. Before releasing the mouse, use the UP and DOWN ARROW keys on your keyboard to increase or decrease the number of spiral segments. To control the decay as you drag, hold down the CTRL (Win) or CMD (Mac) key. Release the mouse to add the spiral to the artboard.

- Click without dragging to set the point of origin for the spiral while opening the Spiral dialog box. Enter the

Figure 3-8 A spiral with ten segments

desired spiral options and click OK to add the spiral to the artboard.

- **Radius**   Set the distance between the center and outer point of the spiral.

- **Decay**   Set the decrease in distance between one spiral and the next.

- **Segments**   Set the number of spiral segments. Each spiral twist is made up of four segments. The selected spiral in Figure 3-8 has ten segments.

- **Style**   Set the direction of the spiral to either clockwise or counterclockwise.

The Rectangular Grid Tool

With the Rectangular Grid tool you can create horizontal and vertical grids with any number of rows and columns. To draw a grid, select the Rectangular Grid tool, click the artboard, and drag out the desired grid shape. Before releasing the mouse, adjust the number of rows and columns using your arrow keys. Press UP or DOWN to add or subtract rows. Press the RIGHT or LEFT ARROW keys to add or subtract columns.

To create rectangular grids with exact proportions, select the Rectangular Grid tool and click the artboard to set the point of origin for the grid and to open the Rectangular Grid Tool Options dialog box. Enter the desired grid settings and when satisfied click OK to add the grid to your artboard:

- **Default Size**   Enter the Width and Height, such as 2.5 in or 72 pt.

- **Reference Point**   Click a square to set the point of origin for the grid.

- **Horizontal Dividers**   Set the number of horizontal dividers to create rows. Enter a Skew number to weight the dividers toward the top or bottom of the grid.

- **Vertical Dividers**   Set the number of vertical dividers to create columns. Enter a Skew number to weight the dividers toward the left or right of the grid.

- **Use Outside Rectangle As Frame**   This option draws the grid frame with a separate rectangle shape rather than with individual divider lines.

- **Fill Grid**   Fills the grid with the current fill color. Leave unchecked for no fill.

The Polar Grid Tool

FIGURE 3-9 Polar grids

The Polar Grid creates elliptical grids. Create a polar grid by selecting the tool and clicking and dragging on the artboard. Before releasing the mouse, adjust the number of circular and radial dividers on the grid using your keyboard's arrow keys. Press UP or DOWN to add or subtract Concentric Dividers. Press RIGHT or LEFT to add or subtract Radial Dividers.

As you can see in Figure 3-9, grids can range from the simple to the complex. To create a polar grid with more exact measurements, select the Polar Grid tool and click the artboard to set the point of origin for the grid and to open the Polar Grid Tool Options dialog box. Enter the desired grid settings, and then click the OK button to add the polar grid to the artboard:

- **Default Size**   Set the Width and Height of the polar grid.

- **Reference Point**   Set the polar grid's point of origin.

- **Concentric Dividers**   Enter the number of the grid's concentric circular dividers. Edit the Skew to make the dividers weighted toward the grid's inner or outer edge.

- **Radial Dividers**   Enter a number for the grid's radial dividers from the center to the edges. Edit the Skew to weight the dividers clockwise or counterclockwise.

- **Create Compound Path From Ellipses**   This option draws each circle with its own compound path and fills every other circle with the specified Fill color.

- **Fill Grid**   Fills the grid with the current fill color. Leave unchecked for no fill.

Editing Lines and Shapes

After drawing a shape, you can change the color of the stroke and fill, the weight of the stroke, and the shape of the line or path of an object. Colors can be applied with swatches from the Swatches and Color Guide panel, as well as from the Color panel. Stroke properties are made with the Stroke panel. In the following, we'll concentrate on color and stroke. When you get to Chapter 4, you'll discover how to edit shapes by selecting their individual paths and points.

Changing an Object's Color

Whether you're editing the color of the fill or stroke, applying the color is the same:

1. Select the object.

2. Make either the stroke or fill active by clicking the Stroke or Fill box at the bottom of the Tools panel, or inside the Color panel.

3. Change the color using one of the following methods:

   - Select a swatch from the Swatches or Control panel.

   - Select a color from the Color or Color Guide panel (both of which you'll learn more about in Chapter 9).

   - Double-click the Stroke or Fill box to open and select a color from the Color Picker dialog box (also covered in Chapter 9). To apply a color, click inside the Select Color area to select a color, and then click the OK button.

The Stroke Panel

The Stroke panel is where you can modify the strokes applied to your objects. To change a selected object's stroke, open the Stroke panel (Window | Stroke) and do any of the following:

- **Weight**   Increase or decrease the number to adjust the thickness of the stroke.

- **Miter Limit**   When the length of a stroke point (join) is greater than or equal to four times the stroke weight, the miter join automatically converts to a bevel join. Adjust the limit, which is set to 4 by default, to override this setting.

- **Caps & Joins**   These six buttons control how stroke caps (ends) and joins (corners) are displayed. Choose from Butt, Round, and Projecting Caps, and from Miter, Round, and Bevel Joins. Figure 3-10 shows examples of each.

FIGURE 3-10 Stroke caps and joins

- **Align Stroke**   These buttons align the stroke to the center, inside, or outside of the path, as illustrated in Figure 3-11.
- **Dashed Line**   Click this checkbox to create a dashed or dotted line instead of a solid line. Use the dash and gap fields to create patterned or irregularly patterned dashed lines. Combine with cap and join buttons to create rounded or flat dash edges. For example, to create a dotted line, like the one shown in Figure 3-12, select Dashed Line, input a 0 pt dash and an 8 pt gap, and then click the rounded caps button.

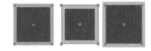

FIGURE 3-11 Align the stroke to the center, inside, or outside of a path

FIGURE 3-12 Create a dashed or dotted line in the Stroke panel

The Cutting Tools

Illustrator has two cutting tools, the Scissors and Knife, which can be used when refining and altering objects. You'll find the Scissors and Knife in the flyout menu under the Eraser tool. (These tools should not be confused with the Slice tools, which are used for creating web graphics and will be covered in Chapter 22.)

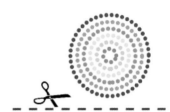

The Scissors Tool

The Scissors tool lets you cut along a segment or anchor point (but not an endpoint) of a selected object and creates open shapes and paths. For example, if you make two cuts along the path of a circle, you can then detach that segment from the whole, as shown in Figure 3-13.

FIGURE 3-13 Use the Scissors tool to cut along a path

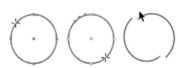

The Knife Tool

The Knife tool cuts into objects and paths, both with and without object selection, and creates closed shapes. Cut objects take on the stroke and fill attributes of the original object. When one or more objects are selected, only those objects can be cut into with the Knife. However, if no objects are selected, the Knife will cut into any object or path that falls under the cut line. Figure 3-14 shows how a set of objects looks before being cut, when none of the objects are selected as the knife slices through them, and when just the star shape is selected as the knife slices through them.

FIGURE 3-14 Knife cuts made to selected and unselected objects

4

Making Selections

How to...

- Work with the Selection tools
- Edit selection preferences
- Use the Eyedropper
- Apply the Select Menu options

Making shapes and paths is generally the first step in creating any illustration. The next step is to learn how to select an object, or part of an object, so you can edit and manipulate it. While it's true that you can make selections through the Layers panel, that's a more advanced topic, which you'll learn about in Chapter 8. In this chapter, you'll discover how to use all of Illustrator's selection tools including the Selection, Direct Selection, and Group Selection arrow tools, the Magic Wand, and the Lasso. You'll also find information about using the amazing Eyedropper tool, along with how to use the various selection options in the Select menu.

The Selection Tools

Each of the Selection tools lets you select an entire object, or part of one, to make edits. The tools are mostly located at the top of the Tools panel, with the exception of the Eyedropper tool, which is located a little further down. The more you work with Illustrator, the more you'll see how often you need to use all of the Selection tools, especially the Selection tool itself. Fortunately, Illustrator has a shortcut that toggles the currently selected tool with the Selection tool, and this shortcut is even more efficient than changing tools from the Tools panel or using the tool shortcut key (such as B for the Paintbrush). Regardless of which tool is active, hold down the CTRL (Win) or CMD (Mac) key to quickly toggle to a Selection tool. In the following section, you'll learn which tools to choose for your various selection needs.

To improve your ability to make selections, especially in files with lots of objects, press CTRL+K (Win) or CMD+K (Mac) to open the Preferences dialog box. Use the dropdown menu or Next button to select the Selection and Anchor Display options and adjust the settings. When finished, click OK to close the dialog box.

The Selection Tool

Use the Selection tool (the black arrow) to select an object in any of the following ways:

- Click the desired object.
- Click and drag a selection marquee around the desired object(s) or path(s) and then release the mouse.
- SHIFT+click an unselected object to add it to the desired selection.
- SHIFT+click a selected object to remove it from the desired selection.

When working with grouped objects, use the Selection tool to select entire groups with a single click, individual objects within groups with a CTRL+click (Win) or CMD+click (Mac), or groups within groups in Isolation Mode.

Isolation Mode

Isolation Mode, which will be covered in greater detail in Chapter 7, is used to modify objects in a group, or grouped objects nested inside another group. To enter Isolation Mode, which actually isolates grouped objects into a special working area in the workspace, double-click with the Selection tool on the grouped object or alternatively right-click (Win) or CTRL+click (Mac) the grouped object to access the context menu, and then choose Isolate Selected Group. Make changes to the objects as needed. To exit Isolation Mode, either double-click with the Selection tool on an empty space of the artboard, select Exit Isolation Mode from the context menu, or click the gray arrow, like the one shown in Figure 4-1, at the top of the document workspace.

FIGURE 4-1 Exit Isolation Mode

The Direct Selection Tool

Clicking with the Direct Selection tool lets you select the anchor points or path segments of any object. You can then reposition those parts separate from the rest of the object. When you click

Selecting and moving an Anchor point

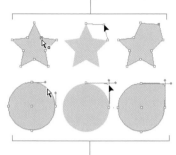

Selecting and moving a Path

FIGURE 4-2 The Direct Selection tool

the path of an object, the object's entire path is selected, giving you the ability to click and drag on any anchor point or segment to modify the shape. However, when you click the fill of a filled object, the entire object gets selected. Figure 4-2 illustrates how a selected anchor point (on a star) and a selected path (on a circle) look before and after being moved with the Direct Selection tool.

A selected anchor point appears as a small solid-blue square. By contrast, unselected anchor points on a selected object appear as hollow blue squares. When selecting multiple paths, unfortunately there may not always be a clear visual indication of which paths are selected. Nonetheless, after selecting multiple paths, you can still click and drag any one of them to move them all at once.

With grouped objects, use the Direct Selection tool to select one or more objects within a group. To select more than one anchor point or path segment on an object, either click the first anchor point or path segment, then SHIFT+click to add or subtract anchor points or path segments to the selection, or click and drag a selection marquee around the desired anchor point or path segment, and then release the mouse.

The Group Selection Tool

The Group Selection tool selects objects within a group, groups within nested groups, or multiple groups in the open document. You can also use it to select individual objects inside a blend, clipping mask, or compound path (more on those in Chapters 15 and 16).

To make a selection with this tool, do one of the following:

- Click an object once in a group to select just that object.
- Double-click an object to select the parent group.
- Triple-click an object to select a nested group's parent group.

FIGURE 4-3 One click selects an object in a group. Two clicks select that object's group. Three clicks select both the nested group and the parent group.

Figure 4-3 illustrates what a single-, double-, and triple-click looks like when selecting an object, group, and nested group with the Group Selection tool. Additional clicks will continue adding groups to the selection. Once all the objects or groups are selected, manipulate them as desired, and then click away from the objects to deselect them. With grouped objects and nested groups, the individual objects remain grouped even after they've been edited or moved!

The Magic Wand Tool

The Magic Wand is a special selection tool that lets you select multiple objects with a single click based on the clicked object's Fill Color, Stroke Color, Stroke Weight, Opacity, and/or Blending Mode. By default, only the Fill Color attribute is enabled as a selection parameter; however, it's easy to customize the settings through the Magic Wand panel.

To open the panel, select Window | Magic Wand or simply double-click the Magic Wand tool. If the panel opens minimized, with just the Fill option showing, click the double-sided arrow next to the panel name to expand the panel. For each of the settings, the tolerance setting determines how similar or dissimilar the individual properties are when making selections. A high tolerance, for example, selects more objects within the range of properties as the original object, while a low tolerance selects fewer objects.

Customize the settings as desired, and when finished, close the panel. All your settings adjustments will remain in place until you change them again.

When selecting with the Magic Wand tool, do any of the following:

- **Create a selection**   Click an object with the properties you desire once, and all objects with matching properties will be selected.

- **Add to the selection**   SHIFT+click another object with different properties to add all similar objects to the existing selection.

- **Subtract from the selection**   ALT+click (Win) or OPT+click (Mac) on an object in the selection and all similar objects will be deselected.

The Lasso Tool

One of the simplest selection tools, the Lasso, selects any objects that fall inside an invisible selection shape or path you draw with this tool. Try it! Just drag across or around any objects and they'll immediately be selected.

The Eyedropper Tool

Like the Magic Wand, the Eyedropper tool works by looking at the properties of the selected object(s). However, unlike the Magic Wand, the Eyedropper has the ability to both pick up and apply object attributes, including character and paragraph styles for text!

To pick up and apply properties from one object (or text) to another with the Eyedropper tool when no objects on the artboard are selected, click an object to copy its properties. As you click, the dropper icon suddenly looks like it has ink inside it! When hovering over text, the dropper icon includes a tiny T. To apply the picked up properties to another object, ALT+click (Win) or OPT+click (Mac) on another object. As you click, the eyedropper icon changes, this time to a reversed full dropper as it applies the "ink."

 To copy a particular color from a gradient, pattern, mesh object, or placed image from one object to another, SHIFT+click the desired color within a gradient, pattern, mesh object, or placed image to sample the exact color under the Eyedropper tip. To apply that sampled color, simply click another object's stroke or fill.

To apply properties from an unselected object (or text) to a selected object, select the object you want to modify and then click the unselected object with the Eyedropper tool to apply that unselected object's properties to the selected object. Alternately, you can ALT+click (Win) or OPT+click (Mac) on a second object to apply the selected object's properties to it.

By default, the Eyedropper copies all the properties in a selection. To refine the selection characteristics, edit the settings in the Eyedropper Options dialog box, which can be opened by double-clicking the Eyedropper tool. When finished, click the OK button to close the dialog box and begin using the new eyedropper options.

 You can sample RGB colors from anywhere outside the open file, even on your desktop. To create a color sample from anywhere on your computer, click anywhere in your document with the Eyedropper tool, and then, *without releasing your mouse*, drag the cursor on top of the object on your computer you'd like to sample, then release your mouse. The sampled color will appear as the stroke or fill in your Tools panel, ready for you to apply it to another object using any of the methods just described.

The Select Menu

Use the items in the Select menu to quickly access objects in your document. Objects can be selected, reselected, deselected, and inverted, as well as saved and reloaded for later use. Platform-specific (Win or Mac) keyboard shortcuts, when applicable, are listed next to the menu options. Here's what all of the Select menu options do:

- **All**   Selects all objects and paths in the open active document.

- **All In Active Artboard**   Selects only the objects and paths on the active artboard in the open active document.

- **Deselect**   Deselects (releases) all objects and paths in the current selection.

- **Reselect**   Reselects objects in the last used selection command.

- **Inverse**   Deselects the selected objects as it selects all other objects.

- **Next Object Above**   Selects the next object above a selected object, relative to their stacking order on the artboard.

- **Next Object Below**   Selects the next object below a selected object, relative to their stacking order on the artboard.

- **Same**   Selects all the objects that have the same attributes as a selected object. Make a selection first, and then choose an option from the Select | Same submenu: Appearance, Appearance Attribute, Blending Mode, Fill & Stroke, Fill Color, Opacity, Stoke Color, Stroke Weight, Graphic Style, Symbol Instance, or Link Block Series.

- **Object**   Selects specific kinds of objects, as chosen from the Select | Object submenu: All On Same Layers, Direction Handles, Brush Strokes, Clipping Masks, Stray Points, Text Objects, Flash Dynamic Text, and Flash Input Text.

- **Save Selection**   To save a selection for later reuse, select any combination of objects in your file and choose this option. When the Save Selection dialog box opens, enter a name for the selection and then click OK. Make and save as many selections as you like. Saved selections are listed at the bottom of the Select menu for easy access.

- **Edit Selection**   Rename or delete any of your saved selections in the Edit Selection dialog box, which opens when you select this option.

5

Pencil, Eraser, Paintbrush, and Blob Brush

How to…

- Use the Pencil, Smooth, and Path Eraser tools
- Edit artwork with the Eraser
- Use the Paintbrush
- Create custom brushes
- Open and use Brush Libraries
- Paint with the Blob Brush

Drawing and painting in Illustrator can be both fast and fun when you take full advantage of all of the available tools. In this chapter, you'll learn about the Pencil, Smooth, and Path Eraser, the regular Eraser, the Paintbrush, and the new Blob Brush tools.

The Pencil Tool

The Pencil tool works just like having a pencil in your hand, only you control it with your mouse (or with a graphics-tablet stylus if you happen to have a nifty graphics tablet, such as the Graphire from Wacom). The pencil can draw freeform (open) paths and closed shapes, both of which can have stroke and/or fill properties.

As you draw with the pencil, before you release your mouse, you'll notice a temporary dotted line appears on the artboard to indicate the shape of the path. After releasing your mouse, the path is drawn with anchor points at the start and end points, as well as along the curves of the path. The actual number of points on the path depends on the intricacy and length of the line and the settings in the Pencil Tool Options dialog box, which can be opened by double-clicking the

Pencil tool in the Tools panel. Paths automatically take on the last-used stroke and fill, though once drawn, the color and other properties of the paths can be altered and refined with the other tools.

To watch a video on drawing with the Pencil tool, visit www.adobe.com/go/vid0039.

Freeform Paths

When drawing freeform paths, a tiny x appears with the tool's icon as you draw. However, when the pencil is in close proximity to another actively selected path, the x will disappear and any new drawing with the Pencil will result in the alteration of that selected path, as illustrated in Figure 5-1.

Closed Paths

To make a closed path, draw out the desired shape with the beginning and end points at roughly the same spot. *Before releasing your mouse,* press and hold the ALT (Win) or OPT (Mac) key. When you see a tiny o appear next to the cursor, Illustrator will close the path with a straight line—regardless of how far your cursor is from the shape's starting point—*if you release the mouse before releasing the keyboard shortcut.* (Otherwise, if you release the ALT or OPT key before releasing the mouse, the path won't close.) Try it and see for yourself how it works. Figure 5-2 shows how the cursor should look when creating a closed path.

Editing Pencil Paths

The Pencil is also a very handy editing tool! With it, you can modify any existing selected path or shape, and even connect two separate paths together:

- **Edit a selected path**   When your Pencil is close to a selected path, you can edit or extend that path when you see the cursor's x disappear.

- **Edit a selected shape**   Draw anywhere on top of the path of a selected shape to redraw that segment of the shape, as in the example in Figure 5-3.

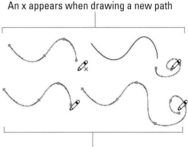

An x appears when drawing a new path

No x appears when altering an existing path

FIGURE 5-1 Freeform paths

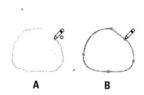

A   B

FIGURE 5-2 Closed paths:
(A) Before releasing the mouse,
(B) After releasing the mouse

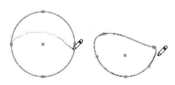

FIGURE 5-3 Editing a shape with the Pencil tool

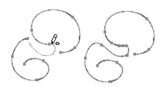

FIGURE 5-4 Connecting paths with the Pencil tool

■ **Connect two paths**   Select the two shapes to be connected, draw a path to connect the two, and then press and hold down the CTRL (Win) or CMD (Mac) key. When a merge icon appears next to the icon (as seen in Figure 5-4), which is a visual indicator that you can successfully connect the paths, release the mouse, and then release the keyboard shortcut.

The Smooth Tool

If the lines you create with the Pencil tool aren't as smooth as you'd like them to be, or you think a particular path has too many anchor points on it, try smoothing them out with the Smooth tool, located in the Pencil tool's flyout menu.

 When drawing with the Pencil tool, pressing and holding the ALT (Win) or OPT (Mac) key before you drag your mouse will temporarily convert the Pencil into the Smooth tool.

Before smoothing   After smoothing

FIGURE 5-5 Using the Smooth tool to simplify paths

The smoothing process is pretty straightforward. Select the object to be smoothed. Then, select the Smooth tool. Draw or drag over the selected path you'd like to simplify and release your mouse. Repeat step 2 until the line has the desired quality. The resulting line will be much smoother and will contain fewer anchor points along the path. Figure 5-5 shows an example of a path before and after smoothing.

To adjust the amount of smoothing, double-click the Smooth tool to open the Smooth Tool Options dialog box. The Fidelity controls the distance the cursor must be from the original path before it adds new anchor points, and the Smoothness dictates how much smoothing the tool applies. Higher values result in a smoother path.

 For an alternate way of smoothing paths without removing anchor points on a selected object, try the command: Object | Path | Simplify. Make sure the Preview option is checked so you can see the results.

The Path Eraser Tool

The Path Eraser tool, located in the Pencil tool's flyout menu, lets you erase parts of any selected path, on both freeform and closed shapes. To use the tool, select the object to be modified, and click and drag across it in the area you'd like to erase. Figure 5-6 shows an example of a path before and after using the Path Eraser tool.

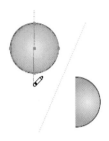

FIGURE 5-6 The Path Eraser used on a path

The Eraser Tool

Unlike the Path Eraser tool, which is really limited to erasing the paths of selected objects, the Eraser tool can erase pretty much anything including paths, fills, objects made up of compound paths or inside clipping paths, and even paths inside Live Paint groups.

The Eraser works slightly differently when objects are selected versus when there are no objects selected on the artboard:

FIGURE 5-7 Erasing part of an object

- **Erasing without selections**   To erase anything on the artboard, regardless of stacking order or placement on individual layers, first make sure no objects on the artboard are selected, and then choose the Eraser tool and drag across the area to be erased.

- **Erasing with selections**   To erase a specific object or set of objects, while leaving all other objects on the artboard untouched, select the object(s) before selecting the Eraser tool, and then drag across them to erase the desired parts. The leaves in Figure 5-7 illustrate how easily objects can be modified with the Eraser.

In addition to erasing freehand with the preceding methods, you can also erase creatively using the following keyboard shortcuts:

- Press and hold the SHIFT key while dragging to constrain the erase line to a 45- or 90-degree angle. Figure 5-8 demonstrates a constrained 45-degree-angle erasure.

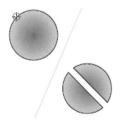

FIGURE 5-8 Erasing diagonally with the SHIFT key

FIGURE 5-9 Erasing with a marquee

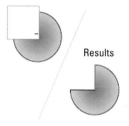

Dragging a marquee around an area

Results

■ Press and hold the ALT (Win) or OPTION (Mac) key while dragging to create a marquee around the desired area, as shown in Figure 5-9. When you release the mouse, everything inside the marquee disappears!

To adjust the angle, roundness, and diameter of the eraser's "head," double-click the Eraser tool to open the Eraser's Tool Options. If you happen to be using a graphics-tablet stylus, you can also adjust additional eraser settings, including fixed, random, pressure, stylus wheel, tilt, bearing, and rotation.

The Paintbrush Tool

The Paintbrush tool lets you add personality and style to your work by stylizing the paths you create. You can use four different types of paintbrushes in Illustrator (shown in Figure 5-10), each of which create unique styles of brush strokes:

- **Calligraphic Brush**   Styles paths with an angled point, like a calligraphic pen. Stroke color is applied evenly along the center of the path.
- **Scatter Brush**   Objects (like confetti or star shapes) are scattered along the path.
- **Art Brush**   An object or shape (such as a decorative banner or watercolor splash) is stretched along the length of a path.
- **Pattern Brush**   Patterned tiles conform to, and are repeated along, the length of a path. Each pattern brush can include up to five tiles, representing the inner and outer corners, start, end, and sides of the pattern.

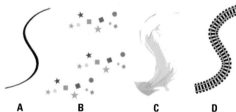

A   B   C   D

FIGURE 5-10 Sample brushes: (A) Calligraphic, (B) Scatter, (C) Art, and (D) Pattern

The style of the brush stroke can either be applied to a path as you draw on the artboard with the Paintbrush tool, or applied separately to any existing selected path through the Brushes panel. To paint with a preset brush stroke, click the desired stroke in the Brushes panel, select the Paintbrush tool from the Tools panel, and begin drawing a path on the artboard. To apply a brush stroke to an existing path, select the object(s) on the artboard and then click the desired brush stroke in the Brushes panel.

The Brushes panel (Window | Brushes), as shown in Figure 5-11, displays the default brush strokes that are loaded into each new document. In addition, the panel has several buttons and menu options to assist you with selecting and applying strokes:

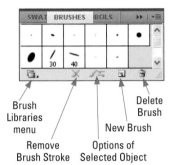

FIGURE 5-11 The Brushes panel

Brush Libraries menu

Remove Brush Stroke

Options of Selected Object

New Brush

Delete Brush

- **Brush Libraries Menu**   Access Illustrator's free Brush Libraries including Arrows, Artistic, Borders, Decorative, Default, and User Defined.

- **Remove Brush Stroke**   Click here to remove a special brush stroke from any selected object or group of objects and replace it with the default 1-pt black stroke.

- **Options of Selected Object**   Click to access the Stroke Options dialog box for any selected object, and change the stroke of that object without updating the original brush. When the dialog box opens, make adjustments as needed to modify the stroke. The dialog box looks slightly different depending on the brush type, and contains the same settings used to create the brush.

- **New Brush**   Click to create a new custom brush.

- **Delete Brush**   Select a brush in the Brushes panel, and then click the trash icon to delete that brush. You may also delete brushes by dragging and dropping them into the trash.

After applying a brush stroke to a path, if you aren't quite happy with the results, or are in the mood to explore the Brush Libraries, feel free to try out other brushes until you find something you like. Everything in Illustrator can be edited and undone, so there's lots of room to explore!

Creating a Custom Brush

You can create four custom brush types, each of which has its own Stroke Options dialog box with custom settings. Before you begin, keep in mind the following:

- For scatter, art, and pattern brushes, you must make the artwork for the brush *before* you create the brush.

- For art and pattern brushes, the artwork for the brushes cannot include working type. They can, however, include type that's been converted to outlines.

■ For pattern brushes, you can create up to five tiles of patterns, for the inner and outer corners, start, end, and sides of the pattern. All the tiles must be added to the Swatches panel as patterns before creating the brushes.

■ For all brushes that use artwork, the art cannot contain gradients, blends, mesh objects, graphs, placed files, bitmap images, masks, or other brush strokes.

■ After a brush has been added to the Brushes panel, you can modify the brush settings through the Brush Options dialog box by double-clicking the brush.

When you're ready to create a custom brush, follow these steps:

1. To create calligraphic or pattern brushes, click the New Brush button on the Brushes panel. To create art or scatter brushes, select the art before clicking the New Brush button.

2. Select a brush type in the New Brush dialog box and click OK.

3. In the Brush Options dialog box, name your new brush and adjust the settings as desired. Click OK to add the new brush to the Brushes panel.

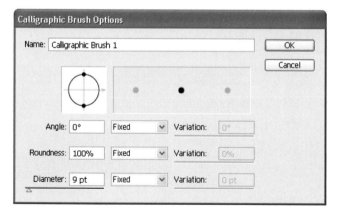

Custom Calligraphic Brush

Create your own calligraphic brush using the settings in the Calligraphic Brush Options dialog box:

■ **Angle**   Sets the brush angle of rotation. Enter a number in the Angle field or drag the arrow in the preview window.

■ **Roundness**   Sets the brush roundness. Enter a number in the Roundness field or drag a black dot in the preview window.

■ **Diameter**   Sets the diameter of the brush. Enter a number in the Diameter field or drag the slider.

■ **Brush Variation Menus**   If desired, select a brush variation (as described in the following) from the popup menu next to the Angle, Roundness, and Diameter options:

■ **Fixed**   The brush has a fixed angle, roundness, or diameter.

■ **Random**   The brush has a random angle, roundness, or diameter. The number entered in the Variation field sets the +/– range of variation between the settings. For instance, a brush with a 10 pt diameter and a 10 pt variation results in a diameter of anywhere between 0 and 20.

■ **Pressure**   (Stylus Users Only) The brush has a varied angle, roundness, or diameter set by the pressure applied by a graphics-tablet stylus, based on the value entered, when applicable.

■ **Stylus Wheel**   (Stylus Users Only) The brush diameter is controlled by settings on the stylus wheel.

■ **Tilt**   (Stylus Users Only) The brush has a varied angle, roundness, or diameter set by tilt of the graphics-tablet stylus.

■ **Bearing**   (Stylus Users Only) The brush has a varied angle, roundness, or diameter set by pressure and tilt applied with the graphics-tablet stylus.

■ **Rotation**   (Stylus Users Only) The brush has a varied angle, roundness, or diameter set by the rotation of the graphics-tablet stylus pen tip.

Custom Scatter Brush

Create your own scatter brush using the settings in the Scatter Brush Options dialog box:

■ **Size**   Controls the size of the objects.

■ **Spacing**   Controls the spacing between objects.

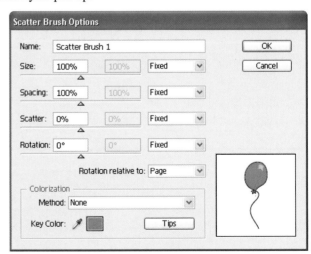

- **Scatter**   Controls how closely objects follow the path.
- **Rotation**   Controls the angle of rotation of the objects.
- **Rotation Relative To**   Sets the angle of rotation for objects, which can be scattered relative to the path or the page.
- **Brush Variation Menus**   If desired, select a brush variation from the popup menu next to the Size, Spacing, Scatter, and Rotation options. These settings are identical to the settings of the Calligraphic brush.
- **Colorization Options**   See the "Colorization Options" section later in this chapter.

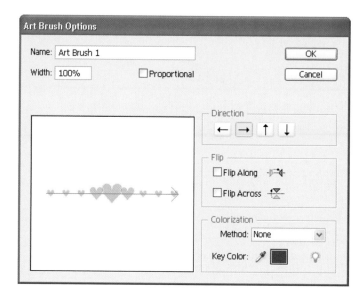

Custom Art Brush

Create your own art brush using the settings in the Art Brush Options dialog box:

- **Width**   Sets how much the width of the art will be adjusted relative to the original.
- **Proportional**   Ensures proportions are maintained when art is scaled up or down.
- **Direction**   Sets the direction the artwork will flow in, relative to the path. Click on one of the arrow boxes to set the direction for the artwork.
- **Flip Along or Flip Across**   Flips the orientation of the art relative to the path.
- **Colorization Options**   See the "Colorization Options" section.

Custom Pattern Brush

Create your own pattern brush using the settings in the Pattern Brush Options dialog box:

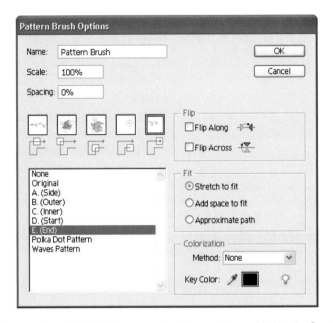

- **Tile buttons** Apply different patterns from the Swatches panel to different parts of a path, as shown in the example in Figure 5-12. Select each tile to set the pattern from the listing below the tiles.

Tip The patterns for the tiles must be rotated in the proper direction and then added to the Swatches panel *before* you create this type of custom brush. See Chapter 12 for more on creating patterns.

- **Scale** Sets the size of the artwork, relative to the original.

- **Spacing** Sets the space between tiles when applied to a path.

- **Flip Along or Flip Across** Sets the direction of the pattern along the path.

- **Fit** Sets how patterns are stretched to fit along the path. **Stretch To Fit** adjusts the length of a pattern to fit the path of the object. **Add Space To Fit** inserts empty space between the tiles so the pattern fits proportionally along the path. **Approximate Path** adjusts tiles to the closest path without altering the tiles by applying the pattern inside or outside the path to keep tiling even.

- **Colorization Options** See the "Colorization Options" section next.

FIGURE 5-12 Tile patterns in a pattern brush: (A) Side, (B) Outer corner, (C) Inner corner, (D) Start, (E) End

Colorization Options

The stroke color appearing in the Stroke box of the Tools panel at the time a stroke is applied with a scatter, art, or pattern brush, along with the colorization method set in the Brush Options dialog box, determines how the stroke appears when it gets applied to a path.

The following options are the same in Scatter, Art, and Pattern brushes:

- **None**   Select this option to keep the colors specified in the brush, rather than overriding them with colorization settings or modifying them using the current stroke color.

- **Tints**   Alters the brush stroke with tints of the stroke color. Black is replaced with the stroke color while all other colors are replaced with tints of the stroke color. This method works well with spot colors.

- **Tints And Shades**   Alters the brush stroke with tints and shades of the stroke color. Blacks and whites in the brush stay black and white, while everything else gets converted to a blend of the stroke color from black to white. Works best with grayscale brushes.

- **Hue Shift**   Uses the color specified in the Key Color box to modify the brush stroke. To edit the key color, click the eyedropper icon and then select a new key color from the art preview area of the dialog box.

For visual assistance in selecting the desired colorization method, click the lightbulb icon next to the Key Color box to open the Colorization Tips dialog box.

Brush Libraries

To view and use any of the brushes in Illustrator's *free* Brush Libraries, select a Brush Library through the panel's Options menu or press the Brush Libraries button on the bottom-left edge of the Brushes panel. Libraries are organized into several different categories to assist you in finding what you need. Categories include Arrows, Artistic, Borders, Decorative, Default, and User Defined, for accessing any custom brushes you create yourself.

Once you select the desired library to open it, the library opens as a floating panel in your workspace. Each successive library opened after that will be added as a tab to that floating library panel. To use a brush from any open library, click the desired brush before selecting the Paintbrush tool. Used brushes are automatically added to the document's Brushes panel for quick future access, which means when you're finished looking through any of the open Brush Library panels, you can close them. Closed panels can then be reopened at any time by using the Brush Libraries button.

The Blob Brush Tool

The Blob Brush is a new tool in CS4 that is really quite remarkable. Different from the regular Paintbrush tool, which creates paths with brush strokes applied to them, the Blob Brush paints objects as a single filled closed path! For example, take a look at the shape in Figure 5-13. What started out as an oval has quickly turned into the beginnings of a little bug shape with the addition of a few strokes applied with the Blob Brush.

FIGURE 5-13 Compound paths created with the Blob Brush

If you're using a graphics-tablet stylus, flip over the pen and try using the eraser to erase parts of the path.

With the Blob Brush tool, each overlapping brush stroke creates new parts to a single combined, or compound, shape. In fact, if you drag the brush over another object with paint attributes similar to the first, all the objects will be combined. What's more, you can use any calligraphic brush with the Blob Brush tool by selecting the desired brush from the Brushes panel before you begin painting with the Blob Brush.

To quickly increase or decrease the diameter of the Blob Brush in 1-pt increments, press the LEFT ([ ) or RIGHT ( ]) bracket keys on your keyboard.

To adjust the tool's settings, including being able to specify the brush size, angle, and roundness, double-click the Blob Brush icon in the Tools panel to open the Blob Brush Tool Options dialog box. Here's an overview of the different settings:

- **Keep Selected**   Keeps the path selected after drawing.
- **Selection Limits Merge**   Limits new paths to selected objects. If left unchecked, the brush will merge paths of objects with similar color attributes.
- **Fidelity**   Enter a number of pixels or adjust the slider to modify the distance between anchor points along the path. The higher the number, the smoother the path. Lower numbers will create curvier paths with more points.
- **Smoothness**   Enter a percentage or adjust the slider to modify the smoothness of the path. The higher the number, the smoother the path. A lower number will make paths conform more to the mouse or stylus' movement.
- **Size**   Controls the point size of the brush.
- **Angle**   Sets the angle of rotation of the brush. Enter a number in the Angle field or drag the arrow in the preview window.
- **Roundness**   Sets the brush roundness. Enter a number in the Roundness field or drag a black dot in the preview window.
- **Brush Variation Menus**   If desired, select a brush variation from the popup menu next to the Size, Angle, and Roundness options. These settings are identical to the settings of the Calligraphic brush.

6

Mastering the Pen Tool

How to...

- Draw straight lines
- Draw curved lines
- Convert lines to curves
- Convert curves to lines
- Edit points and paths

The Pen tool is probably the most maddening and rewarding tool in the Tools panel! Maddening because it takes a little bit of practice to master—and rewarding because once you do understand how it works you can use it to draw or trace nearly anything! When you need a tool to draw straight lines, curved lines, and artwork with complex paths, reach for the Pen tool.

The Pen Tool

The Pen tool creates *paths* that are composed of *anchor points* and *line segments*. The true emphasis in understanding the Pen tool is not in understanding the *line segments* but in understanding the rules to the *anchor points* that determine a line segment. All paths contain at least two anchor points—one at the beginning and one at the end—though paths may include as many anchor points and paths as needed to create the chosen shape. Paths can be open (like a line), closed (like a circle), or compound (like an object composed of two or more open or closed paths—like a doughnut shape created with a closed circle outer shape minus the closed circle inner shape).

On straight lines, the anchor point appears as a tiny box along the path. By contrast, the anchor points on curved paths (sometimes called Bézier curves, after the French engineer, Pierre Bézier, who invented the mathematical model for drawing curved vector graphics) include *direction lines*, which help determine the direction and arc of the paths on either side of the anchor point. Figure 6-1 shows the structure of a path with straight and curved line segments.

The anchor points, as illustrated for the letters L, O, V, and E, in Figure 6-2, are like corners that can support both smooth (straight) and curved paths. There are three basic types of anchor points that define a path segment and these point types break down as follows:

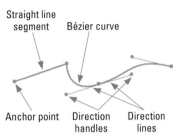

FIGURE **6-1** The structure of a straight and curved line segment

- **Corner**   Path segments flowing from these anchor points are straight. The paths that connect through corner anchor points do not have any direction lines or "handles" extending from the anchor point. The letter L in Figure 6-2 demonstrates straight paths with corner points.

- **Smooth**   Path segments that connect through these anchor points are generally smooth curves (as the name implies), and include one set of direction lines or "handles" (visible on each side of the point) that steer the path on both sides of the point simultaneously— similar to the behavior of a seesaw in which the handle movement on one side of the point causes the handle on the other side of the point to respond in the opposite direction. The letter O in Figure 6-2 illustrates how curved paths are connected with smooth corner points.

FIGURE **6-2** Letters created with different anchor points

- **Cusp**   Path segments that connect through these anchor points may have curves that abruptly change direction, therefore the direction lines or handles that control the path segment function independently on each side of the point. In other words, the handle on one side of the point affects only the segment path on that side (and does not affect the segment path or the movement of the handle on the other side of the point). The letters V and E in Figure 6-2 show combination straight and curved paths with corner and smooth points, and curved paths with smooth corner and cusp corner points, respectively.

Once drawn, lines can be infinitely edited with many of Illustrator's other tools, as you'll learn in a section later in the chapter. Here, we'll concentrate on the Pen family of tools, located in the Pen tool's flyout menu, which are useful for modifying and refining paths:

- **Pen tool**   Creates straight and curved lines by strategically placing anchor points on the artboard to create the desired path.

- **Add Anchor Point**   Adds an anchor point in the desired location to any path. Use extra points sparingly, since the fewer the points, the smoother the lines will appear both onscreen and in print.

- **Delete Anchor Point**   Removes a specific anchor point from a selected path. Once removed, the path is redrawn to the new configuration of segments and anchor points.

Points can also be deleted by selecting them with the Direct Selection tool and clicking the Remove Selected Anchor Points icon on the Control panel.

- **Convert Anchor Point**   Converts a corner point to a smooth point, and vice versa. The Convert Anchor Point tool can also convert a smooth point into a cusp point by moving the handle of a smooth point—an action that automatically converts the handle into one that operates independently.

Drawing Straight Lines

FIGURE 6-3 Open and closed paths with fills

Straight lines can be used to create both open paths and closed shapes, and can be as short or long, simple or complicated, as needed. Paths may cross over one another; however, the resulting shape may have unusual looking fills since fills are created between every two end points regardless of whether the shape is opened or closed, as illustrated in Figure 6-3.

When creating a straight line, you'll be setting down a series of anchor points, between which paths will automatically be drawn. The direction and location of the anchor points is entirely up to you.

To draw straight-lined paths and closed shapes with the Pen tool, follow these steps:

1. Click once on the artboard to set an anchor point. This point will be represented on the artboard as an "invisible" blue anchor point in that it is not an actual "dot of ink."

Be careful not to click and drag because this will create a curved corner with direction lines. If direction lines appear, select Edit I Undo, and start over.

2. Click another spot on the artboard to set down the second anchor point. The path between the two points now appears.

 Press and hold the SHIFT key as you set down anchor points to constrain the lines to a 45- or 90-degree angle.

3. Repeat Step 2 to insert additional straight paths between anchor points.

4. To close the shape, hover your cursor directly over the opening (first) anchor point. When you see a tiny o appear in the cursor, click directly on the anchor point. Figure 6-4 shows how to close a path created with straight lines.

FIGURE 6-4 When a tiny circle appears, click to create a closed path with straight lines

Deselecting an Active Path

Following each click with the Pen tool, the resulting anchor points and paths remain selected. To deselect the active path and begin drawing a new line, CTRL+click (Win) or CMD+click (Mac) anywhere on the artboard away from the active path to deselect it. This keyboard action temporarily toggles your cursor to the Selection tool or Direct Selection tool (determined by whichever of these tools was most recently accessed before using the Pen tool). Once the keyboard shortcut is released, the cursor toggles back to the Pen tool and is ready for you to draw a new path. Paths can also be deselected by choosing Select I Deselect or by selecting any of the other tools from the Tools panel.

 **How to. . .**   # Move Anchor Points As You Draw

To reposition an anchor point as you draw, keep the MOUSE depressed and hold down the SPACEBAR to drag and reposition the anchor point. Release the SPACEBAR and then the MOUSE to set the anchor point.

Drawing Curved Lines

Creating curved lines with the Pen tool takes a little extra concentration at first because you must think about your drawing one step ahead of what you actually see on your monitor. In other words, you must learn to anticipate the direction of the next curve as you set down each anchor point. To do that, you'll be creating curved line segments by clicking and dragging as you set down each anchor point, rather than just clicking to draw straight lines. When you drag you'll create direction lines out of each anchor point, which will be used to determine the arc shape and height of each curved path.

To draw a simple wave-shaped curve, follow these steps:

1. Click the artboard with the Pen tool and drag upwards about one inch. As you drag, the direction lines for the curve are essentially pulled out of the anchor point.

2. Release your mouse. Notice that the ends of the direction lines contain direction handles. You'll use the handles later to adjust the curves, if needed.

 The display size of anchor points and direction handles on your paths can be adjusted in the Selection & Anchor Display Preferences dialog box. Press CTRL+K (Win) or CMD+K (Mac) to open the Preferences dialog box and click the Next button once to see the Selection & Anchor Display settings.

3. To the right of the first anchor point, click and drag again on the artboard to set the anchor point, this time dragging downwards about one inch. Paths are drawn between two anchor points.

4. Release your mouse. The line segment between the first and second anchor points is now drawn, as defined by the length and direction of the direction lines.

5. Repeat steps 1–4 to create a curvy line, like the example shown in Figure 6-5. To deselect the line, CTRL+click (Win) or CMD+click (Mac) away from the active path.

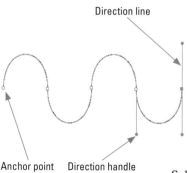

Direction line

Anchor point   Direction handle

FIGURE 6-5 A curvy line

To alter the shape of the curves, switch to the Direct Selection tool and try dragging the handles at different angles. Also notice the seesaw action of the handles as you drag and alter the path segment shape.

To understand the concept of the cusp point, where the anchor points may have curves that abruptly change direction, take a look at the scalloped line in Figure 6-6. Notice how the curves in this path repeat in the same direction. To draw the scalloped shape, you'll need to convert the direction of the handles using the Convert Anchor Point tool. Here's how to do it:

1. Click the artboard with the Pen tool and drag upwards about one inch and release your mouse.

2. To the right of the first anchor point, click and drag downwards about one inch to set the second anchor point.

3. Next, either before or after you release your mouse, press and hold the ALT (Win) or OPT (Mac) key and hover your Pen tool over the direction handle of the down-facing direction line. When the pen cursor turns into the Convert Anchor Point Tool icon, *click the direction handle* and drag it so the direction line is pointing upwards and falls directly on top of, or near, the other upward-facing direction line from the previous curve, as illustrated in Figure 6-6.

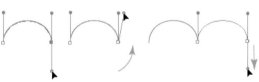

FIGURE 6-6   Create scalloped paths with the help of the Convert Anchor Point tool

4. Release your mouse and then the ALT (Win) or OPT (Mac) key.

5. Repeat steps 2–4 to add additional scalloped curves to the line, and then press CTRL (Win) or CMD (Mac) as you click away from the active path to deselect it.

How to. . .   Reposition Direction Lines

Direction lines can be repositioned any time after the line is drawn by dragging one of the direction handles with either the Convert Anchor Point tool to create a cusp point or dragging with the Direction Selection tool to maintain a smooth point.

Combining Straight and Curved Lines

Some shapes (like an ice cream cone) are created with a combination of both straight and curved lines. Now that you understand the rules of the three types of anchor points, you can consider combination corner points with a smooth point or cusp point, where one side contains a direction line with a handle, while the other side has none. You can convert any corner point to support straight lines and curves on-the-fly as you draw your shapes, or adjust them after you've set the anchor points and paths of your desired shape.

The real secret in going from lines to curves, and vice versa, is to use the Pen tool effectively. When you hover your mouse over the last drawn anchor point, the convert-point icon appears next to the Pen tool, allowing you to quickly and easily transform that anchor point's properties.

FIGURE 6-7 Drawing a curved line after a straight line

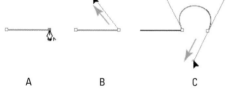

A   B   C

Straight to Curved Lines   Click (without dragging) to set a few anchor points and straight line segments. (See Figure 6-7.) To convert the last anchor point from a smooth to a curved corner point, hover over the last point and when you see a convert icon appear next to the cursor (A), click and drag the anchor point to pull out a single direction line (B), and position it so it points in the direction of the next desired curve (C). The next anchor point you set will create a path that will be curved.

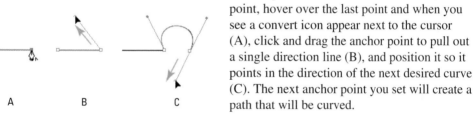

A   B   C

FIGURE 6-8 Drawing a straight line after a curved line

Curved to Straight Lines   Click and drag on the artboard to set down a few anchor points with curved line segments. (See Figure 6-8.) To convert the last anchor point from a curved to a smooth corner point, click once with the Pen tool on the last anchor point created (A). Immediately, one of the two direction lines for that anchor point disappears (B), setting the stage for drawing a straight line between this anchor point and the next (C).

Tip   Corner points can also be converted from a curved path to a straight path by dragging the direction line into the anchor point.

Editing Paths

In a perfect world, we'd all draw our straight and curved lines exactly as we want them the first time around. Fortunately, in the world of Illustrator, not being perfect is perfectly acceptable, and we can edit our paths over and over again until we get them just right.

That said, having a good starting shape to work with helps get the job done more efficiently, so use the following tips with the Pen tool:

- When drawing line segments and shapes with the Pen tool, try to concentrate on the placement of the anchor points more than the angle or curve of the line segments between them. You can always go back into the path with the other tools to refine the line after it's drawn.

- Use the fewest possible anchor points. The fewer the points, the smoother the line will be, both onscreen and in print.

- Place the anchor points at the beginnings of each new turn in the path, where the path either gets bigger or smaller, changes from straight to curved (or vice versa), or flows in another direction.

- When drawing curved segments in particular… drag the direction line handle in the direction you want the next curve to go in, drag the direction line handle about $1/3$ further than the height of the desired curve, and try to set the anchor points where you need them and not worry so much about the angle, height, and direction of curves (you can fix these after the path is drawn).

Adding Anchor Points

To add anchor points on paths that need to be curvier or longer than originally drawn, select the path, choose the Add Anchor Point tool, and click in the desired spot along the path.

Deleting Anchor Points

To remove anchor points from paths to make them less curvy or differently shaped than originally drawn, select the path, choose the Delete Anchor Point tool, and click the desired anchor point.

Add and Subtract Anchor Points

When drawing with the Pen tool, you can quickly add and subtract anchor points without having to change tools in the Tools panel. To add an anchor point to a selected path, hover the Pen tool over a path segment and click when you see the Add Anchor Point Tool icon. To remove an anchor point from a selected path, hover your Pen tool over an anchor point and click when you see the Delete Anchor Point Tool icon.

Editing with the Direct Selection Tool

The Direct Selection tool can do more than simply select parts of an object or group. Use it to select and reposition anchor points, move paths, and adjust the handles of smooth or cusp anchor points.

Repositioning an Anchor Point

To reposition a single anchor point, simply click and drag the point to the desired location. To reposition more than one anchor point on a path, select the first anchor point and then SHIFT+click to select additional points. Once selected, click and drag on any of the selected path segments to move them into the new location. You may also adjust their position incrementally after selecting them by pressing the ARROW KEYS on your keyboard.

Repositioning a Path

To reposition one or more line segments on a path, regardless of whether they are curved or straight, select the first path and then SHIFT+click to select additional paths. Once selected, you can either click and drag any of the selected paths to move them all at once, or alter their position incrementally by pressing the ARROW KEYS on your keyboard. Keep in mind this will move the selected path segments *only* around the anchor points, which will remain stationary if they are not selected.

You can reposition any combination of points and paths at the same time. Simply select the desired points and paths, and then click and drag any one of them to move them into the new position. For more precise adjustments, use the arrow keys.

Remember, you can also use the Pencil and Smooth tools to refine a line drawn with the Pen tool. To redraw or smooth a segment of a path, select the path with the Selection tool and then draw over or drag across that line segment with the Pencil or Smooth tool. Repeat as needed, or combine with other editing techniques, until the line looks the way you want it to.

Adjusting the Direction Lines of a Curve

To adjust the direction lines of a smooth or cusp anchor point, select the anchor point with the Direct Selection tool to activate the direction lines, then click and drag the direction line handle to the new desired position, as shown in Figure 6-9.

Converting Anchor Points with the Control Panel

When the Pen tool is active (and also when particular anchor points of an object are selected with the Direct Selection tool), the Control panel includes tools for converting the selected anchor points of a selected path, as shown in Figure 6-10. These tools will not appear when an entire object is selected, so be sure to select only the anchor points that need converting. (Note: The other Control panel tools are covered in Chapters 7 and 11.)

To use these tools, first select the anchor points to be converted, and then do any of the following:

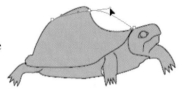

FIGURE 6-9 Adjusting a curved line's direction handles

- To convert one or more corner points into smooth points, click the Convert Selected Anchor Points To Smooth button.

- To convert one or more smooth points into corner points, click the Convert Selected Anchor Points To Corner button.

- To remove selected anchor points from a path, click the Remove Selected Anchor Points button.

FIGURE 6-10 Control panel anchor point tools

Convert selected anchor points to corner   Convert selected anchor points to smooth   Hide handles for multiple selected anchor points   Connect selected anchor points

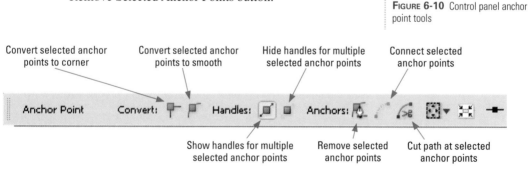

Show handles for multiple selected anchor points   Remove selected anchor points   Cut path at selected anchor points

- To show the anchor point handles for multiple selected points, click the Show Handles For Multiple Selected Anchor Points button.

- To hide the anchor point handles for multiple selected points, click the Hide Handles For Multiple Selected Anchor Points button.

- To connect any two selected anchor points, click the Connect Selected Anchor Points button.

- To cut a path, whether opened or closed, at any one or more selected anchor points, click the Cut Path At Selected Anchor Points button.

To watch an Adobe training video on using the Pen tool, go to www.adobe.com/designcenter/ video_workshop/?id=vid0037.

7

Arrangement, Alignment, and the Pathfinder Panel

How to...

- Change the order of objects
- Group and ungroup
- Copy and paste
- Align and distribute objects
- Use the Pathfinder panel
- Work in Isolation Mode

As you create your illustrations, you may not necessarily draw the individual objects in the order and configuration they ultimately need to be in. That's where the tools in this chapter come in. Here you'll learn about arranging objects, aligning and distributing them, copying and pasting, combining and dividing shapes with the Pathfinder panel, and how to work on individual parts of larger images in Isolation Mode. We'll also take a look at some of the tools that become available on the Control panel when one or more objects are selected.

 Tip Remember, you can always use the rulers, artboard rulers, grids, guides, and smart guides in the View menu to help with evenly positioning, aligning, and distributing objects on your artboard.

Arranging Objects

In Illustrator, every path or shape is drawn separately, and each new one is positioned on top of the last, as shown with the set of shapes in Figure 7-1. This overlapping of shapes is called the *stacking order*, where the object at the top of the stack is the front-most object, closest to the viewer. Fortunately, this ordering is completely flexible and easy to change using the arrange options.

To illustrate, take a look at the objects in Figure 7-2. The object on top needs to be sent further back in the stacking order so all the objects that were drawn are visible.

FIGURE 7-1 Objects are stacked on top of each other

One way to rearrange objects is by changing an object's stacking order through the options in the Arrange menu:

- **Bring to Front** Brings the selected object(s) to the front (top) of the stacking order. Choose Object | Arrange | Bring To Front, or press CTRL+SHIFT+] (Win) or CMD+SHIFT+] (Mac).

- **Bring Forward** Brings the selected object(s) one step forward in the stacking order. Choose Object | Arrange | Bring Forward, or press CTRL+] (Win) or CMD+] (Mac).

- **Send Backward** Sends the selected object(s) one step backward in the stacking order. Choose Object | Arrange | Send Backward, or press CTRL+[(Win) or CMD+[(Mac).

Before arrangement　　After arrangement

- **Send to Back** Sends the selected object(s) to the back (bottom) of the stacking order. Choose Object | Arrange | Send To Back, or press CTRL+SHIFT+[(Win) or CMD+SHIFT+[(Mac).

FIGURE 7-2 Change the stacking order using the Object | Arrange menu

- **Send to Current Layer** Sends the selected object(s) to the currently selected layer in the Layers panel. Choose Object | Arrange | Send To Current Layer.

Tip　The Arrange menu options can also be accessed through the context menu by right-clicking (Win) or CTRL+clicking (Mac) the desired object.

Group and Ungroup

The fastest way to move and manipulate several objects at once is to combine them into a single *group*. Groups can be created from any two or more selected objects. Groups can also be *nested*, or grouped with other objects or other groups, to help you in the organization of your work. For example, the eyes of the frog illustration in Figure 7-3 are grouped.

FIGURE 7-3 Grouped objects

Once a group is created, selecting any of the objects in the group with the Selection tool selects the entire group. To select a part of a group, use the Direct Selection or Group Selection tools, as described in Chapter 4.

To create a group, select the individual objects to be grouped and choose Object | Group, or press CTRL+G (Win) or CMD+G (Mac). To ungroup the objects in a selected group, choose Object | Ungroup, or press SHIFT+CTRL+G (Win) or SHIFT+CMD+G (Mac).

As the grouping takes place, the paths of grouped objects are stacked in sequence in the same layer in the Layers panel. When the selected objects come from different layers, the grouping may inadvertently jumble their stacking order. If that happens, you'll need to rearrange the objects using the options from the Object | Arrange menu.

Objects and groups can also be rearranged through the Layers panel, which you'll learn about in Chapter 8.

Copy, Paste, Cut, and Clear

At the top of the Edit menu, you'll find several commands to help you cut, copy, paste, and clear objects on your artboard. Use these commands to quickly make duplicates of your work and rearrange them in the desired locations.

Copy and Paste

The Copy and Paste commands in the Edit menu work together to help you create quick copies of any selection. Copied selections are temporarily placed on the computer's clipboard in anticipation of being pasted.

Illustrator's clipboard can also be used to copy objects and then paste them into other Adobe applications, including Adobe Photoshop, Adobe InDesign, and Adobe GoLive.

In addition, when you paste, the object(s) being pasted appear at the top of the stacking order for the entire document. Use your mouse to select the Copy and Paste commands from the Edit menu, or for faster results, use the keyboard shortcuts by selecting the object(s) you'd like to copy and pressing CTRL+C (Win) or CMD+C (Mac) to copy the selection to Illustrator's clipboard, and CTRL+V (Win) or CMD+V (Mac) to paste a copy of the selection onto the center of the artboard.

Dragging Copies

For an even faster way of making copies use the *click and drag* method:

1. Select the object(s) to be copied.

2. Hover your mouse over the selection and press the ALT (Win) or OPT (Mac) key. When the cursor turns into a double arrow, as shown in Figure 7-4, keep pressing the keyboard shortcut as you drag the object(s) to pull a copy out of the original.

3. Still pressing the keyboard shortcut, release the mouse to add the copy in the desired location. Then, release the keyboard shortcut.

Cursor changes
to drag a copy

The results

FIGURE 7-4 Duplicate by dragging

Paste in Front/Back

Included in the copy and paste section of the Edit menu are the special Paste In Front and Paste In Back commands for quickly moving objects in front or in back of one or more selected objects after cutting or copying. When objects are pasted using both commands, only the stacking order changes, while their relative position on the artboard is maintained.

Paste in Front

1. Select the desired object(s).

2. Copy or cut the selection using the Edit | Copy or Edit | Cut command.

3. Do one of the following:

   ▢ Choose Edit | Paste In Front.

   ▢ Press CTRL+F (Win) or CMD+F (Mac).

Paste in Back

1. Select the desired object(s).

2. Copy or cut the selection using the Edit | Copy or Edit | Cut command.

3. Do one of the following:

- ▪ Choose Edit | Paste In Back.
- ▪ Press CTRL+B (Win) or CMD+B (Mac).

Cut and Paste

For times when you need to move an object instead of making a copy of it, use the *cut and paste* method instead:

1. Select the object(s) you'd like to cut.

2. Press CTRL+X (Win) or CMD+X (Mac) to cut the selection.

3. Press CTRL+V (Win) or CMD+V (Mac) to paste the cut selection onto the artboard at the top of the stacking order.

 To paste the cut object into a particular position within the stacking order, you can select the object in front of, or in back of, where you'd like the pasted image to go and then choose one of the paste commands. Paste and Paste In Front will paste in front of the selection, while Paste In Back will paste in back of the selection.

Clear

To completely remove a selection from the artboard, select the object(s) and choose Edit | Clear. Of course, you can also use the Edit | Cut option, but that places the cut object(s) temporarily on the clipboard until you replace the clipboard's contents by copying or cutting something else, so really it's more efficient to use the Clear command.

 Selections can also be deleted by pressing the DELETE (Win or Mac) or BACKSPACE (Win) key on your keyboard.

Align and Distribute

The Align panel helps organize selected objects (including groups, paths, and type) by aligning them relative to one another, either along the object edges or selected anchor points. To open the panel, select Window | Align. If you don't see the full panel, click the double-arrows next to the panel's tab once or twice until it completely expands.

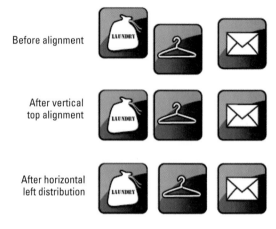

Before alignment

After vertical top alignment

After horizontal left distribution

Selected objects can be aligned and/ or distributed horizontally and vertically along the selected objects' centers, or along their left-, right-, top-, or bottom-most edges. Further, objects can be aligned and/or distributed relative to the boundaries of the entire selection, to a key object within that selection, or to the artboard. Figure 7-5 shows a few objects before and after vertically aligning their tops, and after horizontally distributing them from the left.

FIGURE 7-5 Aligned and distributed objects

Aligning or Distributing to a Selection

Follow these steps to use the Align panel:

1. Select the objects to be aligned and/or distributed.

2. Click the desired button on the Align panel to align or distribute relative to the bounding box around the selected objects:

- **Align**   From left to right, these buttons are Horizontal Align Left, Horizontal Align Center, Horizontal Align Right, Vertical Align Top, Vertical Align Center, and Vertical Align Bottom.

- **Distribute**   From left to right, these buttons are Vertical Distribute Top, Vertical Distribute Center, Vertical Distribute Bottom, Horizontal Distribute Left, Horizontal Distribute Center, and Horizontal Distribute Right.

Tip

When two or more objects are selected, the Align and Distribute buttons also appear on the Control panel.

Aligning or Distributing to a Key Object

To align or distribute relative to a *key* (particular) object within a set of selected objects, follow these steps:

1. SHIFT+click to select all the objects, including the object you wish to target as the key object.

2. Release the SHIFT key and click once on the previously selected object that will be the key object. All the objects remain selected; however, the key object will now have a bolder outline, as shown in Figure 7-6. To deselect the key object, choose Cancel Key Object from the Align panel option menu, or simply click the key object again.

3. Press the desired Align or Distribute button on the Align panel or Control panel.

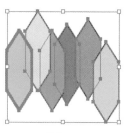

FIGURE 7-6 Selecting a key object and using alignment and distribution

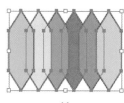

Before   After

With key objects, you can also set the exact distance between selected objects when distributing them vertically or horizontally. Start by SHIFT+clicking to select all the objects (including the key object). Then, release the SHIFT key and click once on the key object to highlight it. At the bottom of the Align panel, select Align To Key Object from the Align To menu and enter the desired distance between selected objects in the spacing value field. Lastly, click the Vertical Distribute Space and/or Horizontal Distribute Space button to distribute the selected objects by the specified distance.

Aligning or Distributing to the Artboard

To align or distribute two or more selected objects relative to the artboard, select the Align To Artboard option from the Align To dropdown menu on the Align panel. This button is also accessible from the same dropdown menu on the Control panel.

For a video on aligning and distributing objects, see www.adobe.com/go/vid0035.

The Pathfinder Panel

The Pathfinder panel contains two sets of powerful path editing tools. The Shape Modes include four tools that combine or create compound shapes, and the Pathfinders consist of six tools that divide, trim, merge, crop, outline, and subtract from any set of selected objects.

The Pathfinder options menu has a few options that may be of interest to you. First, the Pathfinder Options dialog box contains settings for temporarily adjusting how the tools on the panel work. The settings in this dialog box automatically reset each time you open Illustrator.

- **Precision**   The number entered here sets the precision of the pathfinder tools. The higher the number, the more accurate the results, but accuracy does take longer to process. For best results, leave the default setting at 0.028 and only increase if working with complex shapes.

- **Remove Redundant Points**   When enabled, this option deletes overlapping points or points that are close together on the same path.

- **Divide and Outline Will Remove Unpainted Artwork**   Enabling this option will force Illustrator to delete unpainted (objects with no stroke and no fill) artwork, which sometimes result when using the Divide and Outline tools.

The second dialog box accessible through the panel's options menu is the Pathfinder Trap. Trapping is a process used by print shops to prevent potential gaps between two adjoining colors by creating a small area of overlap. Here you can adjust the thickness, height/width, and tint reduction for the trap, as well as options for trapping with process color or reverse traps.

The last option in the panel's option menu is not a dialog box, but rather a Repeat command that repeats the last performed action when adding a new object to an existing selected object or shape that has just been modified with one of the Pathfinder panel's tools. To illustrate, the two squares in Figure 7-7 were first combined with the Pathfinder panel's

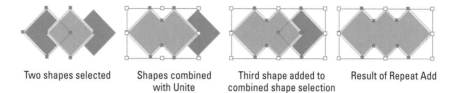

Two shapes selected   Shapes combined   Third shape added to   Result of Repeat Add
                              with Unite   combined shape selection

FIGURE 7-7 The Pathfinder panel's
Repeat command

Unite button. The third square was then added to the selection before choosing the Repeat Add command from the panel's options menu, which resulted in the final shape.

Shape Modes

The Shape Modes buttons have been slightly modified in CS4. In previous versions, the buttons would create compound shapes from selected objects, where the original shapes would be retained so each object within the compound shape could be

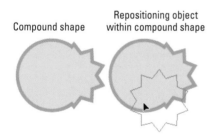

Compound shape   Repositioning object
                      within compound shape

FIGURE 7-8 Compound shapes

moved or edited with the Direct Selection tool, without breaking the compound interaction, as in the example in Figure 7-8. Users could choose to leave the objects in the compound shape or expand the objects into a single new shape by pressing the Expand button.

Now, in CS4, the Shape Modes buttons automatically create these expanded shapes, *unless* you ALT+click (Win) or OPT+click (Mac) the buttons on the panel to create compound shapes, which can then be expanded into a single new shape, if desired, by clicking the Expand button.

To use the Shape Modes, select the desired objects on your artboard and click one of the buttons on the Pathfinder panel:

- **Unite**   Combines selected objects into a single new object. The top-most object's attributes define the properties for the new shape.

- **Minus Front**   Subtracts the top-most objects from the bottom object in the selection.

- **Intersect**　Creates a new shape by subtracting any parts of the shapes within the selection that are not overlapping; only the overlapping parts remain as a single shape.

- **Exclude**　Creates a new shape by subtracting any overlapping shapes within the selection. The resulting shape is a grouped shape made up of the resulting shapes. To move the individual pieces apart, ungroup the shape first.

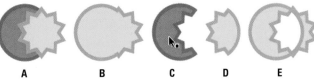

FIGURE 7-9　Objects combined with Shape Modes: (A) Original, (B) Unite, (C) Minus Front, (D) Intersect, and (E) Exclude

- **Expand**　Expands compound shapes into a single new shape.

Figure 7-9 illustrates how each of these Shape Modes buttons performs its task.

A　　B　　C　　D　　E

Tip　If you accidentally press the wrong button on the panel, undo the last command by pressing CTRL+Z (Win) or CMD+Z (Mac) and try again.

Pathfinders

The Pathfinders are the path alteration tools that create new shapes based on the overlapping shapes within a selection. Figure 7-10 shows an original set of objects and how they look when applied with each of the pathfinders.

To use the Pathfinders, select the desired objects and click one of the buttons:

- **Divide**　Divides all the overlapping shapes into individual closed paths. The object can then be ungrouped and the individual shapes rearranged or edited.

- **Trim**　Removes strokes, if any, while cutting away any parts of objects that are hidden by overlapping objects. The resulting shapes may then be ungrouped for editing.

- **Merge**　Removes strokes, if any, as it merges objects filled with the same color.

- **Crop**　Cuts artwork at overlapping edges, removes all strokes, and deletes any shapes behind the top-most object. The resulting grouped object can be ungrouped and edited.

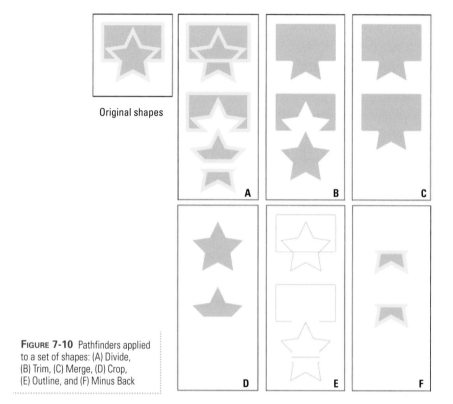

Original shapes

A   B   C

D   E   F

FIGURE 7-10 Pathfinders applied
to a set of shapes: (A) Divide,
(B) Trim, (C) Merge, (D) Crop,
(E) Outline, and (F) Minus Back

▪ **Outline**   Divides all selected objects into line segments
with a 1pt stroke and no fill, cutting the individual paths
where they intersect. The resulting grouped paths can be
ungrouped and edited.

▪ **Minus Back**   Cuts away all artwork behind the top-
most object. The resulting shape retains its original
stroke and fill attributes.

A similar set of Pathfinder options is available through the Effect I Pathfinder menu; however,
these effects can only be applied to groups, layers, or text objects. By contrast, the tools in the
Pathfinder panel can be applied to any combination of objects, groups, and layers. For more on
Effects, see Chapter 18.

Isolation Mode

When editing objects within a group, Illustrator automatically goes into what's called *Isolation Mode*, where the selected group objects (or sublayers of an object made up of multiple layers) become secluded so editing work can focus on just those objects or object parts. The remaining work on the artboard becomes temporarily inaccessible and appears slightly dimmed, like the plate and background of the cake image seen in Figure 7-11, allowing you to concentrate on the isolated objects without disrupting the grouping.

FIGURE 7-11 Isolated art in Isolation Mode

Cake before isolation   Selected cake art in isolation

Entering Isolation Mode

To enter Isolation Mode, select the desired artwork and do one of the following:

- Double-click the grouped object with the Selection tool.
- Right-click (Win) or CTRL+click (Mac) the grouped object and select Isolate Selected Group from the context menu.
- Click the Isolate Selected Group button on the Control panel.
- Select Enter Isolation Mode from the Layers panel options menu.

Tip To watch a video on working with selections in Isolation Mode, visit www.adobe.com/designcenter/video_workshop/?id=vid0041.

Exiting Isolation Mode

To exit Isolation Mode, do any of the following:

- Double-click an empty space of the artboard with the Selection tool.

- Right-click (Win) or CTRL+click (Mac) the grouped object and select Exit Isolation Mode from the context menu.

- Select Exit Isolation Mode from the context menu.

- Click the Exit Isolation Mode arrow button in the Isolation Mode bar at the top of the document workspace.

- Click the Exit Isolation Mode button on the Control panel.

When deeply nested inside grouped objects in Isolation Mode, you may need to click the Back One Level arrow button on the Isolation Mode bar at the top of the document workspace a few times before the Exit Isolation Mode arrow button appears in its place, allowing you to finally exit Isolation Mode.

8

Working with Layers

How to...

- Create new layers
- Set layer options
- Use the Layers panel
- Make template layers
- Trace artwork manually
- Reorganize and target layers

Layering in Illustrator is a powerful way to organize your work, especially when you have multiple objects that can sometimes get hidden behind one another, making it difficult to find those objects, let alone select them.

Essentially, layers are like a standard filing system where each layer represents a folder that contains specific items. In this chapter, you'll learn how to use the Layers panel to create multiple layers with unique labels, organize objects and groups on individual layers and sublayers, create template layers for manually tracing artwork, quickly select targeted paths and groups on layers for faster editing, and even lock, hide, and edit the appearance attributes of objects on each layer.

Understanding Layers

Simply put, a layer in Illustrator is a level of organization that contains an unlimited number of paths, groups, and sublayers (which can also contain an infinite number of sublayers, paths, and groups). Create as many layers as you like, labeling each one with a different name and color code to help with the organization of your work, such as one layer for text, one for borders, one for backgrounds, and so forth. Layers are endlessly flexible, so you can rearrange the layers and their contents as often as needed until everything is ordered as you like. Figure 8-1 shows the Layers panel of a file with several visible layers, one of which has been expanded to reveal the expanded group and paths within it.

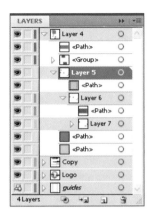

FIGURE 8-1 Use layers to organize your work

Creating a New Layer

By default, the first layer of any new document is named Layer 1. As subsequent layers are created, each will be placed above the currently selected layer, and will be generically named Layer 2, Layer 3, and so forth in numerical sequence until you decide to rename them.

To create a new layer, select the layer inside the Layers panel you'd like to have the new layer placed on top of, and then click the Create New Layer button at the bottom of the Layers panel. The button looks like a tiny page with the bottom left corner turned up. Immediately after clicking, the new layer appears with a default layer name, such as Layer 2.

Renaming a Layer

To change a layer's default name into something more meaningful and descriptive, double-click the layer to launch the Layer Options dialog box. Type in a new name in the Name field and click the OK button to accept the change.

Setting Layer Options

In addition to being able to change a layer's name in the Layer Options dialog box, you can also modify many other layer settings, including the color assigned to appearance attributes of selected objects on the layer, the layer's editability, and more. The following is an overview of all the settings in the dialog box:

- **Name** Specifies the name of the layer (or sublayer) that displays in the Layers panel.
- **Color** Indicates the color code of the layer. The color is set by default but can be changed by selecting a different color from the color dropdown menu or by double-clicking the color swatch to the right of the menu to pick a different color.

Template   Converts the selected layer into a nonprinting template layer, which automatically locks and dims the layer's contents.

Lock   When enabled, the contents of the layer cannot be edited. When disabled, the contents are completely editable. Toggles the same lock that displays in the Edit column.

Show   When enabled, the contents of the layer will be displayed on the artboard. When disabled, the layer's contents will be hidden. Toggles the same eye icon in the visibility column.

Print   Determines whether the layer's contents are printable or not. By default, all layers except template layers are printable. Nonprinting layers display the layer name in italics.

Preview   Shows the contents of a layer in full color with both stroke and fill. When disabled, the layer's contents are displayed as outlines.

Dim Images To   Dims the visibility of linked and bitmap images placed on the layer, but does not alter the visibility of any vector art (unless that vector art has been rasterized).

The illustration in Figure 8-2 shows examples of a dimmed bitmap image with additional layers displaying outline and preview modes.

FIGURE 8-2 Layer options

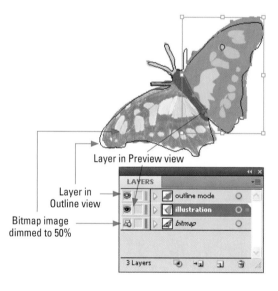

Layer in Preview view

Layer in Outline view

Bitmap image dimmed to 50%

Using the Layers Panel

Using the Layers panel is fairly intuitive; however, there are several buttons and features that warrant a brief explanation. To start, the Layers panel is divided up into several columns of information, as indicated in Figure 8-3, each one performing a slightly different function:

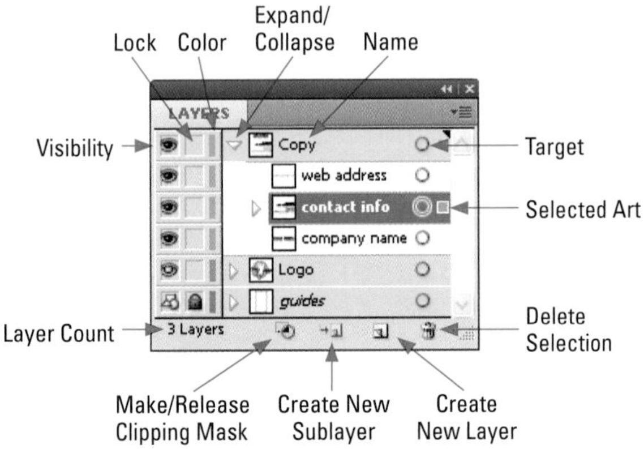

FIGURE 8-3 The Layers panel

- **Visibility column**   Use this column to toggle layer visibility. The eye icon is active by default, meaning the layer's contents are visible on the screen. To hide a layer temporarily, click the eye icon once. To show the layer, click there again. You can also use the following keyboard shortcuts to alter layer visibility:

  - ALT+click (Win) or OPT+click the eye icon to toggle all other layers on and off.

  - CTRL+click (Win) or CMD+click (Mac) the eye icon to toggle the layer's contents between Preview and Outline mode. In Outline mode, the eye icon appears hollow (refer to Figure 8-3).

  - CTRL+ALT+click (Win) or CMD+OPT+click (Mac) the eye icon to toggle all but the selected layer to Outline mode.

- **Lock column**   Use this column to toggle between locking and unlocking the editability of the layer's contents. When empty, the contents of the layer are fully editable, and when displaying a lock icon, the layer becomes temporarily uneditable.

- **Color column**   This column indicates the color being used to highlight selections on the layer, including the bounding boxes, paths, and anchor points. Each layer uses a color from the dropdown menu, in the order they appear. For example, Layer 1 is always light blue, Layer 2 is red, Layer 3 is green, and so forth. However you can choose a different color, if desired, in the Layer Options dialog box.

- **Expand/Collapse column**   This column displays a small gray triangle that indicates whether the layer is expanded or collapsed. A right-facing arrow designates collapsed mode, and a down-facing arrow indicates expanded mode.

■ **Name column**   Use this column to give each layer a unique name. To change the name of a layer, double-click the layer to bring up the Layer Options dialog box, where you can type in a custom name.

■ **Target column**   Use the target icon in this column to quickly select everything on a particular layer, sublayer, group, or path. When selected, the target icon displays with a double ring (like a donut).

■ **Selection column**   The Selection indicator (selected art) column serves two functions. First, it shows when a layer, sublayer, object, or group is selected. You can tell a layer is selected when the layer is shaded a different color than the other layers and/or when a tiny black triangle appears at the top right edge of the layer (see Figure 8-3). Second, when a layer, a sublayer of a layer, or an object on a layer or sublayer is selected, a small colored square appears in this column. The color of the selection indicator square matches the color shown in the Color column, indicating the color used for that layer's selections.

You can modify any of the column settings for any layer at any time. For example, you might decide to lock layers after you're finished working on them to help ensure you don't accidentally move their contents when editing objects on other layers. You may also want to place different versions of projects on separate layers and then modify the visibility of those layers to help determine which version is best. The possibilities are endless!

Layers Panel Buttons

Along the bottom of the Layers panel are several buttons (refer again to Fig 8-3) to help you quickly create new layers and sublayers, create and release layer masks, and delete selections. There's also a handy layer count indicator along the left, so you can see at a glance the number of layers in your file. Here's what each of the buttons does:

■ **Make/Release Clipping Mask**   Creates clipping masks from any two or more selected overlapping objects, and releases objects contained within a selected clipping mask. See Chapter 16 to learn about clipping masks.

- **Create New Sublayer**   Adds a sublayer inside of the selected layer or sublayer. Each new sublayer is capable of displaying additional sublayers, paths, and groups. Sublayers are indented to help identify them quickly.

- **Create New Layer**   Adds a new layer above the selected layer. To make a duplicate of an existing layer and all of its contents, drag that layer onto the Create New Layer icon and the duplicate layer will be added above that layer, without altering the original.

- **Delete Selection**   Deletes any selected layer, sublayer, path, or group. When art is on the layer or sublayer, a warning dialog box appears giving you a chance to cancel or proceed with the deletion. You may also drag and drop items from the Layers panel directly into the mini trash to delete them without having to see the warning dialog box.

The Layers Panel Options Menu

In addition to all the buttons and settings on the Layers panel, there are also more than 20 commands available in the Layers panel options menu.

The following gives a quick overview of each of the options in the menu:

- **New Layer**   Creates a new layer directly above the currently selected layer.

When you ALT+click (Win) or OPT+click (Mac) the options menu icon, the first item reads New Layer Above "Layer Name." When you CTRL+click (Win) or CMD+click (Mac) the options menu icon, the first item reads New Top Layer.

- **New Sublayer**   Creates a sublayer within the currently selected layer.

- **Duplicate "Layer Name"**   Creates a duplicate of the currently selected layer.

- **Delete "Layer Name"**   Deletes the currently selected layer and all of its contents.

- **Options for "Layer Name"**   Opens the Layer Options dialog box for the selected layer.

- **Make/Release Clipping Mask**   Creates or releases a clipping mask from two or more selected objects.

- **Enter/Exit Isolation Mode**   Enters or exits Isolation Mode when a grouped object or layer is selected on the artboard or through the Layers panel.

- **Locate Object**   Helps locate a corresponding item in the Layers panel when the object is selected in the Document window and can be helpful in locating items in collapsed layers.

- **Merge Selected**   Merges all artwork within selected layers or groups into a single layer. CTRL+click (Win) or CMD+click (Mac) to select multiple layers or groups and merge them into the last selected layer or group. Does not merge objects or preserve clipping masks or other layer-level attributes.

- **Flatten Artwork**   Moves artwork inside all visible layers into a single layer, and provides the option of discarding or keeping artwork on hidden layers. Does not, however, preserve clipping masks or other layer-level attributes.

- **Collect In New layer**   Moves selected objects on the artboard to a new layer.

- **Release To Layers (Sequence)**   Moves each object on a selected layer to its own separate layer, as illustrated in Figure 8-4.

- **Release To Layers (Build)**   Moves each object on a selected layer to its own layer *and* duplicates objects to create a cumulative animation sequence, as shown in Figure 8-5.

- **Reverse Order**   Reverses the stacking order of layers, sublayers, or paths selected within the Layers panel.

FIGURE 8-4 Release to Layers (Sequence) puts each object on a separate layer

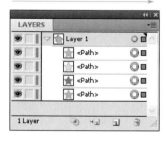

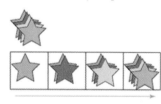

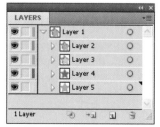

FIGURE 8-5 Release to Layers (Build) creates a cumulative animation sequence

- **Template**   Creates a template layer, which automatically locks and dims the layer's contents and hides the layer's contents when the file is printed.

- **Show All Layers/Hide Others**   Toggles the visibility of all but the selected layer.

- **Preview All Layers/Outline Others**   Toggles the view mode of all but the selected layer from Preview to Outline view. In Outline view, the eye icon becomes hollow to differentiate it from the solid eye icon shown in Preview view.

- **Unlock All Layers/Lock Others**   Toggles between locking or unlocking the editability of all but the selected layer.

- **Paste Remembers Layers**   This option will determine where copied artwork will be placed when pasted back into a file, or pasted into another file. By default, this option is disabled, which allows copied items to be pasted into the currently active layer in the Layers panel. When enabled, copied items are pasted back into the original layer of origin. Also, when this layer is turned on, items copied from multiple layers in one file will retain their multilayer structure when pasted inside of another file.

- **Panel Options**   Opens the Layers Panel Options dialog box for adjusting the row size and thumbnail visibility of a selected layer.

To watch an informative video on creating and using Layers, go to www.adobe.com/designcenter/video_workshop/?id=vid0041.

Making a Template Layer

A template layer is a special layer used for tracing different kinds of artwork in Illustrator, such as hand-drawn logos, clippings from a magazine, or technical drawings created in another application. A template can help ensure that you create consistent angles and proportions in your work, and otherwise guide you to create something greater than you could have done without it.

Template layers are set to display with dimmed visibility and locked editability, so you can see through the artwork to trace it but not edit the layer's contents. Template layers are also set not to print, so you won't accidentally print a template layer along with the artwork created from it.

To create a template layer, place the artwork you'd like to trace into a blank layer by choosing File | Place and navigating to the artwork file. Any kind of *bitmap* artwork (sometimes referred to as *raster* artwork) can be placed in the layer. To use vector artwork, select and rasterize the artwork by going to Object | Rasterize before converting the layer into a template layer. Double-click the layer with the placed file to open the Layer Options dialog box. Name the layer (optional) and select the Template option. This grays out the Show, Preview, Lock, and Print options, leaving only the Template and Dim settings. If desired, edit the value in the Dim Images to: % field. The default number is 50%, which is suitable for most tracings. The higher the number the darker the template; the lower the number, the lighter the template. Figure 8-6 shows a placed image before and after dimming. Click OK to apply the changes.

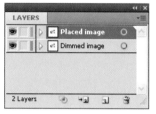

FIGURE 8-6 A placed image before (left) and after (right) dimming with template settings

Template layers display a little differently than regular layers in the Layers panel, making them easy to identify at a glance. Specifically, the name of a template layer is italicized, by default, a lock icon appears in the edit column—but this lock can be toggled off if you need to do so, and instead of the eye icon in the visibility column, a template icon displays there (see Figure 8-7).

FIGURE 8-7 An image traced on top of a template layer

Tracing Artwork

Once your artwork is placed and locked down as a template layer, if necessary, create a new layer above the template layer and start tracing the image manually using any combination of the Pen and Pencil family of tools, and then refine the path using the Direct Selection tool to smooth out curves, adjust angles, and reposition anchor points and paths, as I've done with the frog illustration in Figure 8-7. Alternately, if you happen to be using a graphics-tablet stylus, you may get better results by tracing the original directly on the tablet rather than tracing onscreen. For even more accurate and precise tracing results than hand tracing, however, you may prefer using the automatic Live Trace command, which is described in full detail in Chapter 20.

 Another method for tracing placed artwork, rather than using a template and tracing on top of it, is to use the Live Trace tool. Turn to Chapter 19 to learn more about working with Live Trace.

Reorganizing Layers

Layers, sublayers, paths, and groups can be easily arranged and rearranged to suit your needs. A few different methods can be used—the most simple of which is the drag and drop technique, described in the following subsection.

Dragging and Dropping

Inside the Layers panel, select the layer, sublayer, path, or group you want to relocate. Then, drag and drop the selected layer, sublayer, path, or group into the new position inside the Layers panel.

Collect In New Layer

Another method for reorganizing layers is to use a command from the Layers panel options menu. Select the object(s) you'd like to move to a new layer. Choose Collect In New Layer from the Layers panel options menu. The objects are then placed inside a generically named new layer (such as Layer 8) directly above the previously selected layer.

Send To Current Layer

To move objects from one layer to another, use a command from the Object menu. Select the object(s) to be moved, click the layer you'd like the object(s) moved to, and select Object | Arrange | Send To Current Layer.

Selection Indicator Drag and Drop

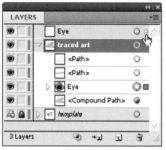

Alternatively, you can also move objects using a version of the drag and drop method that involves dragging a layer's selection square. Select the object(s) to be moved. This activates the colored selection indicator square in the Selection indicator column of the selected object(s) layer. Next, drag and drop this color selection indicator square to another layer to move the selected objects to that layer, as illustrated in the example in Figure 8-8.

FIGURE 8-8 Moving a selected object to another layer

Targeting a Layer

In addition to the four methods described above for moving objects through the Layers panel, you can also adjust the position of any layer, sublayer, path, or group using the Target method. The Target column of the Layers panel provides a visual cue when one or more items on that layer, sublayer, path, or group are selected, or *targeted*, by displaying a double ring icon (looks like a donut) instead of the single ring icon, which displays when no items on a layer are selected. Figure 8-9 shows examples of both targeted and untargeted layers.

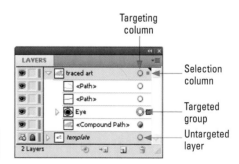

FIGURE 8-9 Targeting a layer

To select an entire layer, sublayer, path, or group, click the corresponding target icon. Technically, items are considered targeted when selected by any method; however, a layer can only be targeted by clicking the target icon in the Layers panel. Once the layer, sublayer, path, or group is selected, the objects within the selection can be edited or manipulated as desired. The following are some things you might do with a targeted selection:

- Move the layer, sublayer, path, or group to a new position within the layers panel or to a new location on the artboard.
- Group the items in the selection.
- Transform (scale, rotate, skew, reflect, distort, and so on) the items in the selection.
- Edit the colors of the items' strokes and fills.
- Enter Isolation Mode to edit just the targeted items.

When you're finished making modifications to the targeted items, click away from the selection on the artboard to deselect everything.

PART II

The Basics and Beyond

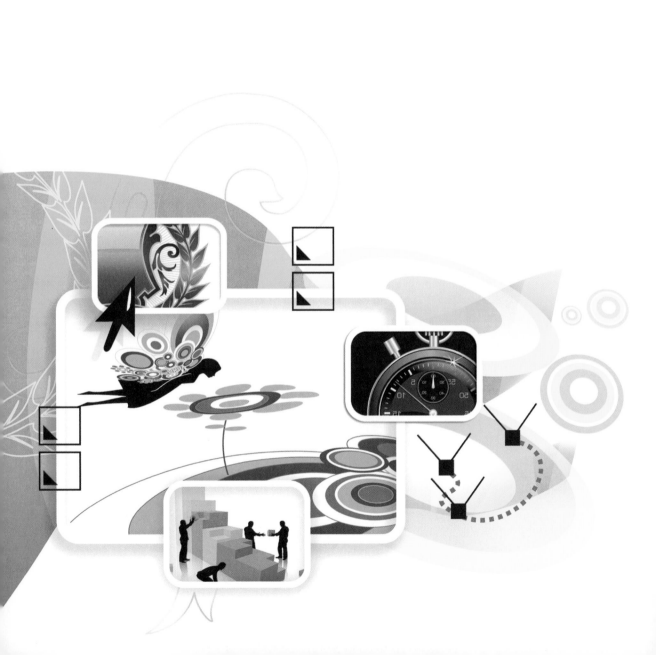

9
Colors, Swatches, and Adobe Kuler

How to...

- Work with the Color, Color Guide, and Swatches panels
- Select color from the Color Picker dialog box
- Use the Swatches panel to create swatches and apply color
- Apply colors from the Pantone color books
- Use Illustrator's built-in color libraries
- Access Adobe's online Kuler service

Working with color can be an exciting and rewarding way to spruce up your illustrations and designs. In Chapter 3, you discovered that it's fairly easy to apply color to the stroke and fill of your objects. In this chapter, you'll learn all the details about working with Illustrator's various color panels, namely the Color, Color Guide, and Swatches panels, as well as how to access and use the Pantone and other color books, use the Color Picker dialog box, and open up Adobe's new *Kuler* (pronounced "color") extension panel, which links you directly to the Adobe Kuler web site where you can interact with the Kuler community to exchange color themes for your projects.

The Color Panel

As you may recall from Chapter 2, when you create a new document in Illustrator, you are prompted to choose a color space, such as CMYK for print projects and RGB for onscreen and web projects.

If you accidentally select the wrong color space when creating your new document, or if you discover you need to change it after you've started to work, you can switch color modes by choosing File | Document Color Mode | CMYK Color or RGB Color.

The color space (or color mode) of your document sets the stage for working with color in that file, and typically the colors appearing in the Color panel will reflect that. For example, when working in a file for a Print project in CMYK mode, the Color panel (as seen in Figure 9-1) will display CMYK sliders that can be adjusted to mix colors with specific color values, such as a deep leafy green with the CMYK values of C=39.61%, M=9.02%, Y=100%, K=22%.

When using the Color panel, keep in mind that as you adjust the color values, you will only be modifying either the Fill or the Stroke color, whichever one happens to be the active setting. You can see which one is active by looking at the Fill and Stroke icons at the bottom of the Tools panel or in the Color panel. If the Fill is active (as in Figure 9-1), it will be on top of the Stroke, and when the Stroke is active, it will appear to be on top of the Fill.

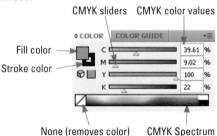

CMYK sliders   CMYK color values

Fill color

Stroke color

None (removes color)   CMYK Spectrum

FIGURE 9-1 The Color panel displaying CMYK values

Changing Color Modes

For best color accuracy when selecting and using colors in your work, try to stick with the one color mode that matches your project. At times, however, you may want or need to alter the color space for individual objects. In those cases, you can use the options menu on the Color panel to select colors from different color modes:

- **Grayscale** This color mode uses a scale from pure white (0%) to pure black (100%). Switch to grayscale mode to convert color objects to black-and-white artwork, or turn grayscale artwork into RGB or CMYK. You could also mix grayscale color using the K channel of CMYK, or the RGB channels in RGB mode so long as you know the correct values, such as R=128, G=128, B=128 for a medium gray.

- **RGB** Red, green, and blue (RGB) are additive colors representing light ranging from 0 (for black) to 255 (for white) that is reflected back to your eyes. When combined, these three colors of reflected light create white light. RGB is the color mode for computer monitors, TV screens, and stage/theatrical lighting.

- **HSB**   Hue, saturation, and brightness (HSB) is the color mode based on our human perception of color. Hue represents the color reflected from or through objects and can be identified by a color name like green or yellow. Saturation (or *chroma*) refers to the strength of a color relative to the amount of gray added to the color proportionate to the hue, from 0%–100%. Brightness is the lightness or darkness of a color from 0% (black) to 100% (white). You'll probably never use this setting.

- **CMYK**   Cyan, magenta, yellow, and black (CMYK) are subtractive colors representing ink pigments from 0% (no saturation) to 100% (full saturation) that are used to reproduce colors in print. (That's where you get the term "four-color process.") While it is possible to combine cyan, magenta, and yellow to obtain a resulting color that is a dark murky gray-black, the color will still lack a necessary density required for a pure black. To compensate for this dullness, a separate black ink (K) is added to the printing process to ensure that the black within your projects prints out nice, dark, and dense as well as adding another component that helps in the mixing process for a wider array of other colors in the spectrum.

- **Web-Safe RGB**   This color mode includes only the 216 RGB cross-platform colors that can be accurately represented on the Web when viewing them on 8-bit monitors. As most systems today use 16-bit or 32-bit displays, however, many designers believe that using the web-safe palette is no longer necessary.

Did You Know?

Working Accurately with Color

Be aware that your computer monitor represents color as RGB, while your printed projects will be using combinations of CMYK inks. This means that some of the colors you see on your screen cannot be reproduced by inks, and some colors you can print cannot be displayed on your monitor. When a color can be produced in one color space but cannot be reproduced in another, we refer to that color as being *"out of gamut."* In other words, the selected color is out of the range of possible colors within the selected color mode. More on that a little later in the chapter.

Drag and Drop to Create Swatches and Modify Objects

You can drag and drop color directly from the Stroke or Fill icons in the Color panel into the Swatches panel to create new swatches. You can also drag and drop color onto any object in your document—whether that object is selected or not—to modify that object's stroke or fill, whichever icon is set to active.

Applying Color from the Color Panel

To mix and apply a specific color to one or more objects, select the object(s) and then adjust the Color panel sliders. As you change the color values, the color of your selection's stroke or fill automatically updates (whichever icon is active in the Tools panel or Color panel). You can also mix colors in the Color panel independent of a selection on the artboard and then save those colors as swatches in your Swatches panel for later use.

To mix a color and save it as a swatch, the first thing you'll need to do is adjust the sliders on the Color panel until you create the desired color. If the Color panel sliders are showing a different color mode that you'd like to be using, select the desired color mode from the Color panel options menu. Next, select Create New Swatch from the Color panel options menu. In the New Swatch dialog box that opens, give your new color a customized name, select Process Color or Spot Color from the Color Type menu, choose a Color Mode from the Color Mode menu if needed, and if creating a Process color, click the Global checkbox to make the color global or leave it unchecked to keep it non-global (see the "Types of Swatches" section later in this chapter for a definition of global versus non-global). Click the OK button, and your new swatch is added to the Swatches panel for later use.

The Color Picker

The Color Picker dialog box is a great color selection tool because it provides you with a view of the color spectrum, making it easy to isolate the hue, saturation, and brightness of the color you want to select and use. In addition to selecting

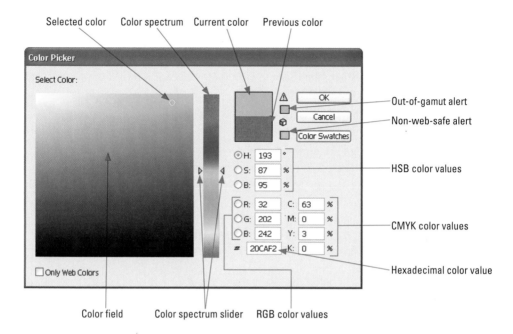

Selected color   Color spectrum   Current color   Previous color

Out-of-gamut alert

Non-web-safe alert

HSB color values

CMYK color values

Hexadecimal color value

Color field   Color spectrum slider   RGB color values

FIGURE 9-2 The Color Picker dialog box

color, you can also preview colors by hue, saturation, brightness, red, green, or blue color spectrums or by a limited web palette; input precise HSB, RGB, CMYK, and Hexadecimal values; and toggle between viewing a spectrum of colors and the swatches appearing in your document's Swatches panel.

Take a look at the Color Picker in Figure 9-2 to familiarize yourself with all the settings. To open and use the Color Picker, double-click the Stroke or Fill icons in the Tools panel or on the Color panel.

Follow these general guidelines to preview and select color with the Color Picker:

- To select a color, adjust the color spectrum sliders and then click or drag somewhere inside the color field. The location of the hollow circle inside the color field determines the color you have selected.

- To adjust the preview of the color spectrum, select one of the H (hue), S (saturation), B (brightness), or R (red), G (green), B (blue) radio buttons. If you're unsure which is best for selecting colors, use the default Hue option.

- To mix an RGB color, enter a number from 0 to 255 in the R, G, and B input fields.

- To mix a CMYK color, enter a percentage from 0%–100% in the C, M, Y, and K input fields.

- To mix a Hexadecimal (web) color, enter the three RRGGBB number/letter pairs, such as 000000 for black, C655C6 for violet, or FF9933 for orange.

- To select a color from the open document's Swatches panel, click the Color Swatches button.

- To return to viewing the Color Picker after clicking the Color Swatches button to view swatches, click the Color Models button.

- To choose a Web-safe color, click the Only Web Colors checkbox and the color field will be restricted to showing only the 216 cross-platform Web-safe color palette.

After selecting a color, the selected color will appear to the right of the color spectrum, directly above the previously selected color. To use the new color and have it replace the currently active stroke or fill, click OK. Otherwise, click Cancel to close the dialog box.

The Out-of-Gamut Alert Triangle

Some RGB and HSB colors inside the Color Picker and Edit Colors dialog boxes cannot be printed with CMYK ink, even though they can appear on your RGB computer monitor. When this happens, Illustrator will display the yellow *out-of-gamut color alert triangle* next to the selected color. When you see this warning icon and your document is a CMYK print project, click the warning icon and Illustrator will automatically shift the selected color to the closest CMYK equivalent that can be printed.

The Non-Web-Safe Alert Cube

The Web-safe palette consists of the 216 RGB common colors that can be accurately represented on both the Mac and PC platforms with 8-bit monitors. While technically there are 256 colors that can be displayed on an 8-bit monitor, 40 of those colors differ from Mac to PC, so the remaining 216 colors make up the Web-safe palette. While working with the Web-safe palette is no longer critical for web projects, you may occasionally still need to use it. For fastest Web-safe color selection, click the Only Web Colors checkbox at the bottom of the dialog box. Otherwise, when you select a color in the Color Picker that falls outside of this Web-safe palette, the gray *non-web-safe alert cube* appears next to the Previous Color area (refer to Figure 9-3). To have Illustrator shift and select the closest Web-safe color, click the non-web-safe alert cube. The non-Web-safe alert cube also appears in the Color panel directly below the Stroke and Fill icons, and the Edit Colors dialog box, which you'll learn about next.

The Color Guide Panel

The Color Guide panel, as shown in Figure 9-3, is a really amazing color aid because it uses a harmony rules algorithm to select colors and create *color groups* based on the first, or *base*, color you choose. A color group is a group of four or more colors that are in harmony with one another. Once created, you can easily add these color groups to your Swatches panel for later use. In addition, for each color group you create, Illustrator suggests alternates to it using variations of tints/ shades, warm/cool, and vivid/muted colors.

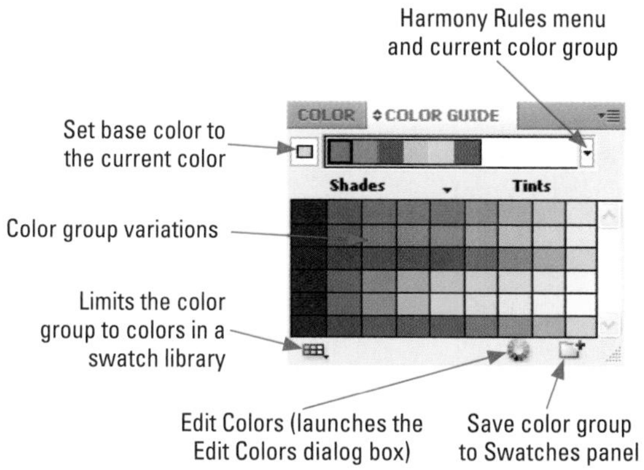

Harmony Rules menu and current color group

Set base color to the current color

Color group variations

Limits the color group to colors in a swatch library

Edit Colors (launches the Edit Colors dialog box)

Save color group to Swatches panel

FIGURE 9-3 Create color groups with the Color Guide panel

The Color Guide works like an enhanced Swatches panel, allowing you to select and apply color to selected objects on your artboard. To set the base color in the panel, select an object and apply a color to that object's stroke or fill, whichever is active in the Tools panel or Color panel. Then, to preview and select color group harmonies using your base color, access the Harmonies Rules dropdown menu. After selecting a new color group, the Color Group variations list updates. To apply a single color from the Color Group variations list to a selected object's stroke or fill, click that color's swatch. Or, to save any of the individual swatches in any of the groups for later use, drag and drop those colors into your Swatches panel. You can also save the active color group (appearing on the Harmony Rules menu) to your Swatches panel by clicking the Save Color Group To Swatch Panel icon or choosing Save Colors As Swatches from the Color Guide panel's options menu.

To learn more about the Color Guide panel and watch a video on creating color harmonies, visit www.adobe.com/go/vid0058.

The Edit Colors Dialog Box

The Edit Colors dialog box (which also goes by the name of Recolor Artwork), shown in Figure 9-4, provides a variety of tools for creating and editing your own color harmony groups. You can also use this dialog box to recolor selected artwork and reduce the colors appearing in your work based on a selected color swatch library.

To launch the Edit Colors dialog box, click the Edit Colors button on the Color Guide panel. You can also open it by selecting two or more objects on your artboard and clicking the Recolor Artwork button on the Control panel, or by double-clicking any of the color group icons in the Swatches panel. Once open, the dialog box has three areas you can work with, depending on your task:

- **Edit** The Edit Colors tab allows you to mix your own colors and alter existing color groups. Play around with the Harmony Rules menu and the color wheel to come up with new color harmonies, and feel free to adjust the color bars and color markers (those circles) within the color wheel by clicking and dragging them. You can also add/subtract colors, change the brightness of the color wheel, save color groups for later use, unlink harmony colors to adjust colors independently (by clicking the Unlink Harmony Colors icon), and preview color changes to selected art (when the Recolor Art checkbox is enabled) before accepting or rejecting the new colors.

- **Assign** The Assign Colors tab lets you select and modify colors from an existing color group and apply them to any selected object(s) on your artboard. Here you can also retain spot colors and reduce the number of colors used in your selected art.

- **Color Groups** This area lists all of the color groups in your open document. You can add, subtract, and modify any existing color group in the list, and these changes will be automatically updated in the Swatches panel. Click the New Color Group button to add a new group to the list, click the Save Changes To Color Group button to save modifications to an existing color group, and click the Delete Color Group button to remove a selected color group from the list.

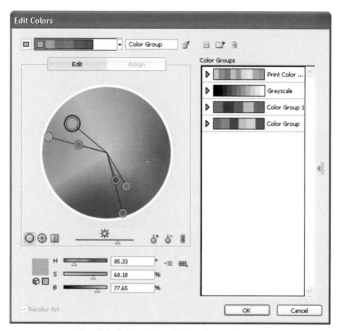

The Edit Colors tab and Color Groups listing

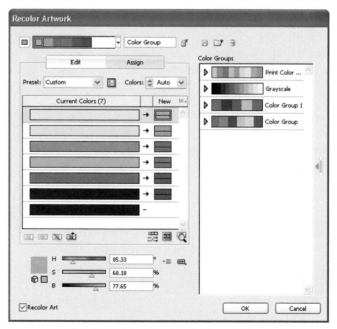

FIGURE 9-4 Create and edit harmony groups with the Edit Colors dialog box

The Assign Colors tab and Color Groups listing

Within each tab there are several buttons and sliders that can further assist you in creating and editing color harmonies. Illustrator identifies each setting with helpful screen tips when you hover your mouse over them so you can quickly grasp the concepts of how each one modifies how color is displayed and how it can be edited.

Tip To learn more about the Edit Colors panel and watch a video about the features of this dialog box, visit www.adobe.com/go/vid0059.

The Swatches Panel

The Swatches panel is where all the colors, gradients, and patterns for your document are stored along with the other file information. This area is fully editable and customizable within each document, giving you ultimate flexibility when working with color. For instance, you can create a limited palette so only colors being used in the file are displayed, or you can construct your own swatch library specific to a particular project or client and then open and use that custom swatch library any time you need it.

The Swatches panel shown in Figure 9-5 has several buttons, options, and menu features:

FIGURE 9-5 The Swatches panel displays all the colors, gradients, and patterns available and/or used in your document

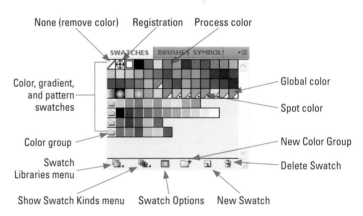

- **Swatch Libraries menu** Provides access to the Swatch Libraries.

- **Show Swatch Kinds menu** Lets you adjust the view of swatches within the panel by kind, such as color, gradient, pattern, or color groups.

- **Swatch Options** Opens the Swatch Options dialog box so you can edit a swatch's name, color type, global setting, color mode, and color values.

- **Edit or Apply Color Group** (Only appears when a color group is selected.) Launches the Edit Colors dialog box.

- **New Color Group**   Creates a new color group based on the colors of a selected object, or creates an empty group folder inside which you may add your own color swatches.
- **New Swatch**   Launches the New Swatch dialog box to create a new swatch in the Swatches panel based on the active color (either stroke or fill) in the Tools panel.
- **Delete Swatch**   Deletes the selected swatch, swatches, or color groups in the Swatches panel. Use the SHIFT+click method to add or subtract from your selection before deleting, or to quickly select all unused swatches, choose Select All Unused from the panel's options menu and then click Delete Swatch.

Applying Color

Use the Swatches panel to apply colors to objects on your artboard by either selecting one or more objects, and then selecting a swatch, or by dragging and dropping a swatch directly onto any object, whether that object is selected or not. The chosen swatch will automatically alter the selection's stroke or fill, whichever is active in the Tools panel.

Types of Swatches

In commercial printing, there are two types of inks used: *spot* and *process*. These colors can be combined in any project, though typically most jobs tend to be either 100 percent process or process plus one or two spot colors, for printing parts of a job like a logo and possibly adding a spot color printing plate for applying varnish over parts of a four-color process document. All spot colors are *global* colors, but process colors can be global or non-global.

Spot Colors

Spot colors are premixed inks that are used instead of, or in addition to, CMYK process inks, and therefore require their own plates during the printing process. Spot colors are more reliable than CMYK process colors because they use a specific mix of inks. They are, however, more expensive to use, and total color accuracy is not guaranteed from one production run to another because of variables like paper and ink quality. Nonetheless, they are more precise than CMYK process inks alone. For the most consistent color accuracy, consider selecting spot colors from one of the color-matching system libraries, such as Pantone (described in the following section).

Process Colors

Process colors are created by mixing some combination of cyan, magenta, yellow, and black inks. Four-color process printing is the least expensive type of printing process and while it is really good for reproducing photographs in color, it also has the greatest likelihood of displaying color shifts from one print run to another. Because your monitor displays color in RGB, for greatest color accuracy, consider referring to process color reference charts for color values before applying those colors to objects in your document.

Global Colors

Global color refers to a color that is linked to its swatch and all instances of its use. All spot colors are automatically global, but process colors can either be global or non-global. When you modify the color values in a global process color, all instances of that color in your artwork will update automatically. By contrast, with non-global colors, when the color values of a swatch are modified, only the swatch itself updates and all instances of the original color remain intact.

Creating a New Swatch

To create a spot, process, or global process color, mix a color in the Colors panel or select a color from the Color Picker dialog box and then click the New Swatch button on the Swatches panel. When the New Swatch dialog box opens, give your new color a name, select Process Color or Spot Color from the Color Type menu, choose a Color Mode from the Color Mode menu, and if creating a process color, decide whether that color will be global or non-global. Click the OK button to close the dialog box and add your new swatch to the Swatches panel. If at any time you need to adjust the properties of that color, double-click the swatch to reopen the Swatch Options dialog box.

Convert Global and Spot Colors

To convert a process global or spot color into a process non-global or CMYK color, click the little square Process Color (or Spot Color) or CMYK buttons on the Color panel below the Tint slider. When the color you're converting is a process color, you'll see the Process Color button, and when the color you're converting is a spot color, you'll see the Spot Color button.

You can easily identify the different swatch types in the Swatches panel by how the swatch squares are displayed. Process colors display as solid squares of color; global colors are shown as solid squares with a white triangle in the lower left corner; and spot colors are like global colors but with a black dot in the center of the white triangle. (Refer to Figure 9-5.)

 To learn how to use the Swatches panel to work with patterns and gradients, turn to Chapter 12.

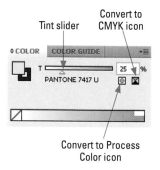

Convert to
Tint slider   CMYK icon

Convert to Process
Color icon

FIGURE 9-6 Adjust the Tint slider to create a tint of any process global or spot color

Creating a Tint of a Color

To create and use a *tint* from any process global or spot color in your Swatches panel, select an object using that color, or select that color from the Swatches panel, and then drag the Tint slider on the Color panel, as shown in Figure 9-6, to adjust the tint range from 0% to 100%. For example, a 25% tint allows only 25% of the ink to pass through a line screen, resulting in a much lighter version of the fully saturated color swatch. If desired, you can save a tint as its own swatch by clicking the New Swatch button on the Swatches panel; that swatch will automatically be named after the original swatch along with the tint percentage, as in Pantone 7417 U 25%.

Swatch Libraries

Illustrator comes preinstalled with several free swatch libraries, each based on different color themes, such as Art History, Earthtone, Metal, Nature, Textiles, and Web. Use these color-themed swatch libraries to assist with applying specific colors to your work.

To access the swatch libraries, click the Swatch Libraries menu button at the bottom of the Swatches panel and select a color theme by name. The colors in that library will then open on your desktop in a free-floating swatches panel, which you can use to apply color to your artwork. You can drag a color from a floating swatch panel into the Swatches panel to add it to your list of available swatches. Feel free to open and close these extra swatch library panels as often as needed.

Pantone and Other Color Books

One important section of the Swatch Libraries menu is entirely devoted to ink color books, like Pantone®, HKS, Trumatch, and Toyo, giving you the option of selecting very specific (and expensive!) spot colors for your print projects.

To access these color books, select Open Swatch Libraries | Color Books from the Swatches panel options menu and select the desired color book from the listing. You can also access the Color Books menu by clicking the Swatch Libraries menu button at the bottom of the Swatches panel.

Like the other swatch libraries, once you select a color book, those colors will open on the desktop inside a floating swatches panel. If you happen to know the number of a color you'd like to use, select Show Find Field from that panel's options menu and enter that number in the Find field. The desired color swatch will come into focus and have a white selection border around it, indicating it is selected and ready for use, as illustrated in Figure 9-7. You may then click the swatch to add it to your Swatches panel for later use.

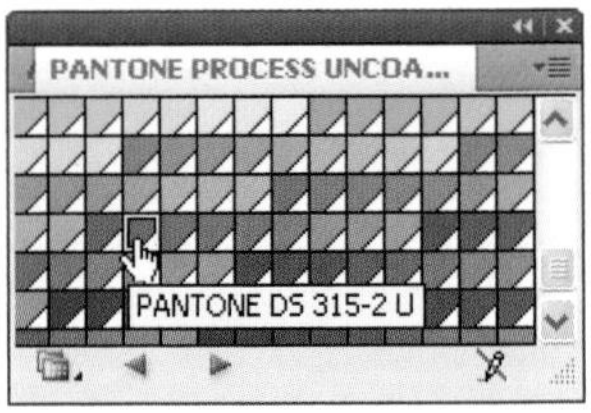

FIGURE 9-7 The selected swatch has a white border

Creating Custom Swatch Libraries

You can easily create and use your own custom swatch libraries for specific projects and clients, and then open up those swatch libraries at any time. To begin, first add, edit, and delete colors in the Swatches panel to your liking. When ready, choose one of the following options from the panel's options menu:

■ **Save Swatch Library As ASE**   Saves your swatch library as an exchangeable file that can be shared with other computers, as well as used in Illustrator, Photoshop, and InDesign.

Only solid colors can be exchanged in this way, so if your swatches include any gradients, patterns, or tints, these will be ignored when opening this file in other programs like Photoshop or InDesign.

■ **Save Swatch Library As AI**   Saves a copy of your swatch library to your computer.

To open and use a custom swatch library, whether ASE or AI, select User Defined from the Swatch Libraries menu at the bottom of the Swatches panel, and choose your custom library by name.

Editing Colors

In addition to all of the color tools mentioned earlier, you can also do some interesting color editing using the color commands through the Edit | Edit Colors menu:

■ **Adjust Color Balance**   This option opens the Adjust Colors dialog box where you can adjust the CMYK, RGB, Grayscale, or Global color values of a selected object's stroke or fill. When you select an object with process global or spot colors, use the dialog box to adjust the Tint slider. You can also convert process global or spot colors into non-global process colors by enabling the Convert option.

■ **Blend Front To Back**   Creates a front-to-back blend from three or more selected filled objects based on stacking order of the objects on the artboard.

■ **Blend Horizontally/Vertically**   Creates a blend from three or more selected filled objects based on stacking order of the objects on the artboard. Select Horizontally to blend objects from left to right or Vertically to blend objects from top to bottom.

■ **Convert to CMYK/Grayscale/RGB**   Converts the colors in your selection from one color mode to another, such as removing color information when switching from RGB to Grayscale, or making grayscale art colorizable by switching from Grayscale to CMYK.

- **Invert Colors**   Inverts the color of the fill or stroke of a selected object, whichever is active in the Tools panel. The inverse color is the opposite color on the color scale and is generally considered a complementary color to the original.

- **Overprint Black**   Select this option to force all black in your file to overprint with black. This setting works only with objects that have black applied to them through the K color channel on the Color panel.

- **Saturate**   Use the Saturate dialog box to increase or decrease the saturation of the selected object's stroke or fill (whichever is active in the Tools panel).

- **Complement**   This option is not accessible through the Edit | Edit Colors menu but rather through the Color panel options menu. When selected, this command converts the fill or stroke of a selected object (whichever is active in the Tools panel) to a complementary color based on the sum of the lowest and highest RGB values of the original color.

Adobe Kuler

Illustrator's *Kuler* (pronounced "color") panel links to Adobe's Kuler web site where you can interact with the Kuler community to exchange color themes for your projects. To use the Kuler panel, select Window | Extensions | Kuler. Before you begin to use Kuler for the first time, you'll be prompted to set up a free account with Adobe.

Once the panel opens and connects with the Kuler web site, you can view color themes by category (Highest Rated, Most Popular, Newest, Random, Saved, and Custom) and time frame (All Time, Last 7 Days, Last 30 Days), as well as search for themes by keyword, tags, title, or creator, by typing in your text in the Search field and pressing ENTER (Win) or RETURN (Mac) on your keyboard. If you find a color theme you'd like to save and use, select it and choose Add To Swatches Panel from the selected theme's flyout menu or click the Add Selected Theme To Swatches button at the bottom of the panel. To view the themes online, select the View Online In Kuler option from the selected theme's flyout menu.

10

Working with Type

How to...

- Add and insert text
- Format type with the Control panel
- Use the Character, Paragraph, and OpenType panels
- Add type to a path or inside a shape
- Use Vertical Type tools
- Wrap text around an object
- Warp type with Envelope Distort
- Fit text with Fit Headline
- Use special Type commands
- Convert fonts to outlines

Illustrator has several different Type tools that let you work freely and creatively with text. In this chapter, you'll discover how to insert, format, and align type; format type with the Control panel; use the Character, Paragraph, and OpenType panels to change the attributes of your text; place type on a path; add type inside a shape; use the Vertical Type tools; make text wrap around objects; warp type using the Envelope Distort command; perform a spell check on your text; insert glyphs; change the case of your text; use Smart Quotes; and convert fonts to outlines.

The Type Tool

When you're ready to add type to your document, you can either *place* a text file into your Illustrator document from another application, or select and use one of the Type tools from the Type Tool flyout menu on the Tools panel.

When any of the Type tools are selected, notice that the Control panel changes to support text formatting, as shown in Figure 10-1. Any word shown in blue underlined type can be clicked to temporarily open that word's corresponding dropdown panel. For instance, click the word Character to view the Character panel. The panel will stay in focus while you use it, and then disappear when you click back to the artboard. Set font characteristics here before adding type to your file, or use the panels to modify existing selected type.

FIGURE 10-1 Apply simple text formatting with the Control panel

In this section, you'll learn about using the Place command to import type, as well as using the Type tool to add Point type and Area type to your files.

Placing Type

To import, or *place*, a text file into your open document, use the File | Place command. When the Place dialog box opens, locate and select the text file you'd like to import and click the Place button. Acceptable file formats for the Place command include .txt, .doc, and rtf. When placing a text file, the Text Import Options dialog box opens, where you can select the encoding platform and choose whether or not to have Illustrator remove extra carriage returns. When placing a Word document (.rtf, .doc, and so on), the Microsoft Word Options dialog box opens, which allows you to choose whether or not to import tables of contents, footnotes, endnotes, and index text, and remove or retain the text formatting.

Your selected text file will then be placed into your document as Area type text, as in the example shown in Figure 10-2. You may then modify the Area type options and format the text as desired. (For more on Area type options, see the "Area Type" section.)

FIGURE 10-2 Placed text is imported as Area type text

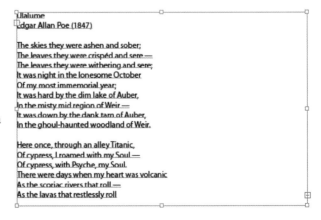

Point Type

Point type, sometimes referred to as the "click and type" method, is the fastest way of adding a word or a line or two of text to your page. To create Point type, select the Type tool from the Tools panel, click the artboard once to set the insertion point (where your text will begin), and start typing. Your type will flow in a single line unless you force a line break by pressing ENTER (Win) or RETURN (Mac) on your keyboard.

Point type can be formatted using any of the tools on the Control panel or in the Character, Paragraph, and OpenType panels. To change the font size of Point type, use the size setting in the Character panel or select the entire text block with the Selection tool and scale it proportionately by holding the SHIFT key while dragging the block by the bounding-box handles.

Area Type

For times when you need to insert a larger block of text or want to ensure that your text sits within a defined space, use the Area type option by creating a text box on your page before you add your type inside it. The box, which can be precisely sized independently of the text within it, holds the type and controls how the type flows within it. You can also set the Area type box to have multiple rows and/or columns, and when more text is in the box than the box can reveal, additional Area type boxes can be added to the page and threaded together so the type flows freely from one box to the next, regardless of where they are positioned on the page.

To create an Area type box, select the Type tool and then click and drag the artboard to create a rectangular shape. When you release your mouse, the type cursor will be inside of the box, ready for you to begin typing. The Area type box can be resized at any time by selecting the box with the Selection tool and dragging it by its bounding-box handles. As the box is adjusted, the type will reflow within it, while the font face, style, size, and other attributes stay as they are.

Like Point type, Area type can also be formatted using any of the tools on the Control panel or in the Character, Paragraph, and OpenType panels. To format the entire Area type box, select the box with the Selection tool before adjusting the formatting. To format a particular word or section within the Area type box, make a selection within the box using the Type tool and then use the Character, Paragraph, and OpenType panels to apply formatting.

Area Type Options

To adjust the width, height, number of rows and columns, gutter size, inset (margin) spacing, first baseline offset (alignment of first line of type within the box), and text flow options in an existing Area type box, select the Area type box with the Selection tool and then double-click the Type tool on the Tools panel to open the Area Type Options dialog box. To preview your changes to the Area type box before accepting them, click the Preview checkbox. When the unit of measure showing in the Area Type Options dialog box is different from the one you want to use, type in the desired number and unit of measure in any of the number fields and Illustrator will convert them. Alternatively, changing the units appearing on your ruler will change the units appearing in the Area Type Options dialog box.

An Area type box need not be rectangular. As illustrated in Figure 10-3, you can adjust the corner anchor point positions of an Area type box by selecting one of its anchor points with the Direct Selection tool and then dragging it into a new position.

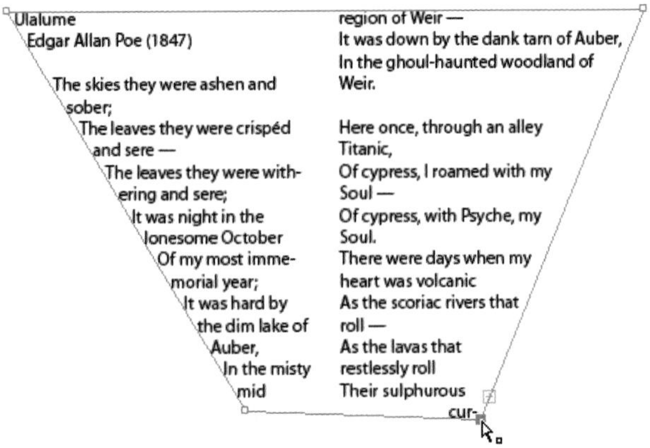

FIGURE 10-3 Reshape Area type boxes with the Direct Selection tool

Ulalume
Edgar Allan Poe (1847)

The skies they were ashen and sober;
The leaves they were crispéd and sere —
The leaves they were withering and sere;
It was night in the lonesome October
Of my most immemorial year;
It was hard by the dim lake of Auber,
In the misty mid

region of Weir —
It was down by the dank tarn of Auber,
In the ghoul-haunted woodland of Weir.

Here once, through an alley Titanic,
Of cypress, I roamed with my Soul —
Of cypress, with Psyche, my Soul.
There were days when my heart was volcanic
As the scoriac rivers that roll —
As the lavas that restlessly roll
Their sulphurous cur-

Threaded Type

If the quantity of type within your Area type box exceeds the dimensions of the box, you'll see a red *overflow text* marker on the Area type box. All Area type shapes contain both an *in port* and an *out port* for linking overflow text. When an out port contains overflow text, it appears as a red box with a red plus sign in the middle. You can thread that text from one Area type box to another, and those Area type boxes can be positioned anywhere on your artboard.

In and out ports appear on the left-top and right-bottom edges of all Area type shapes. For example, in Figure 10-4 you can see an empty in port on the top box, threaded in and out ports with arrows to the other boxes, and an empty out port on the last box.

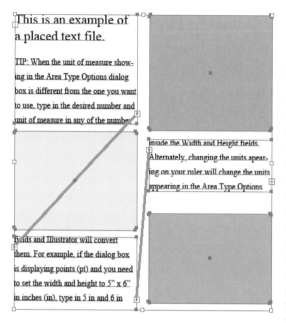

This is an example of
a placed text file.

TIP: When the unit of measure showing in the Area Type Options dialog
box is different from the one you want
to use, type in the desired number and
unit of measure in any of the number

inside the Width and Height fields.
Alternately, changing the units apear-
ing on your ruler will change the units
appearing in the Area Type Options

fields and Illustrator will convert
them. For example, if the dialog box
is displaying points (pt) and you need
to set the width and height to 5" x 6"
in inches (in), type in 5 in and 6 in

FIGURE 10-4 Use the in and out ports on an Area type shape to thread text

To accommodate any overflow type, an Area type box can either be resized using the Selection tool or you may prefer to pick up the overflow type to relocate it to another Area type box. To pick up overflow type, click the red overflow out port icon with the Selection tool. Your cursor will change from a black arrow to what looks like a square corner of a page with text, indicating that the cursor has "picked up" the overflow text. Then, to place the overflow text onto the artboard, either click the artboard once and release your mouse to create a threaded Area type box in the same size as the original, or click and drag to make a new Area type box in the desired size. When you release your mouse, the overflow text will be threaded to that new box. Create as many threaded Area type boxes as needed, and feel free to reposition the boxes at any time by selecting and moving them with the Selection tool.

To remove or break threading between one or more Area type shapes, select an Area type box with the Selection tool and then choose Type | Threaded Text | Release Selection. The text flows into the next object (or reverts to the first object if another object isn't available to the threading). Alternatively, to remove all threading from two or more threaded Area type shapes, select an Area type box and choose Type | Threaded Text | Remove Threading. The text stays in place (within the current Area type shapes) but the threads between these objects are removed. If you want to break threading between two shapes, double-click the in or out port between, and the text flows back into the first object.

Formatting Type

When the Type tool is selected, you can use the limited formatting options on the Control panel to adjust the color of type as well as the type's character, style, size, and alignment. To access the full range of text formatting options, use the Character, Paragraph, and OpenType panels by selecting Window | Type | Character.

The Character Panel

Use the Character panel to adjust the font settings for selected text. The panel displays three types of fonts: Adobe PostScript, TrueType, and OpenType. PostScript fonts are platform-specific and require two files to display and print them, while TrueType and OpenType fonts only need a single file to render the fonts onscreen and in print and can either be platform-specific or platform-independent. OpenType fonts also tend to have a lot more special characters than TrueType and Postscript fonts.

When you open the Character panel, be sure to click the panel's double arrows (next to the panel tab) to view all the options inside it, as shown in Figure 10-5.

The following is an overview of all the Character panel's settings:

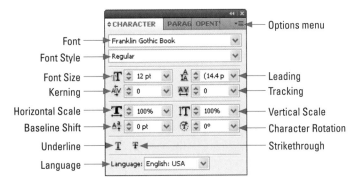

FIGURE 10-5 Use the Character panel to edit font settings

- **Font** Use the Font menu to select a font family from a list of available fonts on your computer.

- **Font Style** Select a font style. Styles are font-specific. Options may include Regular, Bold, Italic, Bold Italic, Semibold, Semibold Italic, Black, Roman, Light, and more.

- **Font Size** Choose one of the preset point sizes from the Size menu or type in your own custom size in the Font Size field.

- **Leading** The leading, or the space between the baseline of one line of type and the baseline of another, is set to 120% of the selected font size, such as 14.4pt leading for a 12pt font. You can adjust this number up or down using the preset sizes in the Leading menu, or type in your own number, positive or negative, in the Leading number field.

- **Kerning** Kerning refers to the space between any two character pairs, such as the space between the T and o in the word Together. To adjust the spacing between any two letters, place your Type cursor between those letters, and either choose a preset number from the Kerning menu or input your own positive or negative number in the Kerning number field.

 Tip You can also adjust the kerning by pressing and holding the ALT (Win) or OPTION (Mac) key, and then pressing the LEFT and RIGHT ARROW keys on your keyboard to increase or decrease the space.

- **Tracking**   The Tracking option uniformly increases or decreases the space between letters and words within any selected block of text. Adjust the tracking with the preset sizes from the menu, or input your own positive or negative number in this field.

- **Vertical Scale**   To increase or decrease the vertical scale of selected type, select a number from the Vertical Scale menu or type your own number in this field.

- **Horizontal Scale**   To increase or decrease the horizontal scale of selected type, select a number from the Horizontal Scale menu or type your own number in this field.

- **Baseline Shift**   Use the baseline shift option to create superscript or subscript characters, like the rd in 3rd or the number 23 in a footnote$_{23}$. After applying the baseline shift, be sure to also reduce the size of the characters.

- **Character Rotation**   Rotates selected text by the number of degrees from 180° to –180° in from the rotation menu. Use any of the presets or input your own number.

- **Underline**   Adds an underline to selected type.

- **Strikethrough**   Adds a strikethrough line to selected type.

- **Language**   Adjust the "proximity language dictionary" for spelling and hyphenation of selected text. By default, the language setting in the United States is English:USA.

- **Options Menu**   Additional character settings, such as Standard Vertical Roman Alignment, All Caps, Small Caps, Fractional Widths, System Layout, and No Break, are offered through the panel's Options menu.

The Paragraph Panel

When you're ready to adjust paragraph settings, open the Paragraph panel, seen in Figure 10-6, by selecting Window | Type | Paragraph. Use the panel to set the alignment, justification, indent, and spacing before or after paragraphs:

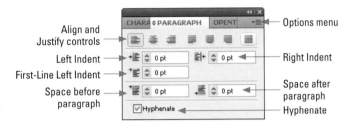

FIGURE 10-6 Adjust paragraph settings with the Paragraph panel

- **Alignment and Justification**   Set the alignment or justification for selected text. Choose Align Left, Align Center, Align Right, Justify With Last Line Aligned Left, Justify With Last Line Aligned Center, Justify With Last Line Aligned Right, or Justify All Lines.

- **Left Indent**   Indents the entire left edge of selected text based on the positive or negative point number entered, such as 2 pt or –10 pt.

- **Right Indent**   Indents the entire right edge of selected text based on the positive or negative point number entered, such as 5 pt or –4 pt.

- **First-line Left Indent**   Adds a first-line indent to the first line of each paragraph.

- **Space Before Paragraph**   Adds extra space between paragraphs directly above the first line of type in each paragraph.

- **Space After Paragraph**   Adds extra space between paragraphs directly below the last line of type in each paragraph.

- **Hyphenate**   When enabled, default hyphenation rules apply. You can adjust these rules in the panel's Options menu.

- **Options menu**   Additional paragraph settings are offered through the panel's Options menu:

  - **Roman Hanging Punctuation**   When on, forces punctuation marks to align outside (either 100% or 50%, depending on the punctuation mark) of the margins of the area type container, as illustrated in Figure 10-7.

"Everyone will be famous for 15 minutes."
—Andy Warhol

"Everyone will be famous for 15 minutes."
—Andy Warhol

FIGURE 10-7 Roman Hanging Punctuation off (top) and on (bottom)

- **Justification**   Use this dialog box to adjust the default justification rules.
- **Hyphenation**   Use this dialog box to adjust the default hyphenation rules.
- **Adobe Single-line Composer**   The way type flows within an Area type shape depends on its *composition* based on the font, style, size, word and letter spacing, and glyph and hyphenation rules. The Single-line composer makes spacing adjustments on a line-by-line basis.
- **Adobe Every-line Composer**   The Every-line composer adjusts the *composition* (see previous sub-bullet) based on the entire text block instead of adjusting type line by line.

The OpenType Panel

FIGURE 10-8 Apply alternate characters to OpenType fonts with the OpenType panel

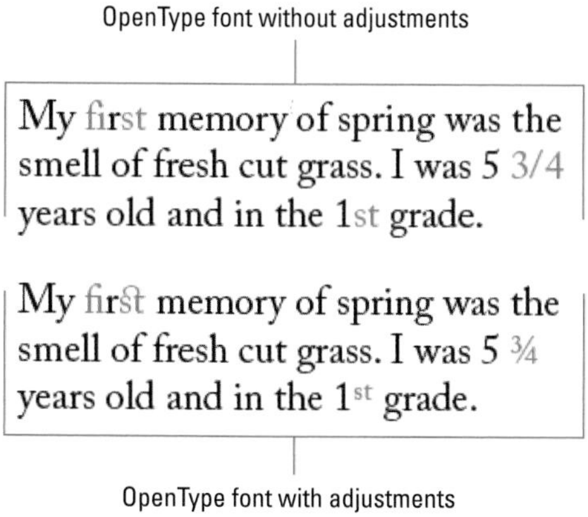

OpenType font without adjustments

My first memory of spring was the smell of fresh cut grass. I was 5 3/4 years old and in the 1st grade.

My first memory of spring was the smell of fresh cut grass. I was 5 ¾ years old and in the 1ˢᵗ grade.

OpenType font with adjustments

Use the OpenType panel when utilizing OpenType fonts to apply alternate characters to your type such as standard ligatures, fractions, and ordinals. You can tell if a font is OpenType by the icon appearing next to the font's name in the Type | Font menu. Mac users can also see the font type icon when selecting fonts from the Character menu on the Control panel and in the Character panel. To use the special features on the OpenType panel, select the text to be modified (either a word or two, or an entire text block) and use the panel's toggle buttons and menus to apply the desired features to the characters. However, keep in mind that not all of the features are offered with every typeface. Figure 10-8 illustrates the use of standard ligatures, discretionary ligatures, ordinals, and fractions.

The Area Type Tool

Use the Area Type tool to add text inside of any closed shape. You can create your shape with any of the shape tools or draw your own with the Pen or Pencil tools. To add text inside a shape, select the shape, choose the Area Type tool from the Tools panel, click the outer edge of the selected shape, and begin typing. Upon clicking, the shape converts into an invisible container rendering its stroke and fill inactive. To create the illusion of text inside a shape that also has a stroke and fill, before you convert the shape into an Area type shape, make a copy of the shape and paste it directly on top of the original (use the Edit | Paste In Front command), and then click the top shape with the Area Type tool. Figure 10-9 shows Area type within a shape positioned on top of another shape with a stroke and fill.

As with any Area type shape, the overflow text can be threaded to other Area type shapes, and those shape(s) can be adjusted with the Area Type Options dialog box. To access the Area Type Options dialog box, select the Area type shape with the Selection tool and then double-click the Area Type tool on the Tools panel. (For details, see the Area Type Options and Threaded Text sections earlier in this chapter for more information.)

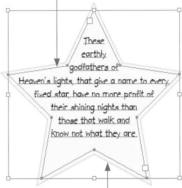

Area Type container with text

Shape behind Area Type container

FIGURE 10-9 Add type inside a closed shape with the Area Type tool

Type On A Path Tool

In Illustrator, text can be added to any path you draw, whether that path is open, like a line drawn with the Pen, Pencil, Paintbrush, Spiral, Line, or Arc tool, or closed, such as a shape created with the Blob Brush or any of the Shape tools. Figure 10-10 shows examples of type on both open and closed paths.

To add text to a path, select your path with the Selection tool, choose the Type On A Path tool from the Tools panel, click the edge of your path, and then begin typing. When you add text to a closed path like a circle, the shape gets converted into a path container rendering its stroke and fill inactive. On an open path, like a spiral, the text flows along that path with the default Rainbow effect and the Path Alignment option set to Baseline. To adjust how the text sits on the path, select your Type On A Path text block with the Selection tool and then double-click the Type On A Path tool on the Tools panel. You'll then see the Type On A Path Options dialog box, inside which you can choose different Effect, Align To Path, Spacing, and Flip options.

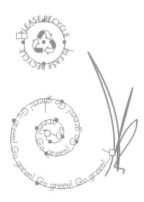

FIGURE 10-10 Add type to an open path like a spiral or a closed path like a circle

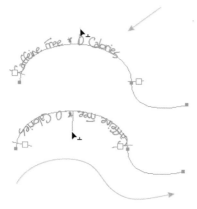

FIGURE 10-11 Flip the direction of text along a path

Once the text is on the path, you can flip and move text along the path using the bracket and midpoint icons. To flip text and make it flow along the opposite side of the path, as illustrated in Figure 10-11, use the Selection tool to click and drag the midpoint icon from one side of the path to the other or select Type | Type On A Path | Type On A Path Options and choose the Flip option from the dialog box.

To move the position of text on the path, as shown in Figure 10-12, select the type with the Selection tool, position your cursor on top of the type's center bracket until you see the small upside down T icon next to the cursor, then drag the center bracket along the path. You can also fine-tune the placement of the text along the path by adjusting the outside brackets with the Selection tool. Furthermore, when the text on the path exceeds the path length, an overflow text port will appear so you can thread the overflow text to another path, extend the path to reveal the overflow text, or adjust the size of the text so it fits on the existing path.

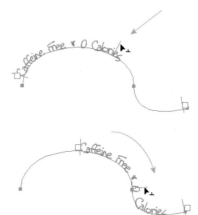

FIGURE 10-12 Move the position of the text on the path

Vertical Type Tools

The Vertical Type tools work exactly like the regular (horizontal) Type tools with one minor difference: With the Vertical Type tools, the type is oriented vertically and flows from top to bottom and right to left (like Japanese characters), instead of from top to bottom, left to right (like Western languages). Use the Character, Paragraph, and OpenType panels to apply formatting.

The Vertical Type Tool

The Vertical Type tool can be used both as a Point Type and Area Type tool, as illustrated in Figure 10-13. To create Vertical Point Type, select the Vertical Type tool, click the artboard to set the insertion point, and begin typing. To create an Area type box, select the Vertical Type tool, click and drag on the artboard to create a rectangular area, and begin typing after you release your mouse.

FIGURE 10-13 Vertical Type can flow in a single line or inside an Area type box

The Vertical Area Type Tool

The Vertical Area Type tool lets you add vertical type inside of any shaped container. To do this, select the shape, choose the Vertical Area Type tool, click the outer edge of your shape, and begin typing. Once you click the shape, the shape converts into a container rendering its stroke and fill inactive. Therefore, if you need the shape with a stroke or fill and want the shape filled with vertical type, make a copy of your shape and paste it directly on top of the original (use the Edit | Paste In Front command) before you click the top shape with the Vertical Area Type tool. Figure 10-14 shows vertical area type inside a shape on top of another shape with a solid fill.

Even though the text is vertical, it still supports threaded text, and because it sits inside of an Area type shape, it also means you can adjust the shape's width, height, number of rows and columns, gutter size, inset (margin) spacing, first baseline offset (alignment of first line of type within the box), and text flow options. To access the Area Type Options dialog box, select the Vertical Area Type shape with the Selection tool and then double-click the Vertical Area Type tool on the Tools panel.

FIGURE 10-14 Use the Vertical Area Type tool to add vertical type inside a shape

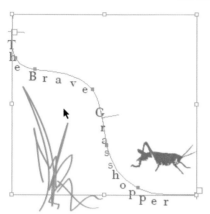

FIGURE **10-15** Adjust Vertical Type On A Path options to control how type flows along a path

Vertical Type On A Path Tool

To add vertical type to a path, you must first draw the path on which it will sit. Paths can be drawn with the Pen, Pencil, Paintbrush, Spiral, Line, Arc, Blob Brush, or any of the Shape tools. Once your shape is drawn, select the Vertical Type On A Path tool, click the edge of your shape, and begin typing.

To adjust how the text sits on the path, select your Vertical Type On A Path text block with the Selection tool and then double-click the Vertical Type On A Path tool on the Tools panel. You'll then see the Type On A Path Options dialog box, inside which you can choose different Effect, Align To Path, Spacing, and Flip options. The vertical type in Figure 10-15 has the Stair Step effect, Ascender Align To Path, and –36pt Spacing.

Wrapping Text Around an Object

To make your text wrap around any selected object, use the Object | Text Wrap | Make command. This effect can be added to any layout with text and you can create an unlimited number of text-wrapped objects. For example, the illustration in Figure 10-16 has four text-wrapped objects (the moon, the witch, the treetops, and the cat). Furthermore, because the Text Wrap is a live effect, you can reposition the text-wrapped object and have the wrapping update automatically, even when the object hangs off the edge of the text block.

To adjust the offset space around the text-wrapped object, choose Object | Text Wrap | Text Wrap Options. When the Text Wrap Options dialog box opens, increase or decrease the number in the Offset field. To make the text wrap inside an object rather than outside it, select the Invert Wrap option. To remove the text wrap setting from any object, select that object and choose Object | Text Wrap | Release.

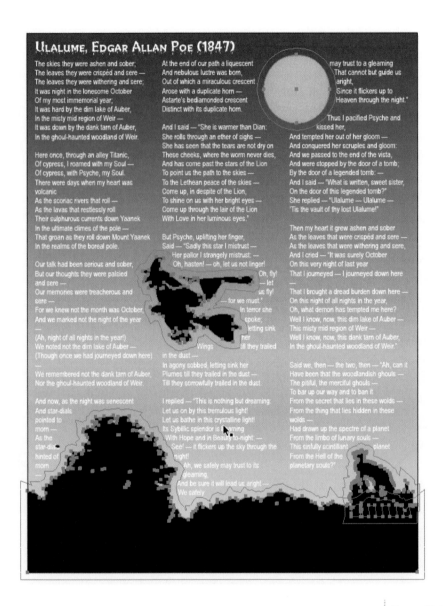

ULALUME, EDGAR ALLAN POE (1847)

The skies they were ashen and sober;
The leaves they were crispéd and sere —
The leaves they were withering and sere;
It was night in the lonesome October
Of my most immemorial year;
It was hard by the dim lake of Auber,
In the misty mid region of Weir —
It was down by the dank tarn of Auber,
In the ghoul-haunted woodland of Weir.

Here once, through an alley Titanic,
Of cypress, I roamed with my Soul —
Of cypress, with Psyche, my Soul.
There were days when my heart was
volcanic
As the scoriac rivers that roll —
As the lavas that restlessly roll
Their sulphurous currents down Yaanek
In the ultimate climes of the pole —
That groan as they roll down Mount Yaanek
In the realms of the boreal pole.

Our talk had been serious and sober,
But our thoughts they were palsied
and sere —
Our memories were treacherous and
sere —
For we knew not the month was October,
And we marked not the night of the year
—
(Ah, night of all nights in the year!)
We noted not the dim lake of Auber —
(Though once we had journeyed down here)

We remembered not the dank tarn of Auber,
Nor the ghoul-haunted woodland of Weir.

And now, as the night was senescent
And star-dials
pointed to
morn —
As the
star-dials
hinted of
morn

At the end of our path a liquescent
And nebulous lustre was born,
Out of which a miraculous crescent
Arose with a duplicate horn —
Astarte's bediamonded crescent
Distinct with its duplicate horn.

And I said — "She is warmer than Dian:
She rolls through an ether of sighs —
She has seen that the tears are not dry on
These cheeks, where the worm never dies,
And has come past the stars of the Lion
To point us the path to the skies —
To the Lethean peace of the skies —
Come up, in despite of the Lion,
To shine on us with her bright eyes —
Come up through the lair of the Lion
With Love in her luminous eyes."

But Psyche, uplifting her finger,
Said — "Sadly this star I mistrust —
Her pallor I strangely mistrust: —
Oh, hasten! — oh, let us not linger!
Oh, fly!
— let
us fly!
— for we must."
In terror she
spoke;
letting sink
her
Wings   till they trailed
in the dust —
In agony sobbed, letting sink her
Plumes till they trailed in the dust —
Till they sorrowfully trailed in the dust.

I replied — "This is nothing but dreaming:
Let us on by this tremulous light!
Let us bathe in this crystalline light!
Its Sybillic splendor is beaming
With Hope and in Beauty to-night: —
See! — it flickers up the sky through the
night!
Ah, we safely may trust to its
gleaming,
And be sure it will lead us aright —
We safely

may trust to a gleaming
That cannot but guide us
aright,
Since it flickers up to
Heaven through the night."

Thus I pacified Psyche and
kissed her,
And tempted her out of her gloom —
And conquered her scruples and gloom:
And we passed to the end of the vista,
And were stopped by the door of a tomb;
By the door of a legended tomb: —
And I said — "What is written, sweet sister,
On the door of this legended tomb?"
She replied — "Ulalume — Ulalume —
'Tis the vault of thy lost Ulalume!"

Then my heart it grew ashen and sober
As the leaves that were crispéd and sere —
As the leaves that were withering and sere,
And I cried — "It was surely October
On this very night of last year
That I journeyed — I journeyed down here
—
That I brought a dread burden down here —
On this night of all nights in the year,
Oh, what demon has tempted me here?
Well I know, now, this dim lake of Auber —
This misty mid region of Weir —
Well I know, now, this dank tarn of Auber,
In the ghoul-haunted woodland of Weir."

Said we, then — the two, then — "Ah, can it
Have been that the woodlandish ghouls —
The pitiful, the merciful ghouls —
To bar up our way and to ban it
From the secret that lies in these wolds —
From the thing that lies hidden in these
wolds —
Had drawn up the spectre of a planet
From the limbo of lunary souls —
This sinfully scintillant   planet
From the Hell of the
planetary souls?"

FIGURE 10-16 Use the Text Wrap command to force text to wrap around an object

Warping Text with Envelope Distort

The Envelope Distort command under the Object menu can be used to distort any object, including text. An envelope is a shape that is used to reshape or distort an existing shape or block of text. With the Envelope Distort tool, you can choose to use either preset warp shapes or mesh grids for the reshaping or distortion. What's more, envelopes can be used on any kind of object except linked objects, graphs, and guides. There are three Envelope Distort commands that work equally well with objects as they do with text: Make With Warp, Make With Mesh, and Make With Top Object. Use the Control panel with each to edit, remove, or expand the envelope and edit the envelope-distorted text.

Make With Warp

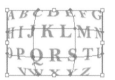

FIGURE **10-17** Text with a Warp Envelope Distort

To make warped text, select your text block with the Selection tool and then choose Object | Envelope Distort | Make With Warp. When the Warp Options dialog box opens, turn on the Preview option. Then, select a Style and adjust the Bend, and Horizontal and Vertical Distortion to your liking before clicking the OK button. Figure 10-17 shows an object with the Fisheye warp style. To edit the warped object envelope, select the warped object and then click the Edit Envelope button on the Control panel and adjust the envelope settings. To edit the envelope contents, select the warped object and then press the Edit Contents button on the Control panel. Both buttons place the warped object in Isolation Mode for editing purposes. When you're finished making changes, double-click the artboard to exit Isolation Mode.

Make With Mesh

FIGURE **10-18** Text with a Mesh Envelope Distort

To make warped meshed text, select your text block with the Selection tool and then choose Object | Envelope Distort | Make With Mesh. When the Mesh Options dialog box opens, select the desired number of rows and columns and click OK. A mesh will then be placed over your type so you can edit it using the Direct Selection tool, as illustrated in Figure 10-18. To edit the envelope mesh object, select the mesh object with the Selection tool and then click the Edit Envelope button on the Control panel, where you can change the number of rows and columns as well as reset the envelope shape. To edit the envelope mesh contents, select the envelope mesh object and then press the Edit Contents button on the Control panel. Editing takes place in Isolation Mode. To exit Isolation Mode, double-click the artboard.

Make With Top Object

To make text warp into a particular shape, place a shaped object on top of a text block, select both the text block and the top shape with the Selection tool, and choose Object | Envelope Distort | Make With Top Object. The text will then flow or wrap itself inside the shape, as shown in Figure 10-19. To edit the envelope top object, select the enveloped text and then click the Edit Envelope button on the Control panel. To edit the top object contents, click the Edit Contents button on the Control panel. Editing takes place in Isolation Mode. To exit Isolation Mode, double-click the artboard.

FIGURE 10-19 Text warped with a top object

Type and shape

Type warped with top object

Fitting a Headline

When you have a headline or paragraph that needs to be adjusted to fit within a fixed size type area, such as an Area type box that is 4 inches wide, consider using the Fit Headline command to automatically track out the letters so they fit evenly within the defined space. Figure 10-20 shows the before and after versions of the Fit Headline command.

Original type in an Area Type box

Type after selecting Fit Headline

SURPRISE

Who:
What:
When:
Where:
IT'S
PARTY
TIME!

SURPRISE

Who:
What:
When:
Where:
IT'S
PARTY
TIME!

FIGURE 10-20 Use the Fit Headline command to make text fit within a type area

To use the Fit Headline command, select the Type tool, click in the line of text you want to fit without selecting any of the text, and select Type | Fit Headline. If you happen to make further adjustments to the type, reapply the Fit Headline command to ensure the type fits snugly.

Performing Other Type Commands

In addition to text formatting tools, Illustrator includes spell check, hidden character, change case, and smart punctuation commands in the Type menu to help you edit and improve the quality of your writing.

Spell Check

To spell check your copy at any time, choose Edit | Check Spelling. When the Check Spelling dialog box opens, click the Start button to begin the spell check process. When questionable words are found, alternatives will appear in the Suggestions area and you'll have the option to Ignore, Ignore All, Change, Change All, or Add the word in question to Illustrator's spelling dictionary. If desired, click the Options expander arrow to reveal additional spell-checking criteria. When no more questionable works are found, the Spell Checker will be complete and you can click the Done button to exit the dialog box.

Show Hidden Characters

Sometimes seeing those hidden non-printing characters—such as soft returns, spaces between words, tabs, and hard returns at the end of paragraphs—can help you with the formatting, alignment, and editing of your text. To toggle this feature on and off, choose Type | Show Hidden Characters or press ALT+CTRL+I (Win) or OPT+CMD+I (Mac) to toggle the hidden characters on or off.

Change Case

Regardless of how type is entered into Illustrator, you can alter the case of type using any of the Change Case commands. To edit the case of any block of selected text to UPPERCASE, lowercase, Title Case, or Sentence case, choose an option from the Type | Change Case menu.

Inserting Glyphs

Each font supports regular letter and number characters along with special glyph characters such as em and en dashes, copyright marks, fractions, and accented letters. You can view the font-specific glyph characters in the Glyphs panel by choosing Type | Glyphs or Window | Type | Glyphs. To add a glyph to your document, position your cursor inside the text area where you want the glyph to go and double-click the desired glyph. At the bottom of the Glyphs panel is a dropdown list for all available fonts, so explore different fonts such as Wingdings to find a wider variety of characters.

Using Smart Punctuation

Inputting text from your own keyboard or from copied content from another program can often result in punctuation that isn't quite as good as it should be. To ensure that your text uses typographically correct punctuation characters, such as proper quotes and fractions, ligatures, ellipses, and en and em dashes, select Type | Smart Punctuation. When the Smart Punctuation dialog box opens, choose the desired Replace Punctuation options, select a Replace In option to replace Selected Text Only or in the Entire Document, and then click OK.

Type converted to outlines

Letter shapes edited with the Direct Selection tool

FIGURE 10-21 Convert type to outlines and edit the letter shapes

Converting Type to Outlines

The more you work on print projects, the more you may get a request from the print house to convert your type to outlines. You may also want to convert fonts to outlines to creatively manipulate individual letter shapes. To convert type to outlines, choose Type | Create Outlines, which converts editable type into grouped editable vector shapes. Those shapes can either be left as is, or ungrouped and individually transformed and reshaped using many of the tools on the Tools panel and all of the commands in the Object | Transform menu. As illustrated in Figure 10-21, you can reactivate a converted letter's shape paths, anchor points, and direction handles and adjust them to create new customized shapes.

11

Transformation and Reshaping Tools

How to...

- Rotate, reflect, scale, and shear art
- Reshape and move art
- Use the Transform menu commands
- Use the Free Transform tool and Transform panel
- Work with the Reshaping tools

Illustrator has a very nice collection of transformation and reshaping tools that can help you modify and manipulate your existing open and closed paths and shapes. While technically all the tools covered in this chapter are considered *reshaping* tools, they're divided here into two categories: the *transformation* tools, which allow you to rotate, reflect, scale, shear, reshape, move, and free transform your objects; and the *reshaping* or *liquefy* tools—Warp, Twirl, Pucker, Bloat, Scallop, Crystallize, and Wrinkle—located in the Reshaping Tools flyout menu on the Tools panel. In addition, you'll learn about the Free Transform tool, the Transform menu commands, and the Transform panel, along with some helpful productivity tips and tricks.

The Transformation Tools

The Transformation tools let you rotate, reflect, scale, shear, reshape, move, and free transform your paths by clicking and dragging selections or by entering exact measurements in a dialog box. You'll find all of these tools in their own section in the middle of the Tools panel. And, because most of these tools work in a similar way, once you learn how to use one of them, you can apply those skills to the rest.

To use the Rotate, Reflect, Scale, or Shear tools, follow these steps:

1. Select the object(s) to be transformed.

2. Select the desired Transformation tool from the Tools panel. As you select one of these tools, notice that a reference point indicator appears in the exact center of the selected object(s). That is the reference point around which the transformation will occur.

3. To transform around this reference point, click and drag anywhere on the artboard. When you release your mouse, the transformation will be complete. Otherwise, you can make the transformation after relocating the reference point. To move the reference point, click in the desired location on the artboard relative to the selected object(s). Once the reference point is reset, you may click and drag your cursor on the artboard to make another transformation. You may repeat this resetting of the reference point and clicking and dragging to transform the selection as often as needed. Furthermore, to make a copy of the original selection with the transformation and leave the original where it is, begin clicking and dragging and then press ALT before releasing your mouse.

When you need to perform more precise transformations, open the desired tool's transformation dialog box by double-clicking the tool on the Tools panel after you've made your selection on the artboard. When the dialog box appears, input the desired distance, angle, and other transformation attributes. You may then click OK to transform your selection or click the Copy button to leave the selection as is and make a copy with the transformation settings.

To precisely set the reference point *before* the transformation *and* open and use the desired tool's dialog box, ALT+click (Win) or OPT+click (Mac) on the artboard where you'd like the reference point to be. The dialog box will open and upon clicking OK, your transformation will occur around the position of the reference point.

The Rotate Tool

Use the Rotate tool to rotate your selection clockwise or counterclockwise relative to the fixed position of the reference

Drawing with Simple Math Equations

Make Illustrator do some math! When you input an equation in the dialog box input field, such as 360/12 (to make a $^1/_{12}$ rotation 360° around the reference point), and click Copy instead of OK, Illustrator will create a rotated copy of your selection. You can then repeat that transformation 11 more times by pressing the keyboard shortcut CTRL+D (Win) or CMD+D (Mac) to get 12 precisely placed objects around the reference.

FIGURE 11-1 Rotate an object around a central reference point

point on the artboard, as illustrated in Figure 11-1. When using the Rotate dialog box, input a positive or negative number in the angle field, such as 36° or –145°, and either rotate the object or make a copy of your object at the specified rotation.

The Reflect Tool

The Reflect tool will flip your selection horizontally or vertically or by an angle based on the position of the reference point of your selection. For example, the right side of the drawing in Figure 11-2 was created by reflecting the left side along the vertical axis and then selecting Copy instead of OK in the Reflect Tool dialog box. When Smart Guides are enabled (View | Smart Guides) you'll see a screen tip with the angle of the rotation as you click and drag your selection. To constrain the reflection to a 45°, 90°, 135°, or 180° angle, press and hold the SHIFT key while you drag.

FIGURE 11-2 Create a mirror image of a selection with the Reflect tool

The Scale Tool

Use the Scale tool to make selections bigger or smaller, relative to the fixed position of the reference point. To proportionally constrain the scaling, press and hold the SHIFT key as you drag the selection. When you scale using the Scale dialog box, you can choose to scale your selection uniformly by percentage, or non-uniformly by inputting a different percentage in the horizontal and vertical scale fields. In addition, you can specify whether or not the strokes and effects on your object will be scaled during the transformation by checking the Scale Strokes and Effects options.

The Shear Tool

The Shear tool skews objects by a shear angle, and either horizontally, vertically, or by a specified angle relative to the position of the reference point, depending on which way you drag your cursor when using this tool. When Smart Guides are enabled, a screen hint will pop up during the shearing to indicate the shear angle and the angle of the axis when applicable. To further understand how the shearing takes place, use the Shear dialog box with the Preview option turned on and try adjusting the different settings before clicking OK or Copy. For example, the rectangle in Figure 11-3 has been transformed with a Shear Angle of 45° and a Vertical Axis.

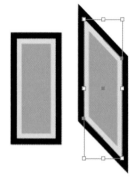

FIGURE 11-3 Shear objects horizontally, vertically, or by a specified angle

The Reshape Tool

The Reshape tool works in two ways depending on whether the shape being adjusted is open or closed. With an open path, use the Reshape tool to reposition existing anchor points or add and reposition new anchor points relative to the entire shape. The whole object actually shifts a little when you click and drag anywhere on it, while at the same time it preserves the general details of the original path. With a closed shape, you must first select the shape with the Direct Selection tool to activate the anchor points before using the Reshape tool to move the anchor points or paths around.

The Move Tool

The Selection tool is your Move tool because you can move any selected object with it. What most people don't know, however, is that the Selection tool also performs move transformations when you access the tool's dialog box. To move a selection with precision, double-click the Selection tool on the Tools panel to open the Move dialog box. There you can set the Horizontal and Vertical position, the Distance, and/or the Angle for the selection's move.

The Free Transform Tool

The Free Transform tool is a three-in-one tool that allows you to scale, rotate, and skew the object(s) in your selection, depending on where you position your mouse, which anchor point you drag on, and which direction you drag in. In addition, when you add some simple keyboard shortcuts to the drag, you can also distort the selection. Selections can include any objects or paths, but not editable type. To edit type shapes, you must first convert the type to outlines.

To use the Free Transform tool, you must always remember three things: First, make sure you select the object(s) you want to transform before selecting the Free Transform tool. Second, begin to drag the selection's bounding box handles before you add any of the keyboard shortcuts. Third, release your mouse before releasing these keyboard shortcuts:

- Drag on a corner anchor point, then press and hold the CTRL (Win) or CMD (Mac) key to distort that anchor point and its connecting paths.

- Drag on a center anchor point, and then press and hold the CTRL (Win) or CMD (Mac) key to distort that entire side of the selection while the opposite side remains fixed.

- Drag on a corner anchor point, and then press and hold CTRL+ALT (Win) or CMD+OPT (Mac) to shear diagonally along the center reference point.

- Drag on a corner anchor point, and then press and hold SHIFT+CTRL+ALT (Win) or SHIFT+CMD+OPT (Mac) to create a perspective distortion.

The Transform Panel

The free-floating Transform panel lets you move a selection to specified X and Y coordinates, resize a selection to precise width and height measurements, and rotate or shear a selection by a specified angle. The X and Y coordinates are relative to the numbers on the document ruler, which by default are set to the bottom left edge of your artboard. All transformations here are made relative to a selection's reference point, which is set, by default, to the center of the selection. You can, however, adjust that point by clicking any of the tiny squares on the Reference Point grid directly below the Transform panel's tab or on the Control panel. This grid can also be used with any of the other transformation and reshaping tools.

Transform Menu Commands

Under the Object | Transform menu, you'll find alternate ways of opening the Move, Rotate, Reflect, Scale, and Shear dialog boxes to perform transformations on your selections. Other options in the Object | Transform menu include Transform Again, which repeats the last performed transformation. You can also use the keyboard shortcut CTRL+D (Win) or CMD+C (Mac); use Transform Each, which opens the Transform Each dialog box for scaling and moving the selection horizontally and vertically, rotating the selection by a specified angle, reflecting the selection along the X and/or Y axis, changing the transformation reference point, and applying a random transformation to the selection; and use Reset Bounding Box, which resets the bounding box into a rectangular shape.

The Reshaping Tools

Illustrator's seven reshaping tools (Warp, Twirl, Pucker, Bloat, Scallop, Crystallize, Wrinkle) are located on a flyout menu under the Warp tool. With them, you can smush and manipulate your selections in an entirely new way. In fact, you'll find that they work a lot like the Liquify tools in Photoshop, if you have any experience with those.

All these tools use a global brush interface along with tool-specific options that can be customized to suit your particular needs. To adjust the settings for any of the reshaping tools, double-click the desired tool's icon on the Tools panel. When the dialog box opens, you can set the width, height, angle, and intensity of the global brush (which can be set up to work with a pressure pen), as well as adjust any tool-specific options. To reshape your selection instead of creating new

How to. . .   Resize Your Reshaping Brush

When working with any of the reshaping tools, the brush size can be interactively resized as you click the desired shape on the artboard by pressing and holding the ALT (Win) or OPTION (Mac) key. To resize the brush proportionally, press SHIFT+ALT (Win) or SHIFT+OPT (Mac) as you click and drag.

original   warp   original   twirl

original   pucker   original   bloat

original   scallop   original   crystallize

original   wrinkle

FIGURE 11-4 Use the Reshaping tools to manipulate your illustrations

shapes on new layers while leaving the original intact, disable the Simplify setting in each of the tools' Option dialog boxes.

The Reshaping tools generally work in the same manner, as described in the following. Figure 11-4 illustrates how each of them can be used to modify your work.

- **Warp tool**   The Warp tool lets you mush, pull, stretch, and model your selection as if you pushed your finger through a blob of paint.

- **Twirl tool**   The Twirl tool twirls your selection in a clockwise or counterclockwise direction based on the setting in the tool's Options dialog box. The amount of twirling depends on how long you press and hold your mouse before releasing it.

- **Pucker tool**   The Pucker tool deflates or pulls the illustration into the point where you click your cursor. The longer you leave your mouse depressed, the greater the intensity of the pucker effect.

- **Bloat tool**   Use the Bloat tool to inflate or puff a selection away from the point where you click your cursor. The anchor points and paths are literally pushed away from your cursor as you click to create a bloating effect.

- **Scallop tool**   Use the Scallop tool to create random scalloped ridges along the outer edges of all the objects in your selection.

- **Crystallize tool**   The Crystallize tool lets you push and pull your selection to turn soft curvy corners into random spiky edges.

- **Wrinkle tool**   When you need to add a bit of uneven wrinkliness to your work, use the Wrinkle tool to apply wobbly, rough wrinkled detail to the outlines of your selection.

12

Making Patterns and Gradients

How to...

- Apply and use patterns
- Access the pattern libraries
- Create your own patterns
- Expand, edit, and transform patterns
- Apply and edit gradients
- Access the gradient libraries
- Use the Gradient panel and Gradient tool
- Create, edit, and save gradients

In this chapter, you'll learn how to work with patterns and gradients in conjunction with the Swatches and Gradient panels. You'll discover how to access and use Illustrator's free pattern and gradient libraries, how to create your own custom patterns and gradients, how to edit and reuse existing patterns and gradients, and how to apply these patterns and gradients to your illustrations.

Patterns

A pattern is any set of repeating elements. Think of the repeating colors, shapes, and objects on fabric, wrapping paper, and wallpaper—all of these are patterns. Patterns are made from a pattern *tile*, or the area on which the pattern sits and has edges that match up with itself on all four sides so when it repeats horizontally and vertically, it tiles seamlessly. Tiles can be any size so long as they are rectangular (or square) in shape, like the ones shown here in Figure 12-1.

In Illustrator, patterns appear in the Swatches panel along with the color and gradient swatches. Though patterns are generally created at the size they were intended to be, they can be transformed in size, rotation, direction, and angle using the Transform tools. You can even save and share your patterns within your own copy of Illustrator or externally with other Illustrator users on different computers and across the Internet.

FIGURE 12-1 Patterns are created from rectangular pattern tiles

Applying Patterns

In Illustrator, patterns can be applied to both the fill and stroke of any open path or closed shape through the Swatches panel. To apply a pattern to a selected object (or objects), simply click the desired pattern swatch in the Swatches panel. If the Fill is active in the Tools panel or Color panel, your pattern will be applied to the selection's fill. When the Stroke is active, the pattern is applied to the selection's stroke. If you can't see the pattern on the stroke, increase the size of the stroke in the Strokes panel.

Patterns fill an object by placing the top left edge of the pattern tile at the top left edge of the object. You can adjust how a pattern sits inside an object by holding down the tilde key (~) (pronounced /til'duh/—it's on the top left side of your keyboard next to the number 1) as you click and drag on the pattern. When you do this, the object stays in place and the pattern moves inside it. Try it a few times to see how it works.

Pattern Libraries

Illustrator comes with a ton of free patterns you can use in any of your documents. To open the pattern libraries, click the Swatch Libraries menu button at the bottom of the Swatches panel, select Patterns, and choose one of the pattern libraries from the Basic Graphs, Decorative, or Nature pattern categories. The swatches in the selected library will open on your desktop in a floating swatches panel. Each time you select a color from a floating pattern panel, that pattern gets added to your list of available swatches in the Swatches panel. Feel free to open and close these extra pattern swatch library panels as often as needed.

Creating Patterns

You can create your own pattern tiles from any object or selection of objects on your artboard, such as a shooting star, a jumble of beach toys, a set of uneven multicolored stripes, or even art with text.

To create your own custom pattern, select the artwork you want to turn into a pattern tile and do either of the following:

- **Choose Edit | Define Pattern.** When the New Swatch dialog box opens, name your pattern and click OK. Your pattern will be added at the end of the regular swatches listing but above any color group swatches in the panel.

- **Drag and drop your artwork directly into the Swatches panel.** This method bypasses the New Swatch dialog box. To name your new swatch, double-click it to open the Swatch Options dialog box, name it, and then click OK.

FIGURE 12-2 Create and use your own patterns

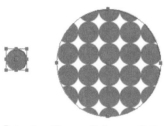

Dot pattern tile   Pattern applied
                        to a shape

New patterns are document-specific and will appear inside your Swatches panel, ready to use at a later time. To access your custom pattern swatches from inside other documents, you'll need to create your own swatch library, which you can then open through the Swatches panel any time you need it. (For further details, see Chapter 9.)

Get creative—your custom patterns can be as simple or as complex as your imagination permits! To illustrate, let's say you wanted to make a polka-dot pattern from a red dot. First you'd draw the dot, next you'd select it and *define the pattern* (described earlier), and then you'd apply the pattern to an object, as in Figure 12-2.

Notice that the space between the dots inside the pattern is rather tight. To add a little bit of breathing room between the dots, add a background shape (like a square) with a solid color fill and no stroke to the pattern design and create a new pattern swatch, as shown in Figure 12-3. If desired, create a see-through pattern by adding a background shape with no stroke or fill.

FIGURE 12-3 Give your patterns breathing room by adding a background shape with a solid fill

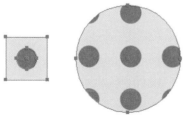

Pattern with larger   Pattern with background
    background   applied to shape

To create a more dynamic pattern, you'll need to think about how the object(s) in the pattern design will tile when repeated. For instance, to create a diagonally flowing dot pattern, position two dots at opposite corners inside a solid square, like the ones in Figure 12-4.

FIGURE 12-4 Create dynamic patterns by strategically spacing objects within the pattern tile

Expanding Patterns

The only real restriction you have when creating patterns is that a pattern cannot be created when it includes another pattern. For example, you might want to make a double-polka-dot pattern where each dot was filled with polka dots. If you applied your pattern to two circles and then tried to define a pattern with those two polka-dot-filled circles, Illustrator would give you an error message that says, "Patterns cannot contain anything painted with a pattern." The workaround is to use the Object | Expand command that releases the pattern from its tile into separate grouped objects, which occasionally may also have a clipping mask applied to them. You would then use a combination of other tools to cut away any unneeded shapes so only the dots inside the dots remain. Then, you can define a new pattern and use it, as illustrated in Figure 12-5.

Dynamic pattern

Dynamic pattern applied to shape

FIGURE 12-5 Use the Object | Expand command to release a pattern from its pattern tile before creating a new pattern

Editing Patterns

All of the patterns you find in the Swatches panel and the pattern libraries can be used as is or edited and then redefined. For example, you may find a black-and-white pattern, like the one shown in Figure 12-6, to which you'd like to add color.

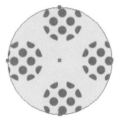

Original pattern

Pattern applied to shape

To edit an existing pattern, drag and drop it from the Swatches panel (or from one of the floating pattern swatch library panels) onto the artboard. When you move a copy of a pattern onto the artboard, it becomes editable artwork detached from the original pattern. Use the Group Selection tool (on the flyout menu under the Direct Selection tool) to isolate individual parts of the pattern to recolor them, and use the Direct Selection tool to select and modify any of the paths and anchor points within the pattern. When you're finished editing a pattern, reselect it with the Selection tool and create a new pattern using the Edit | Define Pattern command, or by dragging and dropping the edited pattern back into the Swatches panel.

Original

Edited

New Pattern applied to object

FIGURE 12-6 Edit patterns to create new ones

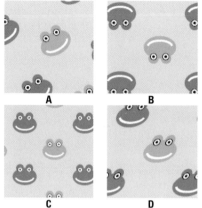

A   B

C   D

FIGURE 12-7 Transform patterns using the (A) Rotate, (B) Reflect, (C) Scale, and (D) Shear tools

Transforming Patterns

When you find or create a pattern you like, occasionally that pattern needs a little tweaking in size, rotation, direction, and angle before it looks the way you want it to. In those times, turn to the Scale, Rotate, Reflect, and Shear tool dialog boxes. Of course, you can use the tools without the dialog boxes, but when you do double-click the tools to open their dialog boxes, you'll get the added option of choosing whether the transformation is applied to the pattern fill, to the object, or to both at the same time.

Take a look at the patterns in Figure 12-7. The first one has been rotated 30°, the second has been reflected horizontally, the third has been reduced in scale by 75%, and the last has been sheared by a 20° angle along the horizontal axis.

Tip   Once you manipulate a pattern inside a shape, all other patterns applied to the same object or new objects will have the same transformations applied to them. To reset the pattern inside any object, set the fill to none or fill it with a solid color. You may then reselect a pattern and that pattern will return to its original state.

Gradients

A gradient is a blend of two or more colors (up to a maximum of 32 colors) that can be applied to the fill of any shape. Gradients can use any combination of process colors and spot colors, and the midpoints between any two colors can be adjusted to control how one color blends into the next. Furthermore, you can create gradients that are either linear (from end to end) or radial (from center to outside), which means that once you select your colors you can create two unique gradient swatches from them—one linear and one radial.

Use any of Illustrator's free gradients in the gradient libraries, or create your own custom gradients using the tools on the Gradient panel. In CS4, you can even edit gradients applied to objects directly on the artboard using the new Gradient widget.

Applying Gradients

To apply a gradient to your artwork, select the object(s) and then choose a gradient from the Swatches panel or any of the floating gradient libraries. Alternatively, you can drag and drop a gradient swatch from the Swatches panel directly onto an object on your artboard as well as drag and drop the Gradient Fill icon from the Gradient panel onto an object on your artboard.

Gradient Libraries

To open and use Illustrator's free gradients libraries, click the Swatch Libraries menu button at the bottom of the Swatches panel, select Gradients, and pick any of the 21 different gradient categories. The gradient swatches in the selected library will open on your desktop in a floating swatches panel. Each time you select a color from a floating gradient panel—whether or not you're applying that gradient to a selection at that moment—that gradient gets added to your list of available swatches in the Swatches panel for later use. Feel free to open and close these extra gradient swatch library panels as often as needed.

The Gradient Panel

When you select a gradient from the Swatches panel, that gradient's attributes are displayed and can be edited inside the Gradient panel, as shown in Figure 12-8. You'll find the Gradient panel grouped with the Stroke and Transparency panels in the panel dock or by choosing Window | Gradient. There are many features on the panel, which has been enhanced greatly in CS4.

FIGURE 12-8 The Gradient panel

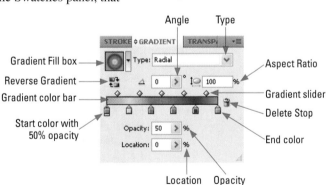

- **Gradient Fill box** Displays the currently selected gradient. Click the menu button to select other gradients appearing in the Swatches panel.

- **Type** Displays the currently selected gradient type, either Linear or Radial. To convert one type to another using the same colors, simply select the desired type.

- **Reverse Gradient**   Toggles the direction of the colors appearing on the gradient color bar as well as any selected object with the gradient applied to it.

- **Angle**   Sets the angle for linear gradients. The default is set to 0°.

- **Aspect Ratio**   Sets the aspect ratio along the vertical scale for radial gradients. The default is set to 100%.

- **Gradient slider**   Adjusts the transition between colors below it on the gradient color bar.

- **Start color**   The left-most color on a linear gradient or the center-most color on a radial gradient.

- **End color**   The right-most color on a linear gradient or the outer-most color on a radial gradient.

- **Delete Stop**   Deletes the selected stop color from the gradient color bar.

- **Opacity**   Adjusts the opacity of the selected color on the gradient color bar. When reduced from 100% (full saturation), the color widget on the gradient color bar has a slightly larger bottom edge (see Figure 12-7).

- **Location**   Adjusts the location of the selected color widget on the gradient color bar relative to the other colors. The 0% setting is at the far left of the gradient color bar, while 100% is the far right. The color widgets can be repositioned anywhere along the gradient color bar by clicking and dragging.

Editing Gradients

To mix your own custom gradients, feel free to edit, add, and subtract colors appearing on the Gradient color bar, as well as adjust the angle, direction, aspect ratio, opacity, and location:

- To edit a color, double-click the color widget you'd like to change and a popup Color panel will appear directly beneath that color widget. Use the color panel to mix a new color or click the Swatches icon along the left edge of the panel to select a swatch color from your document's Swatches panel. Make your color selection and then click the Gradient panel tab or press the ESC key on your keyboard to return the focus to the panel.

- To add a color, place your cursor in the area under the gradient color bar and click when the cursor turns into a white arrow with a plus sign.

- To remove a color, click and drag the color widget off the gradient color bar, or select it and click the Delete Stop (mini trash) icon.

- To adjust a color stop's location, click and drag it into a new position on the gradient color bar or select it and adjust the Location percentage.

- To adjust a color stop's opacity, select it and change the opacity percentage.

- To flip the direction of the colors on the gradient color bar, click the Reverse Gradient toggle button.

Saving Gradients

After you make adjustments to a gradient on the Gradient panel, you can apply that gradient to an object by selecting the object and then clicking the gradient fill box on the Gradient panel; however, that does not mean you've saved the gradient. To save the gradient for future use, either drag and drop the gradient from the gradient fill box on the Gradient panel into the Swatches panel, or choose New Swatch from the Swatches panel options menu. Remember, too, that any time you switch from Linear to Radial and vice versa, you're essentially creating a new gradient blend and will need to save both versions as separate swatches to reuse them elsewhere in your document.

The Gradient Tool

Gradients are applied to your objects exactly as they were created. So, for example, if the gradient you select is linear with a 0° angle, it will flow across your selected object from left to right. You can change that, however, by selecting the Gradient tool in the Tools panel and using the tool's gradient widget, like the one shown in Figure 12-9.

Like the Gradient panel, the Gradient tool widget has color stops and sliders for adjusting color. You can also adjust the length and rotation of the gradient widget, and thus the gradient on your object, by dragging and rotating the widget. To reset

FIGURE 12-9 Use the Gradient tool widget to adjust gradients directly on top of an object

Original gradients   Adjusted gradients

FIGURE 12-10 Adjust the
direction of the gradient using
the Gradient tool

how a gradient flows across a selected object, use the
Gradient tool to click and drag across the selection in the
direction you want the gradient to flow. For example,
the linear and radial gradients in Figure 12-10 have been
changed using this technique.

In addition to applying gradients and being able to
adjust their flow on individual objects, gradients can
also be applied across several objects within a selection,
like letter shapes, as illustrated in Figure 12-11.

To apply a single gradient across multiple shapes,
select all the objects and apply the desired gradient
by selecting its swatch from the Swatches panel or
from one of the gradient libraries. Then, select the
Gradient tool and drag the Gradient tool widget across
the selection to reset the flow of the gradient in the
desired direction uniformly across all the objects
within the selection.

Multiple gradients applied to several individual objects

FIGURE 12-11 Gradients can flow
across one or several objects

Single gradient applied across several objects

13

Symbols, 3D Mapping, and Flash Integration

How to...

- Use the Symbols panel
- Open symbol libraries
- Create custom symbols
- Edit and delete symbols
- Use the Symbol tools
- Map symbol art to 3D objects
- Use Illustrator symbols in Flash

A symbol is any piece of artwork that can be reused over and over again without increasing the size of your document. Think of a symbol like a rubber stamp where you make the original design and then create multiple instances of it to your page. Every instance of a symbol is tied to the original through the Symbols panel. You can adjust the look of symbol instances independent of the source symbol, adjust an instance and update the original, or edit the original and have all the instances of it automatically update. Pretty handy stuff!

Like patterns, symbols can be created from any object or illustration and can be reused over and over again. Illustrator also comes with a fantastic library of free symbols, accessible through the Symbols panel, that you can open and use in your work. Symbols can be scaled, moved, rotated, tinted, made transparent, and have styles applied to them using the family of Symbol tools. Even more amazingly, symbols can be used to map art to objects using 3D effects!

If you happen to work with Flash, you'll love how easily Illustrator's symbols can be copied and imported into Flash and used in your SWF and SVG Flash movies. In fact, since CS3, Illustrator has begun treating symbols in the same way Flash does, which makes Illustrator the perfect tool for creating illustrations that will be converted into Flash animations.

In this chapter, you'll learn everything you need to know about working with symbols, mapping symbols to 3D art, and integrating Illustrator symbols into Flash.

The Symbols Panel

The Symbols panel (Window | Symbols) contains a default set of six symbols, as shown in Figure 13-1.

Use the buttons at the bottom of the Symbols panel and/or the commands in the panel's options menu to perform the following actions:

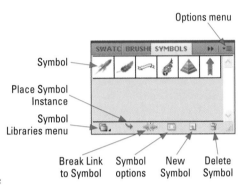

FIGURE 13-1 The Symbols panel

- **Symbol Libraries Menu**   Provides access to all of Illustrator's free symbol libraries.

- **Place Symbol Instance**   Places an instance of the selected symbol onto the artboard.

- **Break Link to Symbol**   Breaks the link between the symbol and the symbol instance and converts the instance into editable vector artwork with no direct connect to the source symbol.

- **Symbol Options**   Opens the Symbol Options dialog box, inside which you can name the symbol, select a symbol type, set the Flash registration, and enable guides for 9-slice scaling.

- **New Symbol**   Creates a new symbol from selected art on the artboard.

- **Delete Symbol**   Deletes the selected symbol(s) from the Symbols panel.

- **Edit Symbol**   Opens the selected symbol in Isolation Mode. Edits made here will be automatically applied to all instances of the symbol on the artboard.

- **Redefine Symbol**   Replaces the symbol selected in the Symbols panel with the selected art on the artboard, thereby redefining that symbol and all instances of it on the artboard.

- **Duplicate Symbol**   Creates an exact copy of the selected symbol in the Symbols panel. To rename the duplicate, select it and click the Symbol Options button at the bottom of the panel. To edit the duplicate, click the Edit Symbol button at the bottom of the panel.

- **Replace Symbol**   Replaces any symbol instance selected on your artboard with an instance of the symbol selected in the Symbols panel.

- **Select All Unused**   Selects all the symbols in the Symbols panel that have not been used in the current document.

- **Select All Instances**   Selects all the artboard instances of the symbol selected in the Symbols panel.

In addition to all these buttons and commands, you can also use the Control panel to name your symbol instances, edit the original symbol tied to the selected symbol instance, break the link between the selected symbol instance and the original, create a duplicate of the selected symbol instance, and alter the opacity of the selected symbol instance. Even cooler, you can use the Replace dropdown menu to swap the selected symbol instance with the instance of another symbol.

Symbol Libraries

Illustrator has an amazing number of free symbols—from martini glasses and satellite dishes to op art and ink splats—that you can open and use in your artwork. To access the free symbol libraries, click the Symbol Libraries menu at the bottom of the Symbols panel and select one of the 32 symbol library options. Like their color, gradient, and pattern cousins, the symbol libraries open in their own floating panels away from the panel dock. Each time you select a symbol from a library, it gets added to the Symbols panel so you can use it again elsewhere in your document.

Creating Custom Symbol Libraries

After you've created a few of your own symbols, you may want to create your own custom symbol library by selecting Save Symbol Library from the Symbols panel options menu. You'll be prompted to save your symbol library in Illustrator's Symbols folder with the name of your choice. To open your library after saving it, all you need to do is click the Symbol Libraries menu at the bottom of the Symbols panel and select your library by name from the User Defined category.

Working with Symbols

To place a symbol on your page, all you have to do is drag and drop one of them from the Symbols panel onto your artboard or select the desired symbol and click the Place Symbol Instance button at the bottom of the panel. If you need three of a particular symbol, drag it over or click the Place Symbol Instance button three times. Or, better yet, drag a new instance of a symbol off an existing instance of a symbol on your artboard—just as you would drag a copy off a regular object—by using the ALT+drag (Win) or OPT+drag (Mac) copy method. The illustration in Figure 13-2 has four instances of a bird symbol, three instances each of two flower symbols and a cloud symbol, and two instances of a grass symbol.

FIGURE 13-2 Use multiple instances of each symbol to create your illustrations

Creating Your Own Symbols

To create your own custom symbol, make your drawing first. Symbols can include any combination of open and closed objects and paths, text, compound paths, mesh objects, grouped objects, and even raster images. When your artwork is ready to be converted into a symbol, select it and drag and drop that selection into the Symbols panel. You can also create symbols from selected artwork by pressing F8, by clicking the New Symbol button at the bottom of the Symbols panel, and by choosing New Symbol from the Symbols panel options menu.

When the Symbol Options dialog box opens, name your new symbol, select a symbol type, and if needed, set the options for using symbols with Flash, which you'll learn about later in this chapter. If you'll only be using artwork in Illustrator, you can leave the default settings as they are and click OK to add the new symbol to your Symbols panel.

Immediately upon creating your new symbol, your original artwork gets relocated into the symbol in the Symbols panel and the selected art on your artboard becomes an *instance* of that new symbol. To create a symbol but keep your original artwork in tact, press the SHIFT key as you create your new symbol.

Editing Symbols

When you go to edit a symbol, what you're actually editing is the original artwork that was used to create it. This means that if your work contains any instances of the symbol, those instances will be immediately updated upon saving the changes to the original.

To edit a symbol, double-click the symbol itself on the Symbols panel and a warning will appear stating that you are about to edit the Symbol. Alternatively, you can select the symbol on your artboard and choose Edit Symbol from the Symbols panel options menu or double-click a symbol instance on the artboard.

The symbol then appears in Isolation Mode where you can make the desired adjustments. For example, the top set of plants in Figure 13-3 was created from the same symbol. The original symbol was then edited in Isolation Mode, and immediately upon saving those edits, all instances of the original symbol were updated, as illustrated in the bottom set of plants.

FIGURE 13-3 Edit a symbol to update all instances of it simultaneously

Original symbol instances

Symbol instances after original symbol was edited

Editing and Redefining Symbol Instances

Editing instances of symbols is more like working with regular objects. You can scale, rotate, shear, reflect, and move symbol instances, as well as apply effects from the Effects menu and settings from the Appearance, Graphic Styles, and Transparency panels. That said, if you want to adjust only a part of a symbol instance without modifying the original symbol, you'll need to expand the instance first by clicking the Break Link To Symbol button on either the Control panel or Symbols panel, or by choosing Object | Expand.

After editing the expanded artwork, you could then create a new symbol or redefine an existing symbol with the new artwork. To redefine an existing symbol, select the new art on your artboard, click the symbol to be redefined on the Symbols panel, and choose Redefine Symbol from the Symbols panel options menu.

Deleting Symbols

To delete any unused or unneeded symbols from the Symbols panel, select the symbol(s) to be deleted and click the Delete Symbol (mini trash) icon. You can also delete by dragging and dropping the desired symbols onto the panel's Delete Symbol icon or by selecting the symbol(s) to be deleted and choosing Delete Symbol from the panel's options menu.

In some cases, an alert dialog box may appear, indicating that one or more of the symbols you're trying to delete is being used and cannot be deleted until the instances of it are either expanded (detached from the symbol and turned back into editable vector art) or deleted themselves. You can then choose to Expand Instances, Delete Instances, or Cancel the deletion of the selected symbol.

The Symbolism Tools

The Tools panel has eight Symbolism tools that you can use to modify how the instances of symbols appear on your artboard. The Symbol Sprayer is the starting point that allows you to create a set of symbol instances. You can then use the other Symbolism tools to change and modify those sets of symbol instances. What makes these tools so robust is that you can modify symbol instances without affecting, or altering the connection to, the original symbol.

Each of the tools uses the same brush head. To modify the diameter, method, intensity, and symbol set density of this brush head, double-click any of the Symbolism tools to launch the Symbolism Tools Options dialog box. Within the dialog box, you'll also see icons that match each of the tools, which can be selected to adjust tool settings or learn more about each tool.

Though you can use the Symbolism tools with individual symbols, they tend to work best with *symbol sets*. A symbol set is a collection of symbols painted onto your artboard with the Symbol Sprayer tool. Symbol sets can include multiple instances of a single symbol or mixed symbols by selecting different symbols in the Symbols panel as you use the Symbol Sprayer tool.

Symbol Sprayer   Symbol Shifter   Symbol Scruncher   Symbol Sizer

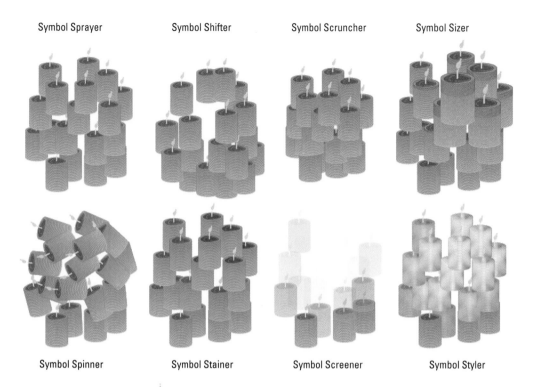

Symbol Spinner   Symbol Stainer   Symbol Screener   Symbol Styler

FIGURE 13-4 Use the Symbolism tools to adjust the symbol instances in your symbol sets

To use any of the Symbolism tools, select one or more symbols or symbol sets on your artboard first, then select the desired Symbolism tool and apply it to your selection. The following is a listing of what each of the tools does. As you read each description, look to the examples in Figure 13-4 to get a visual idea of how each tool can modify your work.

- **Symbol Sprayer tool**   Like a can of spray paint, this tool sprays a *symbol set* of the original selected symbol in your Symbols panel as you click and drag your cursor across the artboard. To create a mixed set, select a different symbol from the Symbols panel and continue spraying with the actively selected set. To delete symbols from a set, press and hold the ALT (Win) or OPT (Mac) key as you click and drag.

- **Symbol Shifter tool**   This tool shifts symbol instances and symbols within symbol sets from their current location in the direction of your mouse movements. In symbol sets, you can also use this tool to adjust the symbol stacking order.

- **Symbol Scruncher tool**   This tool moves symbol instances away from or closer to each other. To move symbols closer together, click and drag your mouse toward the focal point of the scrunching and release when the symbols are at the desired distance. To move symbols away from each other, press and hold the ALT (Win) or OPT (Mac) key as you click and drag your mouse, then release when symbols are at the desired distance.

- **Symbol Sizer tool**   This tool adjusts the size of symbol instances. To make symbols larger, click and drag across those symbols. To make symbols smaller, hold down the ALT (Win) or OPT (Mac) as you click and drag.

- **Symbol Spinner tool**   This tool spins or rotates symbol instances on the artboard as you click and drag in the direction you want the objects to spin.

- **Symbol Stainer tool**   Use this tool to adjust the color of symbol instances. You can help determine the outcome of the color stain created by this tool by selecting a fill color before applying the tool. To remove the stainer color and revert a symbol to its original coloration, press and hold the ALT (Win) or OPT (Mac) key as you click and drag.

- **Symbol Screener tool**   This tool can alter the opacity of symbol instances creating semi- to full-transparent effects. Click and drag across the selection to apply transparency, or press and hold the ALT (Win) or OPT (Mac) key as you drag to remove transparency and restore the symbol instances to 100% opacity.

- **Symbol Styler tool**   Use this tool to apply a selected style from the Graphics Styles panel to symbol instances. You can use any of the styles in the Graphic Styles panel or Graphic Styles libraries or create your own (see Chapter 18 for details). To apply a graphic style, select a symbol set on the artboard and a style from the Graphic Styles panel, and then drag across the symbol set. Press and hold the ALT (Win) or OPT (Mac) key to gradually remove the style from the symbol instances.

Mapping Symbol Art to 3D Objects

Creating 3D objects in Illustrator has never been easier. You can create 3D objects from any shape and then set the rotation, extrude, bevel, revolve, surface shading, and lighting options to further enhance the 3D effect. Even more amazingly, you can map symbols onto 3D images for more realistic renderings of your artwork.

To illustrate how simple it is to convert a regular shape into 3D and map art onto it, take a look at the two objects in Figure 13-5. One has been turned into a 3D object using the Extrude & Bevel effect, the other has become 3D using the Revolve effect, and both have been mapped with custom symbols.

Extrude & Bevel, Revolve, and Map Art

To turn a 2D object into a 3D object using the Extrude & Bevel effect, which extends the object along its z axis, or the Revolve effect, which revolves the object in a vertical circle along its y axis, and then map symbol artwork to it, follow these steps:

1. Select your object on the artboard.

2. Choose Effect | 3D | Extrude & Bevel or Effect | 3D | Revolve.

FIGURE 13-5 Use effects and symbols to create 3D images

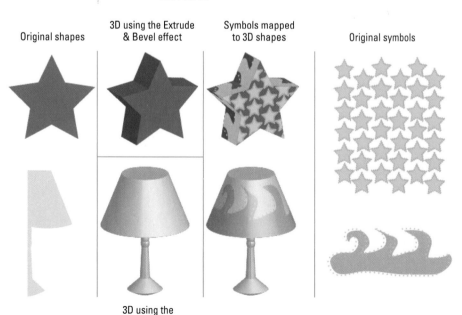

Original shapes

3D using the Extrude & Bevel effect

Symbols mapped to 3D shapes

Original symbols

3D using the Revolve effect

3. Choose the desired settings in the dialog box. To preview your object before accepting the Extrude & Bevel effect, click the Preview box. Click the More Options button to see a full set of 3D options:

- **Position** Determines your object's rotation and perspective. Run through each of the options to see how the 3D preview cube changes. Set the x, y, and z coordinates between −180° and 180° if you know them, or click and drag on the 3D cube until your object looks right. If desired, adjust the perspective percentage.

- **Extrude & Bevel** Sets your object's extrude depth, cap, and bevel.

- **Revolve** Sets your object's angle (number of degrees to revolve between 0 and 360), cap (solid or hollow), offset (distance between the revolve axis and path), and from left or right edge as the axis.

- **Surface** Adds a surface texture to your object, from matte to shiny. Options include Wireframe, No Shading, Diffuse Shading, and Plastic Shading. Select Plastic Shading for the most realistic 3D effect.

- **Lighting** Applies lighting to your object as well as alters the object's shading color. Click the light icon on the lighting sphere to reposition the lighting. Click the New Light button to add additional light sources or the Delete Light button to remove unwanted selected light sources. The default shading color is black, but you can change it to any color in your Swatches panel by selecting Custom from the Shading Color menu.

4. To map symbol art to the surfaces of your 3D object, click the Map Art button. In the Map Art dialog box, select a symbol from the Symbol dropdown menu for each of the object's surfaces. Click the Next and Previous Surface buttons to toggle between the object's different surfaces, which will be outlined in red to assist you in selecting the right symbols for each surface. To shade the artwork with a shading color, click the Shade Artwork option. When finished, click the OK button.

Integrating Illustrator Symbols with Flash

Since Illustrator CS3, Illustrator's symbols have worked identically to symbols in Flash, making the process of sharing artwork between the two programs a snap, so long as you prepare your symbols in Illustrator to work properly with Flash. This can be done in the Symbol Options dialog box as you create each symbol, or later as part of a pre-flight workflow before importing or exporting symbols into Flash.

To set your symbols for Flash integration, double-click a symbol in the Symbols panel to open the Symbol Options dialog box. Start by giving your symbol a name, such as Button or Cloud, and then setting the symbol type to MovieClip. You can reset this later in Flash if needed. Set the Flash Registration for the symbol using the registration icon. Click the square in the registration grid that best represents the area of the symbol you want to use as its registration mark, such as the top left edge or in the very center. If you plan on creating a symbol that is scalable, check the Enable Guides For 9-Slice Scaling option to ensure that your symbols scale properly along with the movie clips.

Tip   To learn more about 9-slice scaling in Flash, see Flash Help. You might also find it useful to watch the video about working with Illustrator, Fireworks, and Flash at www.adobe.com/go/vid0205.

Another step you'll want to take before you send your Illustrator artwork to Flash is to name all the instances of your symbols on the artboard. You can do this by selecting each instance on your artboard and adding an instance name in the Instance Name field on the Control panel.

The last thing you may want to do is set up all your symbol instances on separate, named layers, such as Landscape, Clouds, Trees, Birds, and so on. When you do this, Flash will preserve your layers when you use the importing and exporting processes described in the following subsections.

After you've created your symbols and named all the instances in Illustrator, you have three options for how to get those symbols into Flash. You can copy and paste symbols from Illustrator into Flash, export your files in SWF format, or import your AI file into Flash, preserving layers, symbols, symbol instance names, and more.

Copying Symbols to Flash

To copy your symbols from Illustrator to Flash, select all the symbol instances on your artboard and choose Edit | Copy to copy the selection to your computer's clipboard, or alternatively press CTRL+C (Win) or CMD+C (Mac). Next, you'll open Flash and select Edit | Paste to paste the selection onto the Flash stage, or alternately press CTRL+V (Win) or CMD+V (Mac). A Paste dialog box will appear prompting you to choose importer preferences such as whether the pasted selection should be brought in as a bitmap or use the AI File Importer and whether the paste should maintain layers. Click the OK button to add the objects to your Flash file on their own layers. If you select the objects in Flash you'll notice in the Library panel and Properties inspector that each symbol has been added to the Library panel and the registration marks and instance names of all of them have been preserved.

Exporting Symbols to Flash

To export your Illustrator files containing symbols, you have the option of saving your document as a Flash SWF file by selecting File | Export and choosing SWF as the file format. When the SWF Options dialog box opens, choose the settings that best suit your SWF Flash needs, such as Export As AI Layers To SWF Frames, Include Unused Symbols, and Export Text As Outlines. You can also click the Advanced button to set things like image format, resolution, and frame rate, as well as features like animating blends and exporting static layers across all frames. If desired, you can preview the SWF file in a browser window or on a particular handheld device by clicking the Web Preview and/or Device Central buttons. To export the SWF, click the OK button.

To learn more about setting up Illustrator files with symbols for export as SWF files for Flash, check out the video at www.adobe.com/go/vid0214.

Importing Symbols in Flash

To import your Illustrator file into Flash, open Flash, set up a new document in the size you need (such as 800×600 pixels), and select File | Import | Import To Stage. Next, you'll browse to and select your Illustrator file, and then in the Import "Filename" To Stage dialog box, you'll select which objects and layers from the Illustrator file you'd like to import. Last, you'll click the OK button to have Flash import all the artwork onto the stage, preserving all the layers and symbols.

For additional tips and suggestions about importing Illustrator files with symbols into Flash, watch the following Adobe video at www.adobe.com/go/vid0198.

14

Graph Tools

How to…

- Use the Graph tools
- Enter and edit graph data
- Import data from a spreadsheet
- Change the graph type
- Customize graph fills, strokes, and fonts
- Create and apply custom graph designs

A chart or graph is the perfect visual aid to assist viewers in comprehending complex numerical and statistical data in a visually meaningful way. Of course, you could use a spreadsheet program like Microsoft Excel to create a graph for you, but to really make a chart or graph unique, let Illustrator help you compile your own or imported data into a customizable graph style. As an added plus, graphs created in Illustrator will reproduce more accurately than their Excel counterpart when placed in a page layout program like Adobe InDesign or QuarkXPress. What's more, each graph can be fully customized with color, fonts, gradients, and even custom graph designs. This chapter will teach you how to import your data, use the nine different Graph tools, and customize your graphs for distinctive visual presentations.

The Graph Tools

One of the key reasons Illustrator's graphs are so powerful is that, besides letting you input your own data or import data from a spreadsheet program, Illustrator's graphs can be modified as you work so your graphs will instantly update with the new information. In addition, customizing your graphs is fairly easy to do, so with a little bit of know-how you'll seem like a visual data genius.

The first thing you'll do when you're ready to create a graph is to select a tool from the Graph tools flyout menu on the Tools panel. Graph types include Column, Stacked Column, Bar, Stacked Bar, Line, Area, Scatter, Pie, and Radar.

The tool you select will determine both how the graph will look initially (though you can change the type later if you need to), like the examples shown in Figure 14-1, as well as how data should be entered into it:

- **Column Graph tool**   Makes graphs that compare data in vertical columns.

- **Stacked Column Graph tool**   Creates graphs in vertically stacked columns rather than present them next to each other to emphasize the relationship between the different parts to the total.

- **Bar Graph tool**   Makes graphs that compare data in horizontal columns.

- **Stacked Bar Graph tool**   Creates graphs in horizontally stacked columns to emphasize the relationship between the different parts.

- **Line Graph tool**   Creates graphs that use lines to join points together for one or more sets of data to show progress over time.

- **Area Graph tool**   Makes mountain-range like graphs that plot data using points and lines but fill in those shapes to emphasize individual and cumulative value changes.

- **Scatter Graph tool**   Creates confetti-like graphs that plot data in points along the graph's x/y coordinates. This type of graph is best used for showing trends and patterns, as well as how different variables in data can affect each other.

- **Pie Graph tool**   Makes circular pie-shaped graphs where each wedge in the pie represents percentage values relative to the whole pie.

- **Radar Graph tool**   Also called a Web Graph, this tool creates circular web-like graphs that compare value sets in special categories or over points in time.

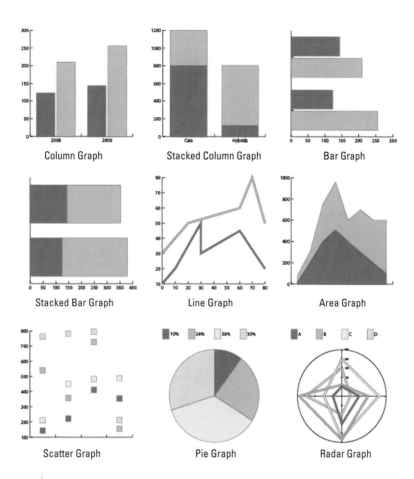

Column Graph

Stacked Column Graph

Bar Graph

Stacked Bar Graph

Line Graph

Area Graph

Scatter Graph

Pie Graph

Radar Graph

FIGURE 14-1 Choose the Graph tool that will best present your data.

With your Graph tool selected, the next step is to drag out a rectangular shape onto the artboard within which your graph will sit. To make a graph with precise dimensions, click the artboard instead of dragging and enter a width and height in the Graph dialog box, then click OK.

As the placeholder graph is added on your artboard, you'll also see your Graph Data window, like the one in Figure 14-2, appear directly below the graph. The Graph Data window looks a lot like a regular spreadsheet with rows and columns, and it is here where you'll input your graph data.

Inputting Data

You have two options when it comes to adding data to your graph through the Graph Data window. You can type in the data yourself or import (or paste) the data from an external spreadsheet file.

Adding Your Own Data

To add your own data, select a cell in the Graph Data window with your cursor and enter your data into the entry text box. If pasting in copied content, select the desired cell and use the Edit | Paste command. The following are some general tips for adding labels to your column, stacked column, bar, stacked bar, line, area, and radar graphs:

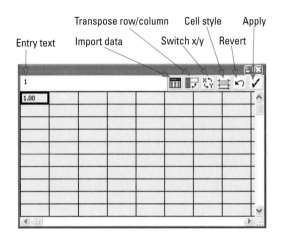

FIGURE 14-2 Enter your graph data in the Graph Data window

- To have a legend on your graph, leave the upper left cell blank, as shown in Figure 14-3.

- When you have more than one data set, enter the labels of the different sets in the top row of cells so they appear in the legend. Otherwise, enter data in the top row.

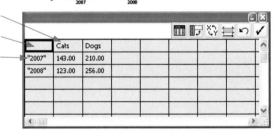

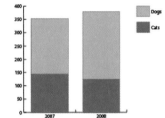

- If you'd like the categories (like months or years) in your graph to have labels along the vertical or horizontal axis, enter those in the far left column.

FIGURE 14-3 Add labels to the Graph Data window

- When your labels use numbers only, such as 2008, surround the numbers with straight quote marks, as in "2008".

- When your labels need line breaks, use the vertical bar key instead of a paragraph return, as in Gallons Used|Summer|2008.

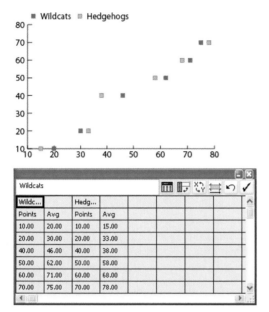

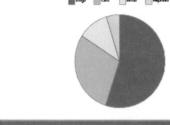

FIGURE 14-4 Scatter graphs require precise input in the Graph Data window

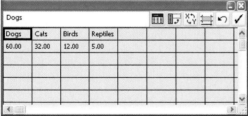

FIGURE 14-5 Enter a single row of data for a pie graph

Scatter and pie graphs require slightly different data input in the Graph Data window. With scatter graphs, you're plotting comparative data from two or more groups at points along the x/y axis. Therefore, enter your data-set labels in every other cell along the top row, add your y-axis data in the first column, and put your x-axis data in the second column. Repeat this process for each data set, as shown in Figure 14-4.

With your pie graphs, if you'd like chart key labels to appear above or alongside the graph, you'll add your data-set category labels across the top row, starting at the left-most cell. If you'd also like to add labels to appear along the bottom of the chart, enter value labels along the left column. For a single pie graph, place your category data below each label using all positive or negative numbers, like the example in Figure 14-5. To create multiple pie graphs, all you need to do is plot additional rows of data below the first row.

Continue selecting cells and entering data as needed. Use the TAB key after inputting data to select the next cell in the same row. To input entered data and move to the cell below in the same column, press the ENTER (Win) or RETURN (Mac) key. Alternatively, you can use the ARROW keys to maneuver to the desired cell location. Keep in mind that each graph type requires your data be entered differently in the row and column cells, which can be a bit confusing at first. Use the dialog box buttons to assist you with sorting and displaying data:

- **Import data**   Opens a dialog box to select and import data from a tab-delimited text file (see the next section for details on importing data).

- **Transpose row/column**   Flips the data from rows to columns and vice versa.

- **Switch x/y**   Toggles the location of the x/y coordinates on the graph.

- **Cell style**   Edits the number of decimals and column width by digits.

- **Revert**   Reverts the data to the state it was in when you first opened or reopened the Graph Data window.

- **Apply**   Applies your data to your graph.

 If at any time you need to adjust the width of the columns in the Graph Data window, position your cursor above the column divider line you want to adjust and when your cursor turns into a double-arrow, drag the handle to the new position.

As you enter your data, you can take a peek at how it will alter your graph by clicking the Apply button. Continue entering your data and making edits to it until you are satisfied. The Data box will remain open on your artboard unless you close it by clicking the Close button.

Importing Spreadsheet Data

When importing data from a spreadsheet program like Microsoft Excel or Lotus 1-2-3, you can input your information in two ways:

- Copy your data from your spreadsheet program, select the top left cell of the Graph Data window, and paste your data into it using the Edit | Paste command, or alternatively by pressing CTRL+V (Win) or CMD+V (Mac).

- Export your spreadsheet program data as a tab-delimited text file, where each row of data is separated by a paragraph return. Data in this format should only include decimal points (like 230.00) but not any decimal commas (as in 23,000). When the text file is ready, click the Graph Data window's Import Data button to select and import that text file.

After your data is in place, click the Apply button to see how your data is revealed in your graph. If needed, use the Graph Data window buttons (as described earlier), make edits, and continue entering data until everything looks right. When you're finished, click the Close button on the dialog box.

Congratulations! You've just created your first graph! At this point, you can leave the graph as is, change the graph type, update graph data, and customize the graph colors.

Editing Graphs

The Graph tool and style you select initially can easily be changed to any of the other graph types. You can also update the data any time you need to, as well as customize the look of your graph with different fonts, colors, patterns, gradients, and even custom graph designs.

Changing the Graph Type

If at any time you want to change your graph from one type to another, use the Graph Type dialog box. To open the dialog box, select the graph you want to change and either double-click any of the Graph tools on the Tools panel or right-click (Win) or CTRL+click (Mac) the selected graph and choose the Type option from the graph's context menu.

The Graph Type dialog box includes three options on its main dropdown menu, each with different settings for controlling how your data gets displayed:

- **Graph Options**   Select this option to choose an alternate graph type by clicking the desired Graph tool icon and adjust that graph's style settings and options. Note: This option is not active if the Graph Data window is still open.

- **Value Axis**   Use this setting to override calculated tick values, adjust the length of your graph's value tick marks and edit the number of tick marks per division, and to add prefix and suffix labels to your graph.

- **Category Axis**   Select this menu option to adjust the length of your graph's category tick marks and edit the number of tick marks per division.

Unfortunately, there is no Preview button in this dialog box for you to see what the different graph types will look like before committing to it, so you'll need to click the OK button before you can see the change to the graph on your artboard. If you're unhappy with the outcome, simply reopen the Graph Type dialog box and select another graph type or press CTRL+Z (Win) or CMD+Z (Mac) to undo the last change.

Updating Graph Data

To edit the data in your graph, select the graph on your artboard, right-click (Win) or CTRL+click (Mac) it to open the context menu, and choose the Data option. You can also access the Graph Data window by choosing Object | Graph | Data. The Graph Data window for the selected graph will reopen in your workspace so you can make your changes. When finished, click the Close button to close the window.

Customizing Graphs

The look of your graphs can be totally customized. As you learned earlier in this chapter, you can alter the placement of graph labels and categories, tick marks, and other features for each graph using the Graph Type dialog box (Object | Graph | Type). But when you really want to take your graph to the next level, use Illustrator's other tools to edit the open and closed shapes within the graph. For example, you can change the color, add drop shadows, reposition the legend, alter the font face, style, size, and color, transform any of the form elements using the Transform tools, apply gradients, blends, and patterns to columns and markers, add brush strokes and graphic styles, and even use the 3D Extrude & Bevel effects on selected parts of your charts for extra dynamic effects!

The objects within your graph are grouped together so they can communicate with the Graph Data window. Within the graph itself, you'll find additional nested groups for objects within each legend.

Tip Do not ungroup the elements in your graph if there's a possibility you will need to adjust the data at any point in the future. If you ungroup the graph, Illustrator treats the elements as separated paths and type, and regrouping does not restore the connection to the Graph Data window.

Selecting and Editing Parts of a Graph

To select the text, columns, markers, paths, or plot points of a graph to change them, use the Group Selection tool, which selects all the parts of a particular group when you click once to select one part and then click that same part again. For example, if you have a graph with two colors, blue and yellow, and you want to select all the yellow elements, click a yellow element once with the Group Selection tool, and then single-click it again and all the yellow parts within that group will be selected and be ready for editing. Alternatively, you could use the Direct Selection tool to choose one element of your graph, and use the Select | Same | Fill Color command to select all similar elements before changing them. To deselect any part of a group, SHIFT+click the object with the Group Selection or Direct Selection tool.

After the parts are selected, go ahead and change the color of the stroke and fill, edit the type, apply a gradient or pattern, and otherwise make adjustments to the selection. Continue selecting and changing different parts until your graph is customized to your satisfaction.

Applying Custom Graph Designs

Believe it or not, you can add illustrations to your graph columns and markers! A graph design can be any drawing or symbol that can be used to represent the values on the graph. You can use any of Illustrator's preset graph designs or create your own and save them in the Graph Design dialog box.

Creating Custom Designs

Before you apply a graph design to the columns and markers of a selected graph, you'll need to import the artwork through the Swatches panel. Click the Swatch Libraries menu button and choose Other Library. Then, navigate to the Cool Extras/en_US/ Sample Files/Graph Designs folder in the Illustrator application folder, select a graph design file, and click the Open button. To import a design from another file, navigate to and select that file and click the Open button. Though you won't see a new panel open, the design will be accessible when you open the Open Column and Graph Marker dialog boxes.

To create your own custom column or marker design, follow these steps:

1. Create your design within a rectangle, which sets the boundary of the design.

2. Select the entire design and rectangle and choose Object | Group to group the selection.

3. With the design still selected, choose Object | Graph | Design.

4. Click the New Design button. Your new design will appear in the preview window.

5. To rename your new design, select it and click the Rename button.

6. Click the OK button to close the Graph Design dialog box.

Applying Custom Designs

To apply your custom design to a column of a graph, select the columns or bars you want to modify (or select the whole graph) and choose Object | Graph | Column. Select your custom design from the listing in the Graph Column dialog box, choose a Column Type, and click OK to apply your design to the graph. Based on the Column Type you select, your design can be vertically or uniformly scaled along the columns, repeated along the column length either with a chopped or a scaled top edge, or stretched along a column at a specified point within the design.

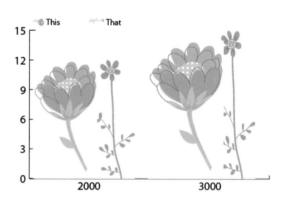

To apply your custom design to a marker on a line or scatter graph, select the markers you want to modify and choose Object | Graph | Marker. Select your custom design from the listing in the Graph Marker dialog box and click OK to apply your design to the graph.

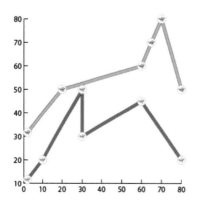

PART III

Special Tools and Techniques

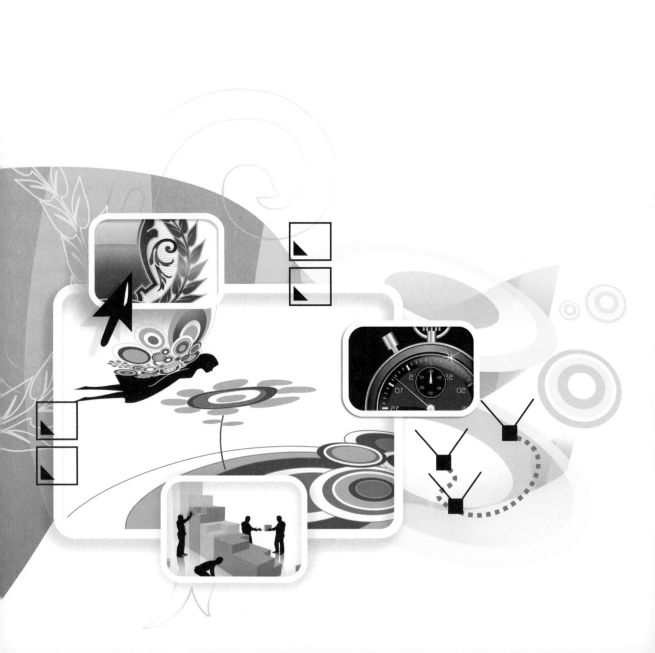

15

Creating Blends

How to...

- Create blends
- Use the Blend tool
- Set blend options
- Edit and manipulate blends
- Use the Blend menu options

In Illustrator, a blend is the resulting set of shapes created between any two or more objects connected with the Blend tool. As amazing as this tool is, blending is a much overlooked feature of Illustrator. Blends can create "tween" or *step* graphics between any two or more lines, shapes, and even text, of any size and color. Plus, you can use the Blend command to have Illustrator do math for you when you need a specific number of evenly spaced duplicate objects. Not only that, because blends are live effects, you can edit the stroke and fill colors of the *key objects*, redraw the spine connecting the shapes, reverse the spine, and even expand the blend to create individual unique shapes from the blend. Consider this chapter your crash course on all things blendy.

Creating Blends

When you're ready to create a blend between two or more key objects, use the Blend tool or the Blend command (Object | Blend | Make). You can create three different kinds of blends, as illustrated in Figure 15-1, each of which distributes shape and blend colors evenly between the key objects.

How to. . .   # Use the Blend Command

To create a blend with the Blend command instead of using the Blend tool, select two or more key objects on your artboard, and then choose Object | Blend | Make. When you use this command, Illustrator decides where within each key object the blend should occur.

The Blend Tool

Blends created from two or more key objects with the Blend tool result in a series of stepped paths where the shapes in the middle of the blend (including their stroke and fill attributes) are morphed. To create a blend with the Blend tool, follow these steps:

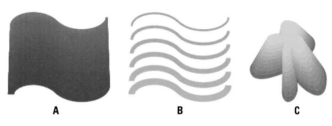

A   B   C

FIGURE 15-1 Create (A) Smooth Color, (B) Specified Steps, and (C) Specified Distance blends with the Blend tool

1. Position your key objects where you'd like them on the artboard.

2. Select the Blend tool from the Tools panel.

3. Click the fill or edge of the first object and then click the fill or edge of the second object to create the blend. To add additional key objects, simply click the fill or edge of the next object. As the blend is generated, Illustrator draws a *spine* between the key objects.

Did You Know?   # Where You Click Changes the Blend

Where you click each key object helps determine the shape and rotation of the blend. For example, the first set of objects in Figure 15-2 were blended from their top left corners, whereas with the second set of objects, the first object was clicked at the top right corner and the second object was clicked at the bottom left, creating an obvious rotation of the blended shapes between the two key objects.

Blend created when both objects
were clicked at top left corners

Blend created when first object clicked
at top right corner and second object
clicked at bottom left corner

FIGURE **15-2** Where you click
objects with the Blend tool
establishes the rotation of the
blend

Blend Options

Blends will automatically be created using the last-used blend style as specified in the Blend Options dialog box. To change the blend type from one style to another, select the blended objects on your artboard and choose a different blend style from the Blend Options dialog box. To open the Blend Options dialog box, double-click the Blend tool on the Tools panel or choose Object | Blend | Blend Options. Here's an overview of the different blend options:

- **Smooth Color**   Makes a smooth blend that uses as many steps as needed to smoothly blend shape and color between the key objects.

- **Specified Steps**   Makes blends that morph the shape and color of the key objects over a specified number of steps, like 254 for a super smooth blend, or 8 for a clearly banded groovy 1970s-style blend.

- **Specified Distance**   Makes blends that morph the shape and color of the key objects over a specified distance using any unit of measure, such as 1 in or 10 pt.

- **Align to Page**   Sets the orientation of the blend to the x axis of the page, as shown in the example in Figure 15-3.

- **Align to Path**   Shifts the orientation of the blend from the page to the path, or *spine*, of the blend (see Figure 15-3).

If you press and hold the ALT (Win) or OPTION (Mac) key as you click the second key object with the Blend tool, the Blend Options dialog box will open so you can modify the blend's style and orientation before it gets added to your artboard.

Editing Blends

A

B

FIGURE **15-3** Objects in a blend
can be aligned to the page (A) or
the path (B)

Illustrator's blends are live effects, which means that any time you change one of the key objects in the blend, the entire blend—and all the steps between the key objects—will update to reflect that change. For example, the object shown in Figure 15-4 started off as a blend between two rectangles. After the blend was created, the yellow object was made larger with the Scale tool, its shape was tweaked with the Warp tool, a 1pt orange stroke was applied to it, and the spine of the blend was redrawn with the Pencil tool.

All blends with two or more paths are treated by Illustrator as a single editable object, which means you can edit the key objects to instantly create different looking blends since the paths between the key objects are redrawn each time you make a change.

FIGURE 15-4 Change the color, shape, rotation, and scale of the key objects in a blend

To edit a blend, try any of the following live editing techniques:

- Select a key object with the Direct Selection tool and edit the shape's fill color, stroke color, and stroke weight, or edit the shape by repositioning anchor points and adjusting direction handles. If needed, add or subtract anchor points using the Add Anchor Point and Delete Anchor Point Pen tools.

- Redraw the spine from the center of one key object to the center of the next using the Pencil tool or adjust the spine by selecting the anchor points or paths with the Direct Selection tool.

FIGURE 15-5 Turn your 3D objects into blends

- Select a key object with the Direct Selection tool and edit it using any of the Transform and Reshaping tools.

- Warp your blends using the Effect | Warp | Arc command.

FIGURE 15-6 Create blends between symbols and objects: (A) blending two of the same symbols, (B) blending a symbol with an object, and (C) blending two different symbols

- Create blends using 3D objects, as illustrated in Figure 15-5, where the size, color, and shape of the spine change.

- Create a blend using symbols, like the ones in Figure 15-6. When the same symbol is used, additional symbol instances will be added to the spine; however, when a symbol and a regular path are used, paths instead of symbol instances are drawn along the spine. If two different symbols are used, paths will also be drawn along the spine.

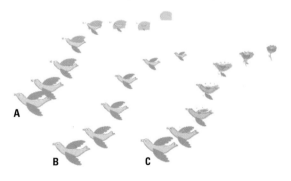

A

B

C

Blend Menu Options

To support the Blend tool's functionality, Illustrator offers a wide set of blend options through the Object | Blend menu. You can create and release blends, expand a blend into individual shapes, replace and reverse a blend's spine, and reverse the order of the blend objects from front to back and vice versa.

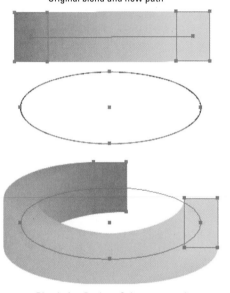

Original blend and new path

Blend after Replace Spine command

To use any of the Blend menu options, select the blend object on the artboard with the Selection tool and choose one of the following commands from the Object | Blend menu:

- **Make** Select this option to create a blend from any two or more selected objects on your artboard. You can also use the keyboard shortcut to access this command: ALT+CTRL+B (Win) or OPT+CMD+B (Mac).

- **Release** Choose this command to release the objects in the selected blend and revert the key shapes to their original unblended state. Access this command by pressing ALT+SHIFT+CTRL+B (Win) or OPT+SHIFT+CMD+B (Mac).

- **Blend Options...** Opens the Blend Options dialog box for changing the style and orientation of the selected blend.

- **Expand** When you want to be able to modify any of the individual paths between the key objects in a blend, choose this command, which results in a series of grouped shapes between and including the key objects. You can then ungroup, move, and edit the individual shapes.

- **Replace Spine** Use this command to replace the spine on a selected blend with a different selected path (like a circle or squiggly line), as in the example in Figure 15-7. You must select both the original blended object and the new path before the Replace Spine option becomes available in the Object | Blend menu.

- **Reverse Spine** Reverses the spine (or more like flips the position of the key objects) within a blend, thereby reversing the sequence of objects between the key objects, as shown in Figure 15-8.

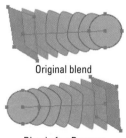

Original blend

Blend after Reverse Spine command

■ **Reverse Front to Back**   Sends the front object to the back or the back object to the front, reversing the order of the objects within the blend, as illustrated in Figure 15-9.

Because you can create blends with multiple objects, experiment with different lines and shapes. You could, for instance, build interesting 3D-like linear and nonlinear blends such as the ones in Figure 15-10, especially if you pay attention to the arrangement of the objects before creating the blend. Have fun and get creative!

Original blend

Blend after Reverse
Front To Back command

FIGURE 15-9 Flip the top-most
object in the blend with the
Reverse Front To Back command

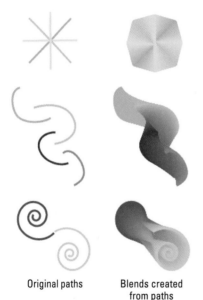

Original paths   Blends created
                          from paths

FIGURE 15-10 Create interesting
linear and nonlinear blends with
multiple objects

16

Clipping Masks and Compound Paths

How to...

- Create clipping masks with objects and type
- Add objects to, edit, and release clipping masks
- Create compound paths
- Edit and release compound paths

In this chapter, you'll learn about two of the more interesting techniques you can perform with your artwork in Illustrator, namely clipping masks and compound paths. With a clipping mask, you can mask away, or hide, portions of your work with another shape, such as making a placed rectangular photograph appear as if it had a rounded rectangle edge. With a compound path, by contrast, you can create any shaped cutouts inside of a larger object, kind of like putting the holes in a wedge of Swiss cheese. What's more, with both of these techniques you can use closed shapes, open paths, text (either editable or outlined letters), photographs, and even artwork in other file formats.

Clipping Masks

In a clipping mask, two objects are combined with a single command so the shape of the top object defines—like a window—the area inside which the other object appears. In other words, everything in the underlying object that falls outside the top object's boundaries will be hidden, both onscreen in Preview mode and in print. For example, the image in Figure 16-1 shows an object (the photo), a mask (the rounded rectangle), and the clipping mask created from them when the mask shape is placed on top of the object using the Clipping Mask command.

The mask can be any shaped object and can be a closed shape, an open path, a compound path, or even text! The mask can have any color fill or stroke and any stroke weight before the mask is applied, however those attributes will be removed when the mask is created since it's the path (or outer edges) of the mask shape that is used to define the area that will be revealed.

There is no limit to the number of objects that can be included in the mask itself. You could, for instance, have 20 different objects beneath the mask shape if you wanted to and only the parts of those shapes that fall directly below the path line of the mask shape will be visible in the clipping mask. Objects that can be masked include single shapes or paths, multiple objects, and even placed images like a JPG, GIF, PNG, TIFF, EPS, PSD, or PDF file.

FIGURE 16-1 Combine (A) an object with (B) a mask shape to create (C) a clipping mask

Creating a Clipping Mask

To create a mask, you need a mask shape and one or more objects to be masked. The mask shape must be a vector shape and always be on top of the object(s) being masked before the mask is applied. When the objects are in position, select the mask and the object(s) below it and choose Object | Clipping Mask | Make, or press the keyboard shortcut, CTRL+7 (Win) or CMD+7 (Mac). This creates what's called a *clipping set*. The mask will then hide any parts of the underlying objects that fall outside the mask shape while showing those objects inside the masked shape.

When working with grouped objects or layers, use the Layers panel to apply clipping masks to your work. Start by moving all the objects and the clipping mask shape into a layer or group. Then, position the mask object at the top of the layer or group. Next, click the name of the layer or group in the Layers panel, and then click the Make/Release Clipping Mask button on the bottom of the panel or choose the Make Clipping Mask command from the Layers panel options menu.

When using the Object I Clipping Mask I Make command, keep in mind that the clipping mask will be created for only the selected items. However, when creating a clipping mask with the Make Clipping Mask button in the Layers panel, all objects in that layer will become part of the mask.

Adding Objects to a Mask

If you discover that you need to add another object to the masked object after you've already created it, position the new object behind the masked object, select the new object and the masked object, and then choose Object I Clipping Mask I Make. You may also add and remove objects from a clipping mask by dragging an object into or out of a clipping mask layer or group in the Layers panel.

The mask will incorporate the new object along with the original masked shapes by releasing the original mask from the masked shapes and creating a new mask. In fact, if you take a peek at the Layers panel, you'll notice that as the mask is created, all the objects in the mask (including the mask shape) are grouped together, making it easier for you to rearrange the objects in that group should you need to edit or move them as a single shape.

Adding a Mask to a Mask

Believe it or not, you can mask a masked object! To create a masked object from a masked object, place the new mask shape on top of the masked object (either by itself or along with other masked and/or unmasked objects), and choose Object I Clipping Mask I Make. It's that easy.

When it comes to printing masked objects with an inexpensive PostScript printer, less is more. In other words, the more complex your masked objects, the more memory it will take for your printer to print it. To keep printing times reasonable, try to limit the number of objects and masks in your masks, and if at all possible, make your mask shapes relatively simple.

Masking Type

Masking type works the same way as masking with an object. Write out the word(s) to be used as a mask and place the type on top of the objects to be masked. Select all those objects, and choose Object I Clipping Mask I Make. The masked objects will be revealed inside the shapes of the letters, like the example in Figure 16-2. And, since this is a live effect you're creating, you can select and edit the type

Text on top of a placed photo

Masked type

FIGURE 16-2 Create masked type with the Clipping Mask command

(this automatically puts the masked object in Isolation Mode for editing purposes) and the masked object will automatically update!

 When working with type that has already been converted to outlines, you may need to create a compound path with the letter shapes before applying the Clipping Mask command. To learn how to create a compound path, see the "Compound Paths" section later in this chapter.

Editing Clipping Masks

To edit the contents of a clipping mask object (such as selecting and modifying the shape of the mask or masked objects' paths with the Direct Selection tool and altering the paths' strokes and fills), there are a few of ways to go about it:

- Select the clipping mask and choose Object | Clipping Mask | Edit Contents. You can then toggle between the clipping path (the mask shape) and the contents of the mask (the masked shapes) by clicking the Edit Clipping Path and Edit Contents buttons on the Control panel.

- Double-click the clipping mask object to enter the object in Isolation Mode. While in Isolation Mode, you can select the different parts of the object on the artboard or through the Layers panel, and make your changes before exiting Isolation Mode (refer back to Chapter 7 for a refresher on Isolation Mode).

- Right-click (Win) or CMD+click (Mac) the masked object to access the context menu and choose Isolate Selected Clipping Mask. To exit Isolation Mode, right-click (Win) or CMD+click (Mac) the masked object again and choose Exit Isolation Mode from the context menu.

Releasing Clipping Masks

If you ever need to separate the mask from the objects being masked, you can release the selected clipping mask by any of the following methods:

- Choose the Object | Clipping Mask | Release command.
- Press the keyboard shortcut, CTRL+ALT+7 (Win) or CMD+OPT+7 (Mac).

- Right-click (Win) or CMD+click (Mac) the masked object and choose Release Clipping Mask from the context menu.

- In the Layers panel, click to select the group or layer with the mask, and then click the Make/Release Clipping Mask button on the bottom of the panel or choose the Release Clipping Mask command from the panel options menu.

If your mask includes multiple masks, repeat the process until all the masks are released. With all four methods, the masked object and underlying shapes are returned, ungrouped, onto your artboard. The only object that will have lost its stroke and fill attributes is the mask shape, which will be displayed as a path with no stroke and no fill. If desired, select the path of the mask shape and apply new stroke and fill attributes.

Creating Clipping Masks from Compound Shapes

FIGURE **16-3** Clipping masks can also be created by masking with compound shapes

In addition to masking shapes with other shapes, you can make a clipping mask from compound shapes, which you'll learn about in the next section. To do this, you'll use the compound shape as the masking shape. Position the compound shape on top of the other object(s), select the compound shape and all the objects below it that you want to be masked, choose Object | Clipping Mask | Make, et voilà! You have a clipping mask made from a compound shape, like the one shown in Figure 16-3.

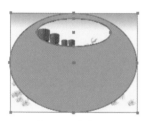

Compound shape
used as mask

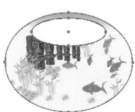

Mask created with
compound shape

Compound Paths

Compound paths are how you can make one or more holes, or cutouts, in a shape from the overlapping paths of multiple shapes, much like a donut or the holes you can make with a fancy shape punch tool. As a matter of fact, when you convert your fonts to outlines, the holes in the shapes of your letters (like in the O or the A) are made from compound paths. The only limitations you have when making compound paths is that the selected objects must be vector artwork and cannot include grouped paths or other compound paths.

To give you an example of what a compound path looks like, take a look at the circles in Figure 16-4. When combined in a compound path, the inner circles become the cutouts in the larger circle, allowing us to see through the shapes to the square behind it.

When smaller shapes are completely on top of one larger shape without overlapping, holes will be created in that larger background shape, and all the objects in the compound path shape take on the stroke, fill, and style attributes of the object furthest back in the selection, as illustrated in Figure 16-5. When multiple overlapping shapes are used to create a compound path (also shown in Figure 16-5), notice that empty areas are created where top shapes overlap the back shape, while overlapping areas outside the back shape will maintain the fill and stroke attributes of the back shape.

Shapes before compound path created with circles

Shapes after compound path created with circles

FIGURE 16-4 Compound paths turn overlapping shapes into holes

Creating a Compound Path

To create a compound path, follow these steps:

1. Position all the shapes on top of one another in the desired stacking order.

2. Select all the shapes.

3. Choose Object | Compound Path | Make or press the keyboard shortcut, CTRL+8 (Win) or CMD+8 (Mac). The objects will be grouped into a compound shape so that when you select any part of the compound the entire compound shape is selected.

4. If desired, move the compound path on top of another object to see through the holes in the compound shape.

Three overlapping shapes with different fill attributes

Shapes in a compound path take on the fill and style of the back object

FIGURE 16-5 When shapes overlap, the compound shape takes on the fill and style of the object at the back of the stacking order

Your compound paths appear grouped together in the Layers panel with the label of <Compound Path>, which, of course, you can change to something else if you like.

Editing a Compound Path

To reshape and move the individual shapes within the compound path, use the Direct Selection and Group Selection tools.

Change the Path Direction

Another thing you can do that a lot of Illustrator users don't know about is change the direction of the paths within the compound shape. The reason you might need to do this is because the holes can only be created when the paths travel in a direction opposite the larger shape. Therefore, if you ever need to control whether an individual shape within the compound path will make a hole or not, try switching the direction of paths in the Attributes panel.

Open the Attributes panel, seen here in Figure 16-6, by choosing Window I Attributes or by pressing CTRL+F11 (Win) or CMD+F11 (Mac). Once open, select any of the individual shapes within your compound path with the Direct Selection or Group Selection tool, and then click the Reverse Path Direction On or Reverse Path Direction Off button in the center of the Attributes panel.

Reverse Path Direction Off
Reverse Path Direction On

Use Non-Zero Winding Fill Rule
Use Even-Odd Fill Rule

FIGURE 16-6   The Attributes panel

The Group Selection tool will select each object within the compound path, while the Direct Selection tool can reactivate the paths and anchor points.

You can also edit the shapes in the compound path in Isolation Mode by doing either of the following with the Selection tool:

- Double-click the compound path object to enter the object in Isolation Mode, where you can select and edit the different objects with the Selection tool or through the Layers panel. (Refer back to Chapter 7 for a refresher on Isolation Mode.)

- Select and right-click (Win) or CMD+click (Mac) the compound path to access the context menu and choose Isolate Selected Compound Path. To exit Isolation Mode, right-click (Win) or CMD+click (Mac) the compound path again and choose Exit Isolation Mode from the context menu.

Changing the Fill Rule

The Attributes panel also contains a few extra buttons that determine how the compound shapes are *wound*:

- **Use Non-Zero Winding Fill Rule**   This is the default setting for compound paths. When enabled, this rule defines the inside and outside of shapes for the overlap.

■ **Use Even-Odd Fill Rule**   This setting uses a more regular algorithm to determine overlapping regions so every other shape is a hole, regardless of the direction of that shape's path.

To illustrate this concept, take a look at the self-intersecting paths in Figure 16-7. The fill rule you choose will determine whether or not the overlapping parts become cutouts when the Compound Path command is applied.

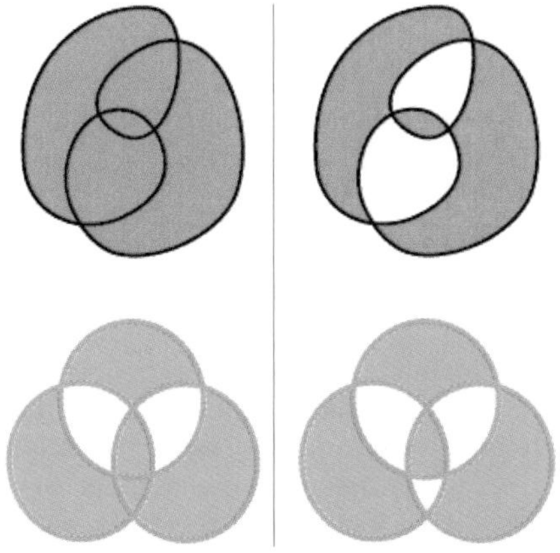

FIGURE **16-7** The fill rule determines how compound paths create holes in self-intersecting and other shapes

Self-intersecting shape with Use Non-Zero Winding Fill Rule

Self-intersecting shape with Use Even-Odd Fill Rule

Releasing a Compound Path

To release the shapes within a compound path back into separate pieces, do any of the following after selecting the compound path:

■ Choose the Object | Compound Path | Release command.

■ Press the keyboard shortcut, CTRL+ SHIFT+ALT+8 (Win) or CMD+ SHIFT+OPT+8 (Mac).

■ Right-click (Win) or CMD+click (Mac) the compound path and choose Release Compound Path from the context menu.

With all three methods, the shapes within the compound path are returned, ungrouped, onto your artboard and all the objects that were formerly the holes take on the stroke, fill, and style attributes of the object furthest back in the selection. For instance, if the backmost object had a black stroke with a yellow fill, all the hole shapes, once released, will also have a black stroke and yellow fill. Likewise, if the back object was green with no stroke, the holes will also be green, making it difficult to see them when unselected. Of course, you can always reselect those shapes and apply new stroke and fill attributes if you like.

17

Transparency and Blending Modes

How to...

- Apply transparency to objects
- Use the Transparency panel
- Create and edit opacity masks
- Flatten artwork for printing
- Use the blending modes

In this chapter, you're going to learn about opacity and blending modes in the Transparency panel. Illustrator, like Photoshop, gives you the ability to adjust the opacity of your objects, grouped objects, and layers to create live transparency effects. This means that your objects can go from being totally solid to fully see-through, like sheets of colored acetate or sheer fabric draped over your work. Also like in Photoshop, Illustrator lets you apply blending modes to your selections, each of which creates rich color interactions between the selected object(s) and the object(s) directly under it. The Transparency panel is where the magic can really happen and it allows your work to take on dramatic effects you never knew possible!

The Transparency Panel

The Transparency panel, shown in Figure 17-1, is where you'll apply transparency and blending modes to your selections, as well as do more fancy advanced techniques like isolate blending, apply opacity masks, and use other commands through the panel's options menu. To access the panel, select Window | Transparency or press the keyboard shortcut SHIFT+CTRL+F10 (Win) or SHIFT+CMD+F10 (Mac). To ensure that you're seeing all the options in the panel, select Show

Thumbnails and Show Options from the panel's options menu or click the tiny double-arrows on the panel tab a few times until the panel completely expands.

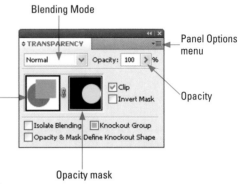

To change the transparency in a selection, adjust the panel's Opacity slider. Transparency can be adjusted on selected single objects, multiple objects, grouped objects, or the objects on one or more selected layers. You can even apply transparency to 3D objects, brush strokes, symbols, patterns, and objects with graphic styles. When transparency is applied to individually selected objects, each object becomes see-through. By contrast, when transparency is applied to a group or to all the objects in a layer, the entire group or layer will have uniform transparency relative to any other shapes under that layer or group, as illustrated in Figure 17-2.

FIGURE 17-1 The Transparency panel

Here's what all the options in the Transparency panel do:

- **Blending Mode** Use this menu to adjust the blending mode of your selection. See the "Blending Modes" section later in this chapter for details about using this feature.

- **Opacity** Adjust the transparency of your selection from 0% (fully transparent) to 100% (fully opaque).

Three objects selected individually and each set to 50% opacity

A targeted layer is set to 50% opacity

FIGURE 17-2 Apply transparency to objects, groups, or layers

Applying Transparency to Layers and Groups in the Layers Panel

When transparency is applied to a group or layer, you can drag new objects into that group or layer through the Layers panel and those new objects will take on the group or layer's opacity settings. Likewise, when you drag an object out of a group or layer through the Layers panel, that object will revert to its prior opacity setting.

- **Preview area**   This area displays a square thumbnail view of your selection on the left. When you apply an opacity mask through the options menu, the right side of the preview area displays the opacity mask.

- **Clip**   When an opacity mask is applied to your selection, this setting turns the mask background black, thereby masking, or hiding, the entire selection. When disabled, the mask background is white, which reveals the entire selection.

- **Invert Mask**   Select this option to reverse the opacity values and luminosity of the masked shape(s). Typically both the Clip and Invert Mask options must be selected for this setting to work properly.

- **Isolate Blending**   This setting limits the blending mode to only the objects in the selected group or layer. When disabled, the blending mode of selected objects will interact with all underlying objects. To isolate the blending mode to a set of two or more objects, first select the objects, group, or targeted layer and choose the desired blending mode from the Transparency panel, then select the target icon next to that group or layer in the Layers panel, and enable the Isolate Blending option in the Transparency panel. Figure 17-3 shows an example of blended objects both with and without this feature.

FIGURE **17-3** Isolate the blending mode to selected objects, a group, or a layer with the Isolate Blending option

Circle and star group with Isolate Blending off

Circle and star group with Isolate Blending on

- **Knockout Group**   This setting prevents the opacity settings within a selected group from affecting one another. When checked, the shapes in a group will not overlap in transparency, and when unchecked, the grouped shapes will have see-through overlapping transparency, as illustrated in Figure 17-4. The third toggle option for this checkbox is the neutral option, which can be used to group objects within a group or layer without affecting the parent group or layer's knockout behavior.

Knockout Group turned on

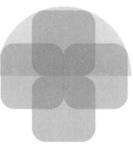

Knockout Group turned off

FIGURE **17-4** Grouped semi-transparent objects

■ **Opacity & Mask Define Knockout Shape**   Enabling this setting when the Knockout Group option is also enabled will make the selected object's opacity mask define the areas that will display transparency. The higher the opacity, the more intense the knockout effect. Gradients can also be used to create a faded knockout effect. Knockout shapes can be either vector or raster. And, when you pair this setting with different blending modes, the effect can become even more dramatic.

The Transparency Panel Options Menu

Some of the options in the Transparency panel will only work when you create an opacity mask, which will hide and reveal portions of your artwork. To create a mask, you'll need to use some of the commands in the Transparency panel's options menu:

■ **Make Opacity Mask**   Adds an opacity mask to selected artwork.

■ **Release Opacity Mask**   Removes an opacity mask from selected artwork.

■ **Disable/Enable Opacity Mask**   Temporarily toggles off an opacity mask on selected artwork by placing a big red X across the mask thumbnail. Click again to toggle the mask back on. You can also toggle the mask on and off by SHIFT+clicking the mask thumbnail.

■ **Unlink/Link Opacity Mask**   Toggles the link between the selected object and its mask. You can also toggle the link by clicking the link symbol (or the gray preview area) between the preview thumbnail and its opacity mask.

■ **New Opacity Masks Are Clipping**   Sets the default Clip option for new opacity masks, which can either be clipped or unclipped. When enabled, all new masks will have the Clip feature turned on giving the mask a black background to hide the selected artwork.

■ **New Opacity Masks Are Inverted**   Sets the default Invert option for new opacity masks, which can either be normal or inverted. When enabled, all new masks will have the Invert Mask feature turned on, which reverses the luminosity values of the mask shape and thereby reverses the opacity of the masked object(s).

■ **Page Isolated Blending**   Toggles on and off the Isolate Blending setting for the entire page.

■ **Page Knockout Group**   Toggles on and off the Knockout Group setting for the entire page.

Creating Opacity Masks

To create an opacity mask to change the transparency of objects below the selected objects, you'll need two parts: the mask and the masking object. The mask can be created from any color, but Illustrator uses black, white, or the grayscale equivalent of the vector object or placed raster image colors in opacity masking objects for the opacity levels in the mask. Keep in mind that a pure black opacity mask completely hides an artwork object, a pure white opacity mask completely reveals an artwork object, and varying shades of gray (or gray equivalents of color) in an opacity mask will create varying degrees of transparency in the artwork.

To create the mask, follow these steps:

1. Select the object(s) you'd like to add the mask to. If more than one object is selected, group the objects by selecting Object | Group or by pressing the keyboard shortcut, CTRL+G (Win) or CMD+G (Mac). Otherwise, without grouping, the top-most object in the selection will be used as the shape for the opacity mask.

2. Double-click the blank area to the right of the selection's thumbnail in the preview area of the Transparency panel to add the mask, or choose Make Opacity Mask from the Transparency panel's options menu. This places a linked mask on the selection, which you can see in the right side of the preview area of the Transparency panel. If you used the top-most object in your selection as the mask shape, the mask thumbnail will take on that shape's appearance. Otherwise, the mask will be either solid white or solid black, depending on whether the Clip option is checked.

Tip

To learn more about working with opacity masks, watch the Adobe video at www.adobe.com/go/vid0056.

Did You Know? Using Masks Between Illustrator and Photoshop

Illustrator's opacity masks can be moved into Photoshop to become layer masks. You can also move Photoshop layer masks into Illustrator, which then become opacity masks!

To illustrate how an opacity mask works, take a look at the objects in Figure 17-5. The letter F is black with a transparency setting of 80%. By selecting both the letter and the background shape, and then choosing the Make Opacity Mask command from the Transparency panel's options menu, the letter becomes the transparent mask area of the background shape. Then, by checking the Clip and Invert options, the mask can be reversed to reveal the letter shape through the mask of the background shape.

When you take a look at the Transparency panel of a masked object, like the one in Figure 17-6, you'll see the shape thumbnail (the opacity mask) linked to the mask thumbnail (the masking object) and the Clip and Invert Mask options checked.

Two objects before adding the opacity mask   Two objects after adding the opacity mask   Two objects with an opacity mask set to Clip and Invert

FIGURE 17-5 The top-most of two selected objects becomes the opacity mask of the underlying shape

Editing Opacity Masks

To further modify an opacity mask once it's been added to a selection, do any of the following:

■ Select the opacity mask thumbnail in the Transparency panel to "enter it." You can also ALT+click (Win) or OPT+click (Mac) the mask thumbnail to enter the mask and temporarily hide all the other artwork on the artboard. Use any of the drawing or painting tools to modify the mask. Opacity mask objects stroked or filled with black will hide the artwork object(s) while opacity mask objects stroked or filled with white will reveal the artwork object(s). The opposite occurs when Invert Mask is checked.

Masking Object thumbnail

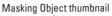
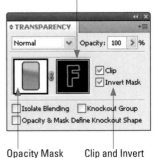

Opacity Mask thumbnail   Clip and Invert options

FIGURE 17-6 Masked objects appear on the Transparency panel preview area as linked mask and object thumbnails

- Select and copy the object(s) on the artboard, such as a word or shape, that you'd like to add to the mask. Then select the opacity mask thumbnail in the Transparency panel to "enter it" (or ALT+click [Win] or OPT+click [Mac] the mask thumbnail to enter the mask and hide all other artwork) and use the Paste command or Paste In Front command to paste the copied artwork into the mask. If needed, select and reposition the mask shape on the artboard.

- To move the mask shape independent of the masked object, unlink the object and mask by clicking the Link icon between their thumbnails on the Transparency panel and then select the thumbnail you'd like to modify. You can then select and reposition the mask or mask shape on the artboard. When finished, click the link area between the thumbnails to relink the mask shape and mask, or select Link Opacity Mask from the panel's options menu.

To exit the mask, select the artwork object thumbnail on the left side of the Transparency panel preview area.

Printing with Transparency

When you work with transparency for print projects, your artwork needs to be *flattened* before it goes to print, which essentially divides up your work by color and transparency. This will ensure that the colors separate accurately and print the way you see them on your screen, which is especially critical for files that include transparency plus more advanced features like complex vectors, spot colors, and extensive use of type.

Of course, you might also need to flatten your artwork occasionally when you save your files in formats that don't support transparency, like a regular PDF file.

 To keep transparency in a PDF without having to flatten the artwork, save the files as Adobe PDF 1.4 (Acrobat 5.0) or later.

Transparency is retained in AI and EPS files in Illustrator 9.0 or later, including all the CS versions. Where it is not retained, however, is where you do things like print a file or save your work in AI or EPS formats in Illustrator versions 8 or earlier.

The only main drawback to flattening is that once you do it and save the file, you can't undo this feature. Therefore, you may want to make a copy of the original file and flatten the copy, just in case you ever need to return to the original file sometime in the future.

Flattening Artwork

To flatten your artwork, select the artwork on your artboard and choose Object | Flatten Transparency. The Flatten Transparency dialog box will appear, inside which you can select the resolution (quality) for the output under the Preset menu.

To assist you in seeing how the artwork will appear when you go to print, turn on the transparency grid by selecting View | Show Transparency Grid.

 To adjust the transparency grid, choose File | Document Setup and adjust the settings in the Transparency section.

The next thing you'll need to do to print your transparency accurately is to set transparency flattening options and use the Flattener Preview panel to ensure your transparencies will separate accurately.

To open the Flattener Preview panel, choose Window | Flattener Preview. To ensure you're seeing the entire panel's options, select Show Options from the panel's options menu. Click the Refresh button to preview the work in your file and select a desired highlight option from the Highlight menu. You can then choose overprint options and choose a preset or customize the resolution of your artwork. Choose the High Resolution option for professionally printed projects, Medium for decent quality from a PostScript printer, and Low for quick proofs on color printers and files for the Web.

To set your transparency flatting options for print, choose File | Print and in the Advanced area choose a flattening preset from the Preset menu or click the Custom button for similar options found in the Flatten Transparency dialog box.

Blending Modes

When you're ready to make some magic happen, try applying some of the different blending modes to your objects:

1. Select the object, group, or layer. To adjust only the stroke or fill of an object, select the stroke or fill in the Appearance panel.

2. Select a blending mode from the Transparency panel dropdown menu. To isolate the blending mode to just the objects in the selection, click the target icon next to the object, group, or layer in the Layers panel and then enable the Transparency panel's Isolate Blending option.

Each blending mode works in a slightly different way to adjust the colors of the selected object(s) and alter how those colors interplay with any objects below the selection's layer or group in the stacking order of objects on the artboard.

Three components of an object are affected when a blending mode is applied, as illustrated in Figure 17-7:

- **Blend Color**   The original color of objects on your artboard before any blending mode other than Normal is applied to any of the objects.

- **Base Color**   The underlying color in an overlapping object(s) before a blending mode is applied.

- **Resulting Color**   The new color produced by the blend and base colors in objects when an overlapping object has a blending mode applied.

FIGURE 17-7 Objects take on new looks when you change the blending mode

Base colors in a pattern with Normal blending mode and 100% opacity

Blend colors (of shirt and pants) on top of base object with Normal blending mode and 100% opacity

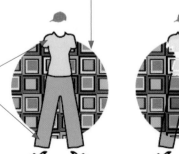

Resulting colors when Lighten (shirt) and Darken (pants) blending modes are applied

To learn more about working with blending modes, watch the Adobe video at www.adobe.com/ go/vid0055.

As you access the blending modes through the menu in the Transparency panel, notice how they're divided into six categories, making it easier for you to select the one that best suits your needs:

- **Normal** (Normal)
- **Darken** (Darken, Multiply, Color Burn)
- **Lighten** (Lighten, Screen, Color Dodge)
- **Contrast** (Overlay, Soft Light, Hard Light)
- **Invert or Compare** (Difference, Exclusion)
- **Color** (Hue, Saturation, Color, Luminosity)

If you're more of a visual than a linguistic person, you'll probably prefer to see what each of the blending modes looks like rather than reading a description of it, like the examples in Figure 17-8 where each of the blending modes was applied to each star shape. On the other hand, if you fancy yourself more of a linguistic person, here's a simple explanation for blending modes to enhance your visual understanding:

- **Normal**   This is the default setting, which leaves the blend color alone without any interaction with the base color of other objects.

- **Darken**   Selects the base color or blend color as the resulting color, whichever one happens to be darker. Areas in the overlapping objects that are lighter than the blend color are replaced, while the darker-than-blend-colors stay as they are.

- **Multiply**   Like Darken, only the base color and blend color are multiplied to create a darker resulting color. When a base or blend color is black, the result is black, and when the base or blend color is white, there is no color change.

- **Color Burn**   Makes the base color darker to reflect the blend color; however, blending with white produces no change.

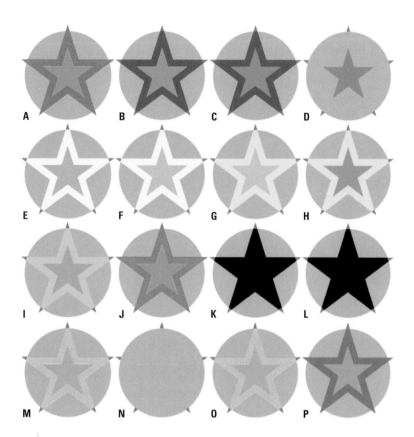

FIGURE 17-8 The blending modes: (A) Normal, (B) Darken, (C) Multiply, (D) Color Burn, (E) Lighten, (F) Screen, (G) Color Dodge, (H) Overlay, (I) Soft Light, (J) Hard Light, (K) Difference, (L) Exclusion, (M) Hue, (N) Saturation, (O) Color, and (P) Luminosity

Lighten   Selects the base color or blend color as the resulting color, whichever one happens to be lighter. Areas in the overlapping objects that are darker than the blend color are replaced while the lighter-than-blend-colors stay as they are.

Screen   Multiplies the inverse colors of the blend and base colors to create a lighter color. Screening with black does nothing, while screening with white creates white.

Color Dodge   Lightens the base color by the blend color, unless the blend color is black, in which case there will be no change.

Overlay   Depending on the base color, this setting will screen or multiply the colors. Highlights and shadows in the base color are typically preserved as the blend colors also mix to reflect the lightness or darkness of the original color.

- **Soft Light**   Depending on the blend color, this setting will lighten or darken the colors to create a soft spotlight effect. Think of the blend color as a light source that is either shining on or dimming down the base color.

- **Hard Light**   Depending on the blend color, this setting will screen or multiply the base colors to create a hard spotlight effect. Use this blending mode to add highlights and shadows to your work.

- **Difference**   Subtracts the base color from the blend color or the blend color from the base color, whichever one happens to have the greater brightness value. Base colors are inverted when blending with white; however, blending with black leaves base colors as they are.

- **Exclusion**   Like the Difference blending mode, only this option produces blends with less contrast. Base colors are inverted when blending with white; however, blending with black leaves base colors as they are.

- **Hue**   Blends the luminance and saturation as the resulting color from the base color and the hue of the blend color.

- **Saturation**   Blends the luminance and hue as the resulting color from the base color and the saturation of the blend color. Gray colors are ignored.

- **Color**   Blends the luminance of the base color with the hue and saturation of the blend color to create the resulting color. Gray levels are preserved. Use this blending mode to apply colors to monochromatic art and to apply tints.

- **Luminosity**   Like the opposite of the Color mode, this mode blends the hue and saturation of the base color with the luminance of the blend color to create a resulting color.

The following blending modes do not blend spot colors: Difference, Exclusion, Hue, Saturation, Color, and Luminosity. Also, when a black color with a 100% K setting is used, it will knock out the color on any layers below it. To prevent this from happening, use a rich black with CMYK values of C: 75%, M: 68%, Y: 67%, K: 90%.

18

Special Effects and Third-Party Plug-Ins

How to...

- Apply Illustrator and Photoshop effects
- Adjust document raster effects settings
- Use the Effect Gallery
- Work with third-party plug-ins

Creating shapes and drawings and placing raster images into Illustrator doesn't need to be the end point for your work. Using the special effects in Illustrator's Effect menu, you can apply fully editable, non-destructive vector and raster style effects to your work from 20 categories and more than 120 different styles. This chapter explains what the effects do and how to use them, the difference between vector and raster effects, how to set up your document for outputting raster effects at the desired resolution, and how to find and use third-party effect plug-ins.

Special Effects

One of the most significant changes in Illustrator CS4 is that the Filter menu has been completely removed from the main menu. Instead, all the special effects and filters have been combined into a single Effect menu that is divided into two sections: one for Illustrator Effects and another for Photoshop Effects.

Another notable change about the effects in CS4 is that all of them now get applied to your selections as non-destructive effects. In fact, not only can you see which effects have been applied to your selected object(s) in the Appearance panel, but you can also reopen each effect's dialog box to edit or remove it from a selection.

Many of the Illustrator Effects in CS4 are vector effects and can be used with any vector objects. These effects will not change your bitmap images unless those images have an extra stroke or fill applied to it through the Appearance panel (which you'll learn about in Chapter 19). The rest of the other Illustrator Effects are raster effects and can be applied to both vector and bitmap objects using the document's global raster effects settings. The Photoshop Effects, by contrast, are all raster effects. Most can be applied to vector and bitmap objects; however, a few can be applied only to bitmap objects.

To help you determine which effect can be used with vector art and which can be used with raster art (especially if you haven't upgraded to CS4 yet), select the object and then choose the Effect menu—when a command is active it can be used on your selection, but when the command is dimmed it cannot.

Applying Effects

To apply an effect, whether it's an Illustrator Effect or a Photoshop Effect, begin by selecting the object, group, or targeted layer you'd like to apply the effect to. To apply the effect to a particular attribute of the selection, such as an object's stroke or fill, select the object and then select that object's attribute in the Appearance panel. Next, choose a command from the Effect menu. When the effect's dialog box opens, adjust the settings (most input fields accept both positive and negative values), and then click OK.

Document Raster Effects Settings

Any time you add special raster effects to your files, you need to be aware of your document's global raster effects settings, which determine the output quality and resolution of your effects. A raster effect is a special effect that uses pixels instead of vector shapes to create the effect, such as a fuzzy drop shadow, an outer glow, or any of the other options in the Effect | Stylize menu.

To check or change the global raster settings in your file, choose the Document Raster Effects Settings command from the Effect menu. When the Document Raster Effects Settings dialog box opens, choose the desired color model, resolution, background, and other settings. The color model should match your project type, such as CMYK for print. For the resolution, choose Screen for your onscreen/web presentation, Medium for printing quick proofs, and High for your professionally printed projects. These settings will remain in effect for the file unless or until you change them again.

Illustrator Effects

The Illustrator Effects in the Effect menu are divided into ten categories. Some of the links in this menu lead to options you've already discovered in other chapters, while others directly apply amazing and wonderful effects to your work.

3D

The 3D option applies three different 3D effects to your selected artwork: Extrude & Bevel, Revolve, and Rotate. To learn more about these effects, as well as how to apply symbol art to a 3D object, refer to the "Mapping Symbol Art to 3D Objects" section in Chapter 13.

Converting to a Shape

Convert any selected object, such as a hand-drawn blob or a star shape, into a rectangle, rounded rectangle, or ellipse. With all these effects, a single Shape Options dialog box opens so you can specify a shape and its width and height using the absolute or relative areas, and when the Rounded Rectangle shape is selected, you may also set the corner radius.

FIGURE **18-1** Apply crop marks to your work with the Effect I Crop Marks command

Crop Marks

The Crop Marks effect adds a set of printer's crop marks around your selection, like the ones shown in Figure 18-1. You may apply this effect to as many objects on your artboard as you like. Crop marks are useful as guides for trimming printed artwork on a cutting board.

Distort and Transform

Tweak out and reshape your vector objects non-destructively using the Distort and Transform menu effects. Refer to Figure 18-2 for examples of each effect.

■ **Free Distort**   Use the interactive preview window to transform the shape of your object by dragging the anchor points of your object into new positions.

- **Pucker & Bloat**   Opens the Pucker & Bloat dialog box where you use a slider to push or pull the anchor points in or out of your object's center to create a sucked in or puffed out version of the original shape.

- **Roughen**   Converts the outer edges of your shape from smooth to jagged based on the size and detail amounts entered in the Roughen dialog box. You can also specify whether the points are smooth or corner (which offers more pointy results).

- **Transform**   Opens the Transform Effect dialog box, which scales, moves, rotates, and reflects, copies, and even applies a random transform to your object.

- **Tweak**   Similar though more random than the Pucker effect, use the Tweak dialog box to adjust the horizontal and vertical edges of your object relatively or absolutely by its anchor points, "in" control points, and "out" control points.

- **Twist**   Twists and turns your object around its center. Enter a positive number to twist clockwise and a negative number to twist counterclockwise.

- **Zig Zag**   Turns the edges of your object into spiky peaks (corner) or wavy lines (smooth) by the size and number of ridges per segment set in the Zig Zag dialog box. Then, set the points on the shape to display with corner or smooth points.

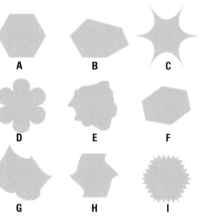

FIGURE 18-2 The Distort and Transform effects: (A) Original shape, (B) Free Distort, (C) Pucker, (D) Bloat, (E) Roughen, (F) Transform, (G) Tweak, (H) Twist, and (I) Zig Zag

Path Effects

The Path effects, which are almost the same as the commands available in the Object | Paths menu, can be used to edit and re-edit the path of the selected object. The only major difference is that the Path menu commands actually transform your selections, while the Path effects apply a non-destructive style to the selection through the Appearance panel.

- **Offset Path**   Offsets (grows or shrinks) the path of the object based on the positive or negative number of points (or other units if you also enter in the unit abbreviation, as in 0.25 in) entered in the Offset dialog box. For objects that have angled lines, select a miter, round, or bevel join, and if needed, adjust the miter limit.

- **Outline Object**   Converts objects with strokes and fills into two separate objects, one for the stroke and one for the fill. You won't be able to see this effect until you expand the appearance by choosing Object I Expand Appearance and then Object I Ungroup The Shape Into Two Shapes.

- **Outline Stroke**   Like the Outline Object effect, only the Outline Stroke also converts the stroke of an object into an identically sized filled shape. To edit the outline as a compound path, select Object I Expand Appearance and then Object I Ungroup The Shape Into Two Shapes.

Pathfinder Effects

Like the Pathfinder and Shape Mode tools in the Pathfinder panel, the Pathfinder effects can be used to make new shapes by combining or dividing overlapping objects, text objects, groups, and targeted layers. What most sets the Pathfinder effects apart from the Pathfinder panel tools, however, is that the effects remain editable after the effect has been applied.

Though you can't modify the settings before they are applied (unless you select the Soft Mix or Trap option), you can preview and adjust the settings and even change the pathfinder type *after* it's been applied through the Pathfinder Options dialog box. To open the Pathfinder Options dialog box after applying any effect, double-click the effect in the Appearance panel.

The Intersect, Exclude, Minus Back, Unite (Add), Divide (Subtract), Trim, Merge, Crop, and Outline commands are the same as the Pathfinder panel options, which you learned about in Chapter 7. In addition, there are three other Pathfinder effects: The Hard Mix effect applies a Darken-like blending mode to the grouped shapes as it strips away any stroke attributes from all the objects; the Soft Mix effect applies a 75% opacity-like transparency effect to the grouped shapes as it strips away any stroke attributes from all the objects based on the opacity or "mixing rate" specified in the dialog box; and the Trap effect creates an overlap area, called a trap, that helps define the print space for adjacent colors.

The Rasterize Effect

The Rasterize effect brings up the Rasterize dialog box, which is almost identical to the Document Raster Effects Settings dialog box described earlier in this chapter. Use this effect to rasterize vector art and choose an appropriate color model, resolution, and background, either with or without the optional anti-aliasing and clipping mask settings.

The Stylize Menu

Use the Stylize menu to apply cool special effects to your selections such as adding arrowheads to paths, applying drop shadows, feathering edges, adding an inner or outer glow, rounding the corners of a hard-edged shape, or applying a scribble effect. Figure 18-3 illustrates some of the things you can do to your objects with the Stylize effects. The Scribble effect is particularly interesting because you can use the Scribble Options dialog box to create your own scribble effects with varying angles, path overlap, variation, and line options, or choose one of the 11 scribble Settings from a preset scribble style list.

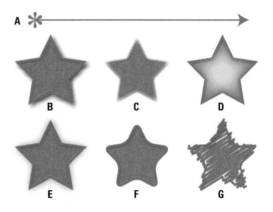

Figure 18-3 The Stylize effects: (A) Add Arrowheads, (B) Drop Shadows, (C) Feather, (D) Inner Glow, (E) Outer Glow, (F) Round Corners, and (G) Scribble

SVG Filters

The SVG filters—from which there are 18 default effects to choose, like BevelShadow, Turbulence, and Woodgrain, and other filters that you can import to extend Illustrator's SVG filter capabilities—can be used to add high-quality vector format, XML-based, resolution-independent SVG effects to your object, group, or targeted layer. To apply a filter using its default settings to a selection, choose a filter from the Effect | SVG Filters menu. Otherwise, to use a filter and customize its settings, choose Effect | SVG Filters | Apply SVG Filter. When the Apply SVG Filter dialog box appears, enable the Preview option and select the desired filter from the list. To edit the filter's properties before applying it to the object (or at anytime thereafter), select the filter from listing within the Apply SVG Filter dialog box and click the Edit SVG Filter button (FX button) at the bottom of the dialog box. This opens an Edit SVG Filter window, inside which you can edit the XML for that filter. Further, if you happen to know XML, you can create your own filter by clicking the New SVG Filter button, entering your code, and clicking the OK button. To delete a filter from the Apply SVG Filter dialog box, select the filter by name and click the Delete SVG Filter button.

The Warp Menu

Warp and distort your objects, text, blends, paths, and bitmap files using one of the 15 preset warp styles from the Warp menu,

including: Arc, Arc Lower, Arc Upper, Arch, Bulge, Shell Lower, Shell Upper, Flag, Wave, Fish, Rise, Fisheye, Inflate, Squeeze, and Twist. When the Warp Options dialog box opens, you can choose any of the different warp styles as well as adjust the sliders to apply bending and distortion. Figure 18-4 shows an object in its original state and as it appears after being warped with the Arc style.

Photoshop Effects

Like their vector-based Illustrator Effects counterparts, the ten raster-based Photoshop Effects also apply non-destructive filter-like effects to your work, which can then be modified as often as you like and even discarded if you happen to change your mind. What makes the Photoshop Effects different, however, is that these effects are raster-based and their quality is therefore controlled by the settings within the Document Raster Effects Settings dialog box (see the Document Raster Effects Settings section earlier in this chapter for details).

If at any time you want to adjust the shape of your object after applying a filter, use the Direct Selection tool to select and adjust the object, or simply expand the object (Object | Expand Appearance) and the effect and then modify the shape.

The Effect Gallery

The Effect Gallery should probably be the first place you check out while exploring all of Illustrator's Photoshop Effects. The gallery is almost exactly like the Filter Gallery in Photoshop in that it uses an interactive dialog box to preview and adjust each effect before applying it.

Though not every effect in the Photoshop Effects section is in the Effect Gallery, many of them are, including everything in the Artistic, Brush Strokes, Distort, Sketch, Stylize, and Texture menus. To use the gallery, select an object, group, or targeted layer and choose Effect | Effect Gallery. The Gallery dialog box is split into three sections: a preview pane, an effect selection pane, and an effect adjustment pane, as seen in Figure 18-5.

Once the dialog box opens, select an effect, adjust its settings, and click the OK button to modify your selection and add the fully editable effect to the object in the Appearance panel.

Artistic

The Artistic effects are all accessible directly through this menu, though you can also select them in the Effect Gallery. When

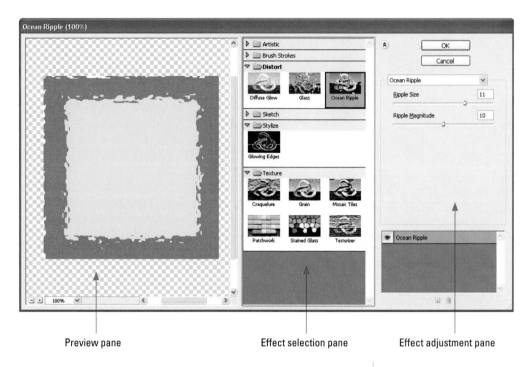

Preview pane   Effect selection pane   Effect adjustment pane

FIGURE 18-5 The Effect Gallery

the Effect Gallery opens, you'll see a preview of your selection with one of the Artistic effects applied, along with preview examples of how each of these effects can modify your work. Artistic effects include Colored Pencil, Cutout, Dry Brush, Film Grain, Fresco, Neon Glow, Paint Daubs, Palette Knife, Plastic Wrap, Poster Edges, Rough Pastels, Smudge Stick, Sponge, Underpainting, and Watercolor.

Blur

Three types of Blur effects can be applied to your artwork (as illustrated in Figure 18-6) depending on your needs. The Gaussian Blur applies a realistic blur to your entire selection based on the specified radius in pixels from 0.1 to 250.0. The Radial Blur creates a radial (or circular) blur in a spin or zoom fashion on a scale from 0 to 100. The Smart Blur performs more of a sharpening effect that is controlled by a radius and threshold, and also includes the option of applying the effect to the object in Normal, Edge Only, or Overlay Edge modes.

Brush Strokes

Brush Strokes effects are accessible both here and through the Effect Gallery. Selecting any of these effects from the menu will

Original   Gaussian   Radial   Smart

launch the Effect Gallery, where you can sample each of the effects in a preview window and adjust them before applying them to your work. Brush Strokes effects include Accented Edges, Angled Strokes, Crosshatch, Dark Strokes, Ink Outlines, Spatter, Sprayed Strokes, and Sumi-e.

Distort

Three distort menu options are available—Diffuse Glow, Glass, and Ocean Ripple—all of which are in the Effect Gallery. The Diffuse Glow applies a grainy glow to your work, Glass makes your work appear as if it were viewed from behind a glass brick, and Ocean Ripple creates a watery ripple effect.

Pixelate

Four great pixelation effects are available from the Pixelate menu, as shown in the examples in Figure 18-7:

- **Color Halftone** Converts the fill and stroke of your artwork into a halftone pattern based on the specified maximum radius and screen angles for up to four channels.

- **Crystallize** Applies a distorted crystallized pattern to the fill and stroke of your artwork based on the specified cell size from 3 to 300.

Original   Color Halftone   Crystallize   Mezzotint   Pointillize

- **Mezzotint**   Turns the stroke and fill of your object into a mezzotint defined by the specified type. Types include fine, medium, grainy, and coarse dots; short, medium, and long lines; and short, medium, and long strokes.

- **Pointillize**   Applies a pointillized (dotted) pattern to the fill and stroke of your artwork based on the specified cell size from 3 to 300.

Sharpen

Use the Sharpen menu to apply the Unsharp Mask effect to sharpen up your blurry vector and raster images by bumping up the contrast. This effect works like Photoshop's Unsharp Mask filter, only as an effect it remains editable through the Appearance panel.

Sketch

All of the Sketch effects are located in the Effect Gallery, and with the exception of Water Paper, each effect adjusts the selection in black and white. Effects include Bas Relief, Chalk & Charcoal, Charcoal, Chrome, Conte Crayon, Graphic Pen, Halftone Pattern, Note Paper, Photocopy, Plaster, Reticulation, Stamp, Torn Edges, and Water Paper.

Stylize

The one and only Stylize effect, Glowing Edges, is also in the Effect Gallery. When applied, it creates a neon-like glow along the outer edges of your selection.

Texture

The Texture effects are also accessible through the Effect Gallery and include Craquelure, Grain, Mosaic Tiles, Patchwork, Stained Glass, and Texturizer. Though some are more realistic looking than others, they all can be used to simulate different surface styles.

Video

The two Video effects, De-Interlace and NTSC Colors, are ideal for processing your files that will be used in film and video projects. Use the De-Interlace effect to smooth vector and raster images and reduce the appearance of interlaced lines, and use the NTSC Colors effect to reduce the colors in the selection to a restricted color space suitable for TV.

Apply Last Effect and Last Effect

One of the cool things about the Effect menu is the two commands at the very top of the menu, which let you repeat the last-used command on any new selection without having to drill down into the menu and submenus to select it. Choose the Apply "Last Effect" option, or press SHIFT+CTRL+E (Win) or SHIFT+CMD+E (Mac), to apply the last-used effect with all its settings to your selection. Alternatively, choose the "Last Effect" option, or press ALT+SHIFT+CTRL+E (Win) or OPT+SHIFT+CMD+E (Mac) to apply the last-used effect and reopen that effect's dialog box so you can adjust the settings if desired.

Third-Party Plug-ins for Illustrator

A plug-in is a special file that you can purchase (or sometimes get for free or as shareware) and download from the Internet and then install into your Adobe Illustrator program to enhance how your software works. The plug-ins are typically created by software developers and Illustrator users who are seeking advanced capabilities in a variety of work areas.

Adding Plug-in Preferences

When using plug-ins, you could install them in Illustrator's default folder or save them to another location. When saving to a folder other than Illustrator's default folder, be sure to specify the location of any additional plug-in folders in the Plug-ins & Scratch Disks category of Illustrator's Preferences.

Finding Third-Party Plug-ins

The first place to look when seeking out third-party plug-ins is on Adobe's own Third-Party Plug-ins for Illustrator page at www.adobe.com/products/plugins/illustrator/index.html. Plug-ins are listed alphabetically and by software company. You'll find tons of interesting and exciting options to choose from like: Artlandia's Artlandia Collection for creating patterns and textile designs; Nineblock Software's BetterHandles, which improves how you can work with and use the Bézier curve handles; and Code Zebra's Symbols for Illustrator, an amazing collection of technical symbols in categories like landscaping, architecture, networking, and people. The plug-ins listed here are free unless you see an Order icon, in which case you'll have to pay for them.

Other great places to look for free, shareware, or pay-to-use third-party plug-ins include:

- Doing a Google search for "Illustrator plugin"

- The Illustrator|World blog at www.illustratorworld.com/forum/

- The PluginsWorld Illustrator listing at http://illustrator.pluginsworld.com/plugin.php?directory=adobe&software=illustrator&category=0

- Rick Johnson's Graffix plug-ins at http://rj-graffix.com/software/plugins.html

- The CNET Illustrator plug-in downloads listing at www.download.com

- The Graphics Software area on About.com at http://graphicssoft.about.com/od/illustratorplugins/Adobe_Illustrator_Plugins_and_Addons.htm

- Adobe's Illustrator Plug-ins Exchange at www.adobe.com/cfusion/exchange/index.cfm?s=5&from=1&o=desc&cat=209&l=-1&event=productHome&exc=17

19

Custom Graphic Styles and the Appearance Panel

How to...

- Use the Appearance panel
- Add extra strokes, fills, and effects
- Duplicate, clear, delete, and edit style attributes
- Work with the Graphic Styles panel
- Use the free graphic styles libraries
- Apply and edit graphic styles
- Create custom styles and style libraries

In this chapter, you'll learn how to use two of the most underappreciated and amazing panels in Illustrator: the Appearance panel and the Graphic Styles panel. The Appearance panel, which you learned about briefly while working with Effects in Chapter 18, shows a list of all the style attributes (like strokes, fills, and opacity) and effects applied to a selected object, group, or targeted layer. From within the Appearance panel you can edit any of those styles and effects, move them around to change their stacking order, make duplicate copies of any of the attributes or delete them, and save an entire *style stack* as a new graphic style in the Graphic Styles panel. Then, in the Graphic Styles panel, you can select and apply well over 200 different free graphic styles to your work from the Graphic Styles Libraries menu, as well as create your own custom styles and save them in your own custom style libraries.

The Appearance Panel

In Illustrator, the objects, paths, and groups you create on your artboard appear in the Layers panel where you can adjust their stacking order, create layers, and otherwise arrange the different elements into an order that suits your needs. However, the appearance attributes of those objects, paths, groups, and layers—things like an object's stroke, fill, opacity, and effects— are listed in the Appearance panel, where you can edit, delete, rearrange, and even add multiple attributes to your selection.

FIGURE 19-1 The Appearance panel

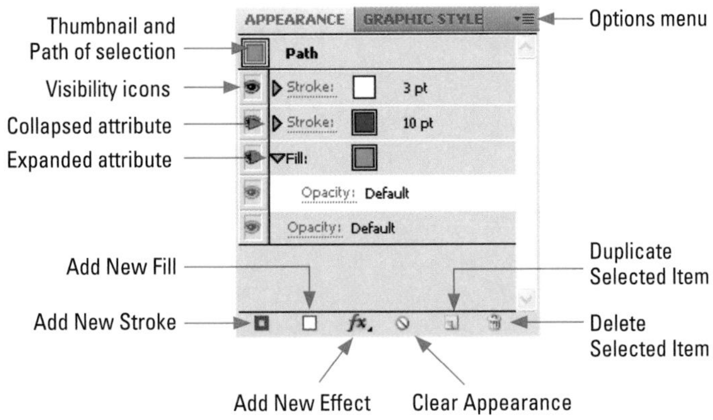

The Appearance panel, as seen in Figure 19-1, is typically grouped in the panel dock with the Graphic Styles panel. To open or bring the Appearance panel into focus, select Window | Appearance, or press the keyboard shortcut SHIFT+F6.

When you select an object on your artboard, the Appearance panel shows that object's default attributes, such as its stroke, stroke weight, fill, and opacity setting. By contrast, when multiple objects, a group, or a targeted layer is selected, the Appearance panel will show only common attributes like a fill color or opacity setting, and when no object is selected, the panel displays attributes of the last selected object. Therefore, to see the attributes of a particular object, select only that object, even if it happens to be part of a group or layer.

Keep in mind, when looking at the attributes of a selected object in the Appearance panel, each attribute in the panel can be displayed in collapsed or expanded mode by clicking the triangle to the left of the attribute name. You can also make each attribute visible or hidden by toggling the visibility icon (eyeball) along the left of the panel. When multiple attributes are hidden, you can quickly turn the hidden items back on by selecting Show All Hidden Attributes from the panel's options menu. In addition, you can use the other commands in the panel's options menu and the buttons along the bottom of the panel to modify the attributes of your selections.

Adding Strokes and Fills

Up until now, the objects you've been creating on your artboard have each had only a single stroke and fill attribute. Not any more! With the Appearance panel you can add multiple strokes and fills to your objects, as well as apply all the special effects from the Effect menu directly to your selections using the Add New Effect button at the bottom of the panel. For example, you can add two strokes to the same object like the rectangle in Figure 19-2. As you can see, the strokes are nested and varied in size to create the dual stroke appearance.

FIGURE 19-2 Add additional strokes to your shapes for dramatic styles

Shape with single stroke   Shape with two strokes   Appearance panel for shape with two strokes at left

To add a new stroke or fill to a selected object, click the Add New Stroke or Add New Fill button along the bottom of the Appearance panel, or choose the Add New Stroke or Add New Fill command from the panel's options menu. To adjust the color and/or stroke weight of the new stroke or fill, select the new stroke or fill layer in the Appearance panel to activate and edit its attributes. These same steps can be used to add strokes or fills to grouped objects and targeted layers. However, keep in mind that when you place the stroke below the fill, the stroke will surround the entire grouped object, whereas strokes placed above the fill will be individually applied to each object in the group.

Clear Appearance Panel Settings for New Objects

How to...

To ensure that any new objects that get created have only a single stroke and fill with no effects or other attribute settings, make sure the New Art Has Basic Appearance option is selected in the Appearance panel's options menu. Otherwise, to apply all the currently selected attributes to any new object created, make sure the New Art Has Basic Appearance option is deselected.

Adding Effects

In Chapter 18, you learned how to use the special non-destructive effects in the Effect menu in your work. What you didn't learn was that you can use the Appearance panel to select and apply those same Effect menu options by clicking the Add New Effect button (*fx*) at the bottom of the Appearance panel.

To add an effect to your selection, click the Add New Effect button at the bottom of the Appearance panel and choose one of the Illustrator or Photoshop effects from the menu listing. Each effect applied to your work will be listed in the Appearance panel along with the object's stroke, fill, and opacity attributes, and, as you'll learn in the following subsections, all the effects are fully editable.

Duplicating Strokes, Fills, and Effects

Another method for altering the appearance of a selected object is to duplicate any of that object's existing attributes. To create a duplicate of any appearance item, begin by selecting the object and then selecting the attribute layer in the Appearance panel that you'd like to copy. To duplicate that attribute, click the Duplicate Selected Item button at the bottom of the panel or choose Duplicate Item from the panel's options menu. If desired, select the new appearance attribute to activate it and make any desired changes.

Each new item you add to the attribute stack will appear directly above the last selected attribute. When no attributes are selected in the Appearance panel, the new attribute will typically be added to the top of the style stack. The top-most item in the stack is the top-most attribute of the selected object, and any remaining attributes of the object are stacked beneath that from top to bottom. If needed, the order of the attributes can be changed at any time by dragging and dropping them into the desired position within the panel.

To change the stacking order of a special effect within the Appearance panel, drag it up or down and drop it into the new position. You can tell when it is safe to "drop" the attribute into its new position when you see a double line appear between the attribute layers. For instance, to move a Scribble effect from a stroke to a fill, drag and drop the attribute into the new position, as illustrated in Figure 19-3.

Scribble effect applied
to the object's fill

Scribble effect moved
to the object's stroke

FIGURE 19-3 Reposition style
attributes in the Appearance panel

Copying, Editing, Clearing, and Removing Strokes, Fills, and Effects

When you select one or more objects, a group, or a targeted layer, all of the attributes that display in the Appearance panel for that selection are editable.

Copying Appearance Attributes

To copy the appearance (or part of the appearance) of one object to another, do any of the following:

- Select the object with the stroke appearance you want to copy and ALT+drag (Win) or OPT+drag (Mac) the target icon of that object in the Layers panel onto the object you want to have the new appearance.

- Select the object with the stroke and fill appearance you want to copy and drag that object's appearance thumbnail from the top of the Appearance panel onto another object on your artboard.

- Use the Eyedropper tool to "pick up" and "apply" a stroke and fill style (but not any effects) from one object to another.

Editing Appearance Attributes

Once the attribute layer is activated, click the Stroke or Fill color icon directly to open a dropdown Swatches panel and select a different color. If the color you need isn't in the Swatches panel (yet), try SHIFT+clicking the Stroke or Fill color icon instead to open a dropdown Color panel, where you can mix and apply your own colors. To adjust the stroke weight, choose another size from the Stroke Weight menu or type in your own number in the Weight field.

In addition, you can edit appearance attributes through their attribute label. Any time the Appearance panel displays a word in blue text with a dotted or solid underline (such as Stroke or Opacity or any of the Effects), you can click that attribute label to open a dropdown version of that attribute's attending panel options, which is faster than having to switch panels to change an attribute.

Clearing and Reducing Appearance Attributes

To completely remove any and all appearance attributes from a selection, click the Clear Appearance button on the bottom of the Appearance panel or choose the same command from the panel's options menu. Immediately after choosing this command, the stroke and fill are set to None, the opacity and blending modes are returned to their default 100% and normal settings, and any previously applied effects will be completely removed.

If you want to clear only some of the attributes, consider using the Reduce To Basic Appearance command from the Appearance panel's options menu. This command removes all effects, blending modes, and opacity settings.

Removing Appearance Attributes

Sometimes trying out an idea is the only way to see if it will work. When the application of an attribute or effect doesn't work, feel free to zap an unwanted attribute by selecting it in the Appearance panel and clicking the Delete Selected Item button along the panel's bottom edge. You can also delete selected attributes by choosing the Remove Item command from the panel's options menu. To select more than one attribute at a time, CTRL+click (Win) or CMD+click (Mac) each item until you have the ones you want selected before deleting them.

The Graphic Styles Panel

The Graphic Styles panel is the panel you'll use to select and apply special multi-attribute/effect styles to your objects. By default, the panel comes preloaded with a set of six default styles. As you hover your mouse over each of them, you'll see the name of the style along with a screen tip, such as Shadow. (ALT+click to add to the existing style. Right-click for a larger preview.)

Along the bottom of the Graphic Styles panel, as well as in the panel's options menu, you'll find several buttons and commands to assist you in using the styles. Here's what several of the commands do:

■ **New Graphic Style** Creates a new graphic style based on the styles applied to the currently selected object, group, or targeted layer.

Duplicate Graphic Style   Creates a duplicate of the graphic style selected in the Graphic Styles panel.

Merge Graphic Styles   When you select two or more styles in the Graphic Styles panel and choose this option, a new merged style will be created from them and added to the panel.

Delete Graphic Style   Deletes the selected style(s) from the Graphic Styles panel.

Break Link to Graphic Style   Separates the instance of a style applied to an object from the master style in the Graphic Styles panel. The style instance can then be modified independently of the master graphic style.

Select All Unused   Selects all unused styles in the panel, should you want to see which styles are not being used and possibly delete them to make your overall file size smaller and your Graphic Styles panel less cluttered.

Sort by Name   Rearranges the graphic styles alphabetically by name, though you can also drag and drop the styles into any desired order.

Use Square for Preview   Displays previews of the styles in the Graphic Styles panel or any of the graphic styles libraries as squares.

Use Text for Preview   Displays previews of the styles in the Graphic Styles panel or any of the graphic styles libraries as text (the letter T).

Graphic Styles Libraries

Illustrator comes with 11 free graphic styles libraries. To open a library, click the Graphic Styles Libraries menu at the bottom of the panel or choose the Open Graphic Style Library command from the panel's options menu, and then select one of the libraries by name. The selected library will open as a free-floating panel. You can then open additional libraries through the Graphic Styles Libraries menu at the bottom of the Graphic Styles or floating styles panel, or use the Load Previous Graphic Styles Library and Load Next Graphic Styles Library buttons at the bottom of the floating panel to scroll through the available styles libraries.

In addition to the Libraries, you can also import styles from other Illustrator files by choosing Window | Graphic Style Libraries | Other Library and selecting the file to be imported.

Styles opened in this way will appear in the graphic style library panel rather than in the Graphic Styles panel.

Applying Graphic Styles

To apply a graphic style to your work, select the object(s), group, or targeted layer on your artboard and then click the desired style in the Graphic Styles, from the Style dropdown menu on the Control panel, or from within any of the floating graphic styles libraries. Each time you click a style from the floating panel—whether you're actively applying the style to a selection or not—that style gets added to the Graphic Styles panel for future use.

Applying a graphic style to live, editable text can sometimes change the stroke and fill attributes of the text. To leave the text attributes as they are, make sure the Override Character Color option in the Graphic Styles panel options menu does not have a checkmark next to it. Alternatively, when you do want your text to fully take on the attributes of a particular style, enable the Override Character Color setting.

Sometimes when you apply graphic styles to groups, the fill doesn't seem to display. If that happens, move the style's fill attribute above the Contents layer in the Appearance panel.

Creating Graphic Styles

When you're ready to create your own graphic styles, the first thing you'll need to do is apply the desired styles to one or more objects, groups, or layers. For example, you could start with a grouped set of simple shapes, set the stroke and fill attributes for them, then add another fill below the first fill, select the new fill in the Appearance panel and apply the offset path effect to it, like the object shown in Figure 19-4.

To turn the style set of your selection into an official graphic style, which you can name and reuse again and again, do any of the following:

FIGURE 19-4 Creating a style set using the Appearance panel

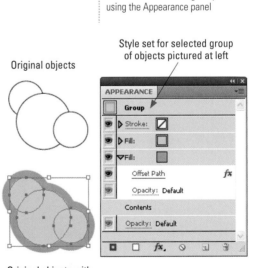

Original objects

Style set for selected group of objects pictured at left

Original objects with multiple attributes

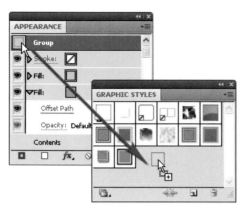

■ Drag and drop the selection's style thumbnail from the top of the Appearance panel into the Graphic Styles panel, as shown in the illustration.

■ Click the New Graphic Style button at the bottom of the Graphic Styles panel. If you ALT+click (Win) or OPT+click (Mac) the button, you can name the style before it gets added to the Graphic Styles panel.

■ Choose New Graphic Style from the Graphic Styles panel options menu.

■ Drag and drop the selection into the Graphic Styles panel.

To name your new graphic style, double-click the style icon or choose the Graphic Style Options from the Graphic Styles panel options menu, enter a name for your style in the dialog box, and click OK.

Saving Graphic Styles

After you've created one or more custom graphic styles, those styles will become part of the saved document; however, they will not be accessible to any other files until you save them in your own custom graphic styles library.

To create a custom library that includes all the styles appearing in the Graphic Styles panel as a custom library, choose the Save Graphic Styles option from the Graphic Styles Libraries menu or the Save Graphic Style Library command from the Graphic Styles panel options menu. When the Save Graphic Styles dialog box opens, it will already be set to save your new library into Illustrator's Graphic Styles folder, so all you need to do is provide a name for your new custom library and click Save.

When you're ready to open and use your custom graphic styles library, select the User Defined option from the Graphic Styles Libraries menu and select your custom library by name. Your library will open in its own free-floating panel or will be added to the existing floating panel in your workspace. Use your custom library just as you would any of Illustrator's free custom libraries, by selecting styles to apply them to your work or add them to your document's Graphic Styles panel.

Editing Graphic Styles

Each time you apply a graphic style to an object on your artboard, you're really only adding an instance of that style rather than the style itself. This fact gives your styles the ultimate flexibility, allowing you to accomplish two totally different things: First, you can modify each style instance without fear of "ruining" the original style. Second, you can modify any instance of a style, update the original style to reflect the changes, and update all instances of that style appearing in your work.

To edit an instance of a style, while leaving the original style intact, select the object and modify the style attributes in the Appearance panel. To edit an instance of a style, update the original style in the Graphic Styles panel, and update all other instances of that style with the update, select the object(s), group, or layer with the style applied to it and adjust the style attributes in the Appearance panel. Then, choose the Redefine Graphic Style command from the Appearance panel's options menu.

Breaking the Link to Graphic Styles

Clicking the Break Link To Graphic Style icon at the bottom of the Graphic Styles panel will permanently separate any instance of a graphic style applied to an object on your artboard from the style displaying in the Graphic Styles panel. This means that the detached style can be modified independently of the original graphic style and would not be affected if the original style was modified.

Deleting Graphic Styles

To delete a graphic style, select it within the Graphic Styles panel and click the Delete Graphic Style button along the bottom edge of the panel. Any objects on your artboard that happened to use instances of the deleted style will still have the same style attributes; however, they will no longer be associated with the original style and therefore cannot be globally updated using the Redefine Graphic Style command.

 To learn more about working with the Appearance and Graphic Styles panels, visit www .adobe.com/go/vid0051.

20

Live Paint and Live Trace

How to...

- Use the Live Paint Bucket and Live Paint Selection tools
- Create a Live Paint group
- Edit and apply color to a Live Paint group
- Create Tracing Objects with Live Trace
- Set custom tracing options
- Convert Tracing Objects into Live Paint groups
- Expand Tracing Objects into editable vector art

In this chapter, you'll learn how to work with Live Paint and Live Trace, two techniques that a lot of new Illustrator users tend to shy away from because they seem too confusing to learn without the help of an expert. This chapter is your expert. Here, you'll learn how to create Live Paint groups and work with the Live Paint tools to paint the various strokes and fills of your objects, including the spaces created by overlapping lines of different paths and shapes. You'll also see how easy it is to trace raster images with the Live Trace command and convert them into either Live Paint groups or expanded, editable, and scalable vector art!

Live Paint

In Illustrator, when you draw each path and shape on the artboard, the objects sit one on top of the next in a bottom-up stacking order. Paths and closed shapes can have strokes and fills, but each object is separate and overlapping, or intersecting areas do not create new closed shapes—that is, unless you turn your drawings into Live Paint groups.

Live Paint is a special Illustrator painting technique that allows you to add colors, gradients, and patterns to the individual *edges* (paths) and *faces* (shapes) within a selected group of objects.

Think of it as like working with a coloring book where you can fill in any of the outlined shapes—including shapes that aren't fully closed—as well as add color to the lines. To use Live Paint, you'll need to first create a Live Paint group, which is a special type of object grouping that isolates the objects for the purpose of applying paint with the Live Paint tools. Once the group is created, you can apply colors, gradients, and patterns to any of the group edge and face areas with the Live Paint Bucket tool, or select multiple areas with the Live Paint Selection tool and then apply edge and face colors, gradients, and patterns to those selections.

The Live Paint Bucket Tool

The Live Paint Bucket tool is the enhanced replacement tool for the old Illustrator Paint Bucket, which used to let you pour fill colors into closed shapes. Not only is the new Live Paint Bucket tool more effective at filling in colors, it can also detect and highlight different paintable areas as you hover your cursor over an image. Even more amazingly, you can use the Live Paint Bucket tool to fill in unclosed areas, such as a shape drawn with a pencil line that includes a 5-pixel gap.

Creating a Live Paint Group

Before you can use the Live Paint Bucket tool, you must first create a Live Paint group. Groups may include paths and shapes, but they cannot include live type, brushes, or bitmap images. Therefore, to include text, brushes, or bitmaps in your Live Paint group, you must first convert those objects into paths by converting type to outlines, expanding special brushes into objects, and tracing bitmap images. Also keep in mind that there are quite a few limitations to Live Paint groups. For instance, some effects and transparency can be lost when you create the groups, and you also can't use a lot of commands and other features on them.

To create a Live Paint group, use the Selection tool to select the desired objects on your artboard, and then convert them into a Live Paint group by selecting the Live Paint Bucket tool and clicking anywhere inside the selection. You can also create Live Paint groups by choosing Object | Live Paint | Make, or by pressing the keyboard shortcut, ALT+CTRL+X (Win) or OPT+CMD+X (Mac).

Once your objects have been converted into a Live Paint group, the corner anchor points of its bounding box, when selected, will have tiny gray starbursts inside them, as illustrated in Figure 20-1.

FIGURE 20-1 Live Paint groups

Original Live Paint group   Live Paint group with   Live Paint group after paint
with bounding box   paint applied   and path adjustments

Objects in a Live Paint group can be edited just like regular objects, so you can use any of the drawing tools to add, delete, adjust, and transform the objects as well as apply colors, gradients, and patterns to the different paths and intersecting shapes. As you adjust the shapes, the strokes and fills also automatically update to reflect the changes to the paths and shapes.

Applying Color to a Live Paint Group

To apply a color, gradient, or pattern to an actively selected Live Paint group, select the Live Paint Bucket tool and hover your cursor over the selection. As you move your cursor, paintable areas and paintable strokes (when strokes are enabled) will be highlighted with a default 4-pt red border, as illustrated here.

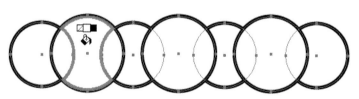

To change the highlighting color and other tool preferences, double-click the Live Paint Bucket tool on the Tools panel to open the Live Paint Bucket Options dialog box. There you can select a different highlight color and thickness (width), toggle highlighting on and off, and choose which parts of your Live Paint group can be colorized by the tool. By default, the tool will paint fills but not strokes; however, you can choose to paint just fills, just strokes, or both fills and strokes. In addition, you can toggle on or off the default Cursor Swatch Preview icon, though it's such a great tool aid that I highly recommend you always leave it on.

When you're ready to apply paint to a single highlighted edge and face area, click a highlighted area and that spot will be filled with the currently selected fill color, gradient, or pattern. To choose a different fill color, gradient, or pattern (or stroke color, gradient, or pattern when the Stroke option is active in the options dialog box and a stroke area is highlighted), use any of the following options:

- Select a color, gradient, or pattern from the Swatches panel, or a color from the Color or Color Guide panel, before clicking inside a highlighted paintable area.

- Use your keyboard's UP, DOWN, LEFT, and RIGHT ARROW keys to alter the swatch preview colors, gradients, or patterns appearing in the Live Paint Bucket tool's Cursor Swatch Preview area. For example, if the Cursor Swatch Preview is displaying the default No Fill/White/Black color scheme, pressing the RIGHT ARROW three times will replace the Cursor Swatch Preview with a Red/Yellow/Green color combination. The center square of the Cursor Swatch Preview represents the color, gradient, or pattern that will be applied when you click the highlighted paintable area.

- Press the ALT (Win) or OPT (Mac) key on your keyboard to temporarily convert your Live Paint Bucket tool into the Eyedropper tool and click to sample a color, gradient, or pattern from another object in your document. After sampling, release the ALT (Win) or OPT (Mac) key so your cursor returns to the Live Paint Bucket tool. You can then click a highlighted paintable area to fill it with that sampled color, gradient, or pattern.

- When the Paint Strokes option is not enabled in the Live Paint Bucket Options dialog box, then pressing the SHIFT key will temporarily toggle your Live Paint Bucket tool into the Live Paint Brush tool, which will allow you to paint stroke segments on your Live Paint group with the color, gradient, or pattern in the center of the Cursor Swatch Preview area.

When the Paint Strokes option is enabled in the Live Paint Bucket Options dialog box, it is not necessary to press the SHIFT key because the cursor should automatically switch from a paint bucket to a paint brush when you hover the cursor over the stroke and fill areas of a Live Paint group.

■ Double-click inside a shape to fill that shape with the color, gradient, or pattern in the center of the Cursor Swatch Preview area as well as any adjacent faces that share the same fill and stroke edges.

■ Triple-click inside a shape to fill that shape with the color, gradient, or pattern in the center of the Cursor Swatch Preview area as well as all faces that share the same fill and stroke edges. For example, if there were four faces that used a green and you wanted to repaint them all purple, a triple-click inside one of the green faces would change all four of them to purple.

 To view onscreen tips about working with Live Paint, open the Live Paint Bucket Options dialog box and click the Tips button.

Editing a Live Paint Group

Once you create a Live Paint group with two or more shapes, you can continue to edit the group by adding new shapes to it, editing or deleting shapes within it, releasing the Live Paint group setting, expanding the selection into editable artwork, and controlling the size of gaps that determine which areas can be painted.

To draw new shapes into a Live Paint group, you must first enter Isolation Mode by double-clicking the Live Paint group with the Selection tool. Once in Isolation Mode, you can draw new paths and objects, delete and edit shapes, as well as select and apply colors, gradients, or patterns to the shapes using the Live Paint Bucket and Live Paint Selection tools. When finished, exit Isolation Mode by double-clicking the artboard with the Selection tool.

To further edit your Live Paint groups, use the commands in the Object | Live Paint menu:

■ **Object | Live Paint | Make**   Turns any two or more selected objects, groups, or targeted layers into a Live Paint group. The paths of objects within a Live Paint group are grouped together in a single layer in the Layers panel and labeled as a Live Paint group.

- **Object | Live Paint | Merge**   Adds additional objects to a Live Paint group when you select the Live Paint group and the new objects before selecting this command.

- **Object | Live Paint | Release**   Removes the Live Paint group setting from a group of objects. Upon release, the strokes and fills of the objects get replaced with the default no fill and 0.5-pt black stroke.

- **Object | Live Paint | Gap Options**   Opens the Gap Options dialog box where you can set the size of gaps in paths of a Live Paint group, choose to close gaps in the selected Live Paint group with paths (by clicking the Close Gaps With Paths button), and adjust the color for the gap preview indicators. For instance, with some drawings, like the one shown here, gaps in a path cause the shape to remain open, rather creating a totally closed shape. The size of those spaces, or gaps, can determine whether Illustrator will recognize the unclosed space as a paintable region. To highlight any gaps in a selected Live Paint group based on your Gap Options settings for that group, choose View | Show Live Paint Gaps.

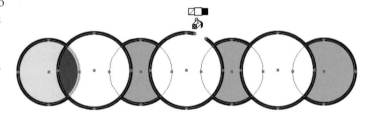

- **Object | Live Paint | Expand**   Removes the Live Paint group setting from a group of objects and slices the shapes into individual objects where each stroke and fill are separated based on the intersection of paths. By default, the expanded shapes will be grouped together, so you may need to ungroup them before being able to select the shapes individually.

The Live Paint Selection Tool

The Live Paint Selection tool is the alternate Live Paint tool you can use to select one or more Live Paint regions without altering them, or to select multiple regions so you can paint them all at once. For example, to increase productivity, you might want to select three different regions first and then apply the same color, gradient, or pattern fill to them. You'll find the

Live Paint Selection tool on the Tools panel next to or directly below the Live Paint Bucket tool depending on the Tools panel configuration.

Like the Live Paint Bucket tool, the Live Paint Selection tool also highlights Live Paint regions as you move your cursor over the Live Paint group. In addition, it also gives you a visual

indication of which regions are selected after you click them by emphasizing the selected regions with a light gray screen effect, as illustrated here.

To edit the highlight color of the Live Paint Selection tool, double-click the tool on the Tools panel to open the Live Paint Selection Options dialog box. There you can adjust the highlight color and width, toggle the highlighting feature on and off, as well as decide whether the tool will select just fills, just strokes, or both fills and strokes.

Selecting a Live Paint Region

To select an entire Live Paint group, click anywhere on the group with the Selection tool. To select an edge and face region in a selected Live Paint group with the Live Paint Selection tool, all you need to do is click along, or inside of, any of the highlighted areas. To select multiple regions, press and hold the SHIFT key as you select each region with your mouse. Alternatively, you can drag a marquee shape around the objects you'd like to select. To deselect any of the selected multiple regions while keeping the other regions selected, press and hold the SHIFT key and again click the region you'd like to deselect.

Painting a Live Paint Region

To paint multiple selected regions within a Live Paint group, do any of the following:

- Select the areas with the Live Paint Selection tool and then select a color, gradient, or pattern from the Swatches panel—or a color from the Color or Color Guide panel—and it will be applied to the highlighted paintable area(s).

- Press the ALT (Win) or OPT (Mac) key on your keyboard to temporarily convert your Live Paint Selection tool into the Eyedropper tool so you can click to sample a color, gradient, or pattern from another object in your document. As you click the other object, the multiple selected areas in the Live Paint group will automatically be painted with that sampled color, gradient, or pattern.

- Double-click to select any adjacent shapes within the Live Paint group that share the same outer stroke and fill areas.

- Triple-click to select similar regions throughout the entire Live Paint group, such as all faces or all edges.

For a video on using Live Paint, see www.adobe.com/go/vid0042.

Live Trace

Live Trace is a powerful Illustrator tool that allows users to quickly trace any raster art or bitmap images and convert them into vector-based drawing! Live Trace is the ideal replacement for stand-alone tracing software programs like Adobe Streamline as well as the old-fashioned trace-it-yourself method, which for many was a tedious and time-consuming task. With the scalable vector artwork created from the Live Trace tool, you can either leave the artwork in its Tracing Object format, convert the Tracing Object into a Live Paint group, or expand the art into fully editable working vector shapes. Figure 20-2 shows a scanned placed bitmap image and the copy of it produced with Illustrator's Live Trace tool.

FIGURE 20-2 The Live Trace command

Original raster image

Vector illustration created with Live Trace

Tracing Options

When the Tracing Options dialog box opens, enable the Preview option and play around with the different Presets, Adjustments, and Trace Settings so you can begin to learn how each feature

How to...   **Choose the Right Tracing Options**

When the Live Trace tool traces your images, it uses the contrast and/or color data in the file to build the paths and lay down the anchor points of the vector-based version. You can control the parameters of the trace through the Tracing Options dialog box, which can be opened by selecting Object | Live Trace | Tracing Options or by choosing Tracing Options from the Tracing preset and options menu button next to the Live Trace button on the Control panel.

modifies the resulting Tracing Object. For instance, if you're tracing a logo from a scanned raster image, you might want to compare the Black and White Logo, Comic Art, and Inked Drawing presets to see which one looks best to you and then fiddle with the Adjustments and Trace Settings until the Tracing Object suits your needs.

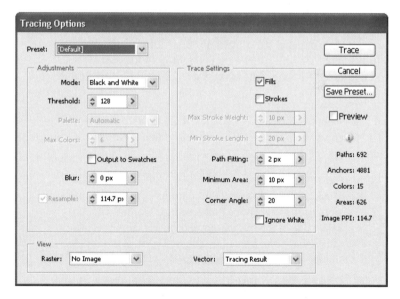

Each of the presets uses specific Adjustments and Trace Settings, but you can enhance the results by modifying any of the dialog box settings. To help you know what to do, hover your cursor over any of the input fields or dropdown menus to read a tool tip about that particular setting. For example, the tool tip for the Strokes Trace Setting is "Create stroked paths in the tracing result."

If you create a custom set of tracing options that you'd like to save for later reuse, click the Save Preset button in the Tracing Options dialog box and you'll be prompted to name and save your custom preset. Saved custom presets will then become accessible at the bottom of the Preset menu. To edit or delete a preset, choose Edit | Tracing Presets to open the Tracing Presets dialog box. Clicking the Edit button will reopen the Tracing Options dialog box for the selected preset so you can change the settings, and clicking the Delete button will completely remove the selected preset. In addition, you can import and export presets through the Edit | Tracing Presets menu.

Creating a Tracing Object

To turn a raster image into a Tracing Object with the Live Trace tool, begin by selecting a placed (File | Place) or embedded (Edit | Paste) bitmap image on your artboard with the Selection tool. Placed files are linked to their original source file, which can be opened and edited by clicking the Edit Original button on the Control panel. To convert a placed file into an embedded file click the Control panel's Embed button. With your bitmap selected, access the Live Trace command in any of the following ways:

- Choose Object | Live Trace | Make to trace your raster image with the Default tracing settings.

- Click the Live Trace button on the Control panel to trace your raster image with the Default tracing settings.

- Click the Tracing preset and options menu button to the right of the Live Trace button on the Control panel to select one of the tracing preset options. Upon releasing your mouse, the bitmap image will be traced with the tracing preset option you selected.

- Choose Object | Live Trace | Tracing Options or select Tracing Options from the Tracing preset and options menu button on the Control panel to set your own custom tracing settings.

To use a custom set of colors for the tracing when the Tracing Options dialog box Mode is set to Color or Grayscale, open the desired Swatch Library in your workspace, select the Tracing Object on your artboard, reopen the Tracing Options dialog box by clicking the Tracing Options Dialog button on the Control panel, select that Swatch Library by name from the Palette menu in the Adjustments section, and then click the Trace button.

After the raster file has been turned into a Tracing Object, you can still modify the tracing options by selecting the Tracing Object and either choosing a different option from the Preset menu on the Control panel, or by pressing the Tracing options dialog button to the right of the Preset menu on the Control panel to reopen the Tracing Options dialog box.

 To release a tracing and go back to the original raster art, choose Object I Live Trace I Release.

Converting Tracing Objects into Vector Art

When it comes to editing a Tracing Object, your options are fairly limited. However, if you really don't need to do anything else to your traced image, leaving it as a Tracing Object is fine. However if you want to be able to paint the different regions of your artwork or be able to edit the traced image as a scalable vector shape, you'll need to either convert the Tracing Object into a Live Paint group or expand it into vectors. Both options are extremely useful and versatile, depending on your needs. The only drawback to converting a Tracing Object into a Live Paint group or expanded editable vector art is that once the conversion is complete, you can't go back and change the tracing options.

Creating a Live Paint Group

To turn your Tracing Object into a Live Paint group, which can then be edited using the Live Paint Bucket and Live Paint Selection tools, select the Tracing Object and click the Live Paint button on the Control panel or choose Object I Live Paint I Convert To Live Paint. To trace and convert your raster image with a single click, choose Object I Live Trace I Make And Convert To Live Paint.

You will know the process is complete when you see the Live Paint bounding box appear on your selection. If you don't see the bounding box, check to see that the Show Bounding

Box option is turned on in the View menu or press the keyboard shortcut, SHIFT+CTRL+B (Win) or SHIFT+CMD+B (Mac). Use the Live Paint tools, as described earlier in this chapter, to select and paint the different paintable areas of the Live Paint group.

Expanding a Tracing Object

To turn your Tracing Object into editable vector art, which can then be modified, tweaked, and transformed with any of Illustrator's other tools and commands, click the Expand button on the Control panel or choose Object | Live Trace | Expand. To trace and convert your raster image with a single click, choose Object | Live Trace | Make And Expand.

Upon converting the Tracing Object into editable art, the placed image will be converted into a single grouped object made up of vector shapes. You may then use the Direct Selection tool to select and modify shapes within the group, or ungroup the object and use the Selection tool to select and edit the different shapes.

For a video on using Live Trace, go to www.adobe.com/go/vid0043.

PART IV

Real World

21

Print and Design: Editorial, Branding, Textiles, Crafts

How to…

- Create logo designs
- Design a postcard
- Make an editorial illustration
- Design a magazine ad
- Create business cards and stationery
- Design a book jacket
- Make a T-shirt design
- Create craft projects for kids
- Design graphics for scrapbooking

Though, technically, Illustrator is an illustration program, not a page layout program, you can certainly use it for your print design projects, such as creating logos; editorial advertisements; decorative borders for Word documents; backgrounds for PowerPoint presentations; postcard design; stationery sets, including business cards, letterhead, and envelopes; textile design; T-shirt design; greeting card design; and even illustrations and designs for fun projects like scrapbooking and kids' crafts. In this chapter, you'll discover new ways of working with Illustrator to produce some of these types of print projects.

Logo Design

If you ever need to design a logo, which is an easily recognized, memorable, and unique graphic symbol, mark, or identifying name that brands a product or represents a company, Illustrator is the only program you should consider using to create it because logos need to be scalable to fit on anything from the side of a pencil to the side of a blimp.

With logos, you need to decide whether the logo will be made up of a *logotype*, which is a stylized text-only logo based on the company name (think Verizon or Coca-Cola), or an *iconic logo* that includes the company name and some kind of graphic element (think Nike or Adobe). Some companies also like to include a *tag line*, or slogan, with their logo, and possibly even a *trademark* or *registered trademark* symbol if they have already registered their company name with the U.S. Patent and Trademark Office (think Budweiser or Taco Bell).

To begin your logo design, start with the name of the company in black. At this stage, you want to focus on the design, so do not add any color to the logo design until the design is approved by the client. In addition, there may be times when a client may need to print in black and white in addition to color. By designing in black and white, you are assured the logo will have appeal under these circumstances and adding color from that point will be like icing on the cake. Choose a font that best portrays the image your client wants to project. For example, if your client's company is called ColorLids and they manufacture modern multicolored plastic-lidded containers, you might want to choose a font that looks modern, hip, and clean.

After you select a font, convert the font to outlines so you can adjust the letter shapes to make the letters more unique, such as changing the shape of the dot on an "i," connecting two letters together, or adding a flourish to the first or last letter. If the logo will also have a tagline, add that in and choose an appropriate font for it.

If the logo design also needs a graphic symbol, start to play around with primitive shapes, such as a circle, star, square, or polygon, as well as non-uniform shapes and irregular hand-drawn shapes.

ColorLids   ColorLids
COLORLIDS   ColorLids
COLORLIDS   **ColorLids**
COLORLIDS   **ColorLids**

When you are finished creating several designs, present the client with your three or four favorite ideas and let them help guide the logo development from there. Ideally, you should only allow up to two to three rounds of revisions to one of the three or four logos you present to the client, which will help keep the project focused and within budget. For example, let's say you show the client three designs. The client should select one design and provide feedback. You'd then work some more on it and present the client with three or four versions of their selected design. The client would then choose one of those revised designs as the official design. For the last round of revisions, you'd add color treatments and other effects (like drop shadows or reflections) to the final design, which would then be presented to the client so they could select one as the final logo design.

Postcard Design

Postcards are great for things like sales promotions, gallery opening invitations, media kit inserts, special announcements, and oversized calling cards. Postcard designs need two sides: one typically for a color image and the other for text and post office indicia. With Illustrator CS4's new multiple artboard capability, you can now design both sides of your postcard in a single document.

One of Illustrator's free templates is a 4" × 6" postcard layout with guides. To use the postcard template, which puts both sides of the postcard on a single artboard with guides and crop marks, choose File | New From Templates to open the New From Template dialog box. From there, open the Blank Templates folder and select and open the file called Promotional 1.ait. This file includes layouts for a Newsletter, Postcard, and Table Tent.

FIGURE 21-1 Lay out both sides of your postcard design on a single layer with multiple artboards

Alternatively, to create your own professional postcard layout in any size, begin by choosing File | New to open a new document in the size of the postcard you need. For example, if you need to design a 5" × 7" postcard, choose the Print option under New Document Profile, set the Number Of Artboards to 2, set the Units to Inches, choose Landscape for the Orientation, set the width and height of the file to 7 in by 5 in, and add a Top/Bottom/Left/Right bleed of 0.125 in. A bleed is an area of the layout that deliberately extends past the edge of the artwork so the artwork can be trimmed off cleanly during the printing and finishing process. The photograph in Figure 21-1 shows an example of an edge bleed. Click OK when you are satisfied with the settings.

Next, lay out your artwork for the front and back of the postcard on the two artboards. Add text, place photographic images, use effects, draw shapes—do whatever you need to do to get the message across. If needed, make your rulers visible so you can drag out guides to assist with the placement of the content on your postcard. Figure 21-1 shows an example of how one postcard can be designed in Illustrator.

Save your work in the Illustrator AI file format and then check with the print provider to see what file format they prefer for artwork submissions. Most production houses, like ModernPostcard and PrintingForLess, can accept many file formats including AI, EPS, PSD, and PDFs.

Tip Order from www.PrintingForLess.com and receive $25 off of your first order. Simply input the unique coupon code RP1T2FU8F in the Promotional Code field of any PrintingForLess order form while completing your order and you will see the discount applied on your receipt.

Editorial Illustration

Editorial illustration, or advertising illustration, is a particular kind of art that is used to convey meaning without words and often helps to illustrate the ideas contained in a particular article, report, or news item in a magazine, newspaper, journal, or other publication. A lot of editorial art is political in nature, but quite a bit of it is also playful, fun, and light.

Typically, when you're asked to make an editorial illustration, you are also provided with an idea, theme, sentence, or an entire article, report, or news item from which you'll glean your inspiration for the illustration, such as "We need an illustration for an article about single women and loneliness of the dating scene," and the title of the piece is "Martini for One." Your job is to make that into an illustration.

With illustration, it is often best to use your own talents and be 100 percent yourself when making editorial art, as all people have their own unique take on life and can use their personal experiences to inspire them and guide them in their work. Start your editorial projects by making quick sketches of your ideas, either on paper or in Illustrator. Don't worry about being perfect at this stage—what you really want to do is quickly come up with at least five to ten idea sketches. From those, select two or three ideas to develop a little further and show as "*roughs*" to your client for selection. The client will often have constructive feedback and art direction that can assist you in creating the final piece. You can then create the final editorial piece in full color and detail.

Magazine Ads

With magazine ads, as with newspaper advertisements, you're often provided with all the copy and graphics that need to go into the ad and it's your job to put all the pieces together in a visually pleasing way. Most ads have spatial constraints and other limitations, such as paper quality and the number of colors that can be used, as well as demographic concerns since you'll want to ensure that the ad you create will appeal to the advertiser's target audience. The best way to prepare for creating a magazine advertisement is to do some research on the magazine in which the ad will appear. You might also want to take notice of what other advertisers for similar products or services have done in their ads to be sure you don't accidentally mimic them.

To begin, create a new blank Print document in the exact size you need, then add all the elements to the page, including text, logo graphics, tag lines, other branding information, and photographs. The project may be as simple as advertising for a local sushi restaurant with a logo, telephone number, and hours of operation, as dull as an ad for prescription sleeping pills, or as fun as a product ad for a wholesome and healthy snack.

When laying out the ad, try not to use more than two or three fonts since more can make the advertisement look busy and unorganized. For instance, select two or three different fonts, or use variations of the same font family, such as regular, bold, and italic versions of Arial. Do the same for colors, picking one primary color for the page, one for fonts, and possibly a third for an accent color. Give your ad lots of breathing space and don't feel as if you need to fill up every inch with content. Oftentimes, a photograph will dominate the ad and text will be used to enhance the photographic message and mood. Whatever your task, make it balanced, interesting, unique, and creative.

Business Card Design

Business card design is actually one of the more challenging things a designer creates because, like a logo, it must convey the image of the company while being a functional advertisement piece. Depending on the client's needs, a business card can contain such things as a logo, tagline, address, URL, telephone, and fax, as well as the name, title, cell number, and e-mail address of the person whose card it is. Color is also a consideration that is often determined by the client's budget. If they have a lot of money, you can do a full color card with a photograph or intricate graphic design on special paper along

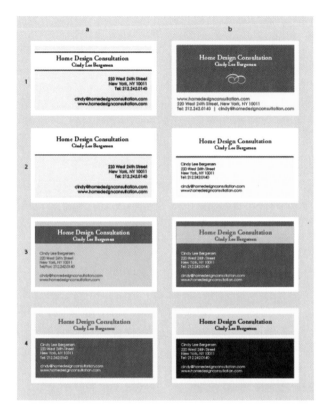

FIGURE 21-2 With business card design, even the slightest layout change can project an entirely different image

with Pantone colors (Pantone is more reliable as far as color accuracy goes, though it is more expensive than CMYK process color). If the client doesn't have a lot of money, you'll be limited to one or two colors of ink and whatever paper is on special at the printer you use.

Business cards can be oriented vertically or horizontally, though most corporate clients will prefer the traditional horizontal layout. If you open the blank business card template (File | New From Template | Blank Templates | Business Cards. ait), you can use any of the four artboards in the file to assist you with your layout. Otherwise, create your own business card file in the appropriate size and orientation. But before you do that, you may want to play around with different layout ideas in a blank letter-sized print document sectioned off to the appropriate size before you settle on the four to eight different options you'll show to your client, like the eight examples in Figure 21-2.

Once the client approves the design, you can set up an appropriately sized document and paste a copy of that design into the new file. Check with the printer who will be printing the business cards to see if they have any special bleed or other preflight printing requirements along with finding out what file formats they accept.

Stationery Design

Stationery design almost always follows the lead of a company's business card design, using the same fonts, colors, and general layout style. Stationery may include a single sheet with logo and contact information, or two pages for the cover sheet with logo and contact information, and the second sheet with branding but no contact info.

To create your own stationery, begin with Illustrator's free stationery template (File | New From Template | Blank Templates | Stationery.ait), which includes artboards for letterhead, envelope, invitation, invitation envelope, and compliment slip, or start with your own blank letter-sized Print document (File | New). Next, copy all the artwork and text from the business card layout and paste it into your file. If you don't have access to the original business card artwork, use Illustrator's tools to re-create them. The last thing to do is try out a few different layout ideas, each of which somewhat mirrors the design of the business card, until you settle on one or two designs to show your client. It is often best to present your ideas along with the business card, like the example in Figure 21-3, so the client can get a feel for the flavor of how their new stationery fits in with the business card design.

FIGURE 21-3 Presenting your stationery design with the business card makes a big impact

Book Jacket Design

Technically speaking, you should be using a page layout program like Adobe InDesign or QuarkXPress to lay out a book jacket design. However, if you really wanted to, you could certainly use Illustrator to do it.

A well-designed book jacket can make the difference between a book that sells and one that is largely ignored. Book jackets convey a book's message and can even create feelings of excitement in the potential reader, so it's important to create a design that will be visually appealing, enticing, and attractive on the front and back covers, and along the book's spine.

Good book jackets should grab the reader's attention on the front cover, entice the reader further on the back cover, reflect the book's content and theme, be targeted toward the audience who will be reading it, and use sans-serif fonts, which are often easier to read from a distance.

Tip Serif fonts are generally easier to read for large amounts of body text due to the extended feet at the tops and bottoms of the letters (to help guide the eye), whereas sans-serif fonts offer a cleaner look for headlines and advertising layouts.

The front of the book should include the title, subtitle, and byline (if any), the author's name, editor's name(s) when applicable, and some kind of photo or graphic to capture the reader's eye. The spine repeats the book title and author name, and sometimes also the publisher's logo, a photo, or some artwork, and since the space is often narrow, consider using all capital letters with extra spacing between each letter for the type. The back of the book jacket may include such things as the author's photo and a short bio, the testimonials from qualified authorities, benefits and features of the book, and the ISBN, bar code, and price. You may also be tasked with laying out the content on the inner flaps of the book jacket, which normally contain a synopsis of, or excerpt from, the book and sometimes biographical information about the author.

Before you do too much work, speak with the client about concepts so you need to develop only one or two ideas for the client to choose from. Then, create a new blank Print document (File | New) in the size to match the book, which should be provided to you by the publisher or author. Because the front, spine, back, and inner flaps of the jacket need to be printed on a single sheet of paper, you'll need to set up guides to assist you with the layout for each area. Once the document is set up, you can go to work assembling all the pieces into a visually pleasing layout.

T-Shirt Design

Almost anything goes when it comes to the world of T-shirt design. Usually designs will cover just the front of the shirt, but you can also create designs that cover the back and sleeves, too. T-shirt designs need to be big enough to fill the space on an XL or XXL shirt, while at the same time not being overwhelmingly too large for an S or M shirt. The other thing you need to consider is how the shirt design will be applied to the shirt material, which might be silkscreen, heat-transfer decal, embroidery, digital printing, or some other process.

To get started, open the Illustrator T-Shirt template (File | New From Template | Blank Templates | Tshirt.ait), which includes a rectangular guide for your artwork along with a t-shirt illustration you can use to visualize the placement of your design on an actual shirt.

Next, start designing! If you plan to use white ink and print your work on a color shirt, consider giving your artwork a temporary background to match the t-shirt color so you can design on top of it. When you're finished with your design, delete the temporary background shape before providing the artwork to your printer. Designs can be as simple or as complex as you like. Figure 21-4 shows a lizard design that would appeal to young males.

FIGURE 21-4 Use the Illustrator T-shirt template to lay out your shirt designs

Kids' Crafts Design

You can design tons of things in Illustrator for kids' craft projects. Create holiday projects, coloring pages, printable stickers, puzzles, and assemblables that follow a particular pattern. To make your craft projects accessible to the widest possible audience, design everything to fit within a standard U.S. letter-sized page (8.5" × 11") so each page can be printed on a home printer.

The following are just a few craft ideas you can design in Illustrator:

■ **Printable stickers**   Create a checkerboard of sticker designs using similar colors, text, and a theme (like a holiday) so children can print the file on sticky paper and easily cut out the designs.

■ **Coloring pages**   Design a coloring book page on a theme such as going to the beach, visiting the zoo, or discovering dinosaurs. Use thick lines, bold shapes, and clear divisions of space to emphasize where children should add colors.

■ **Puppet crafts**   Design a puppet shape that can be printed, colored in, cut out, and taped to a drinking straw to create fun and playful stick puppets.

■ **Word search and crossword puzzles**   Construct your own kid-themed word search and crossword puzzles complete with text and illustrations.

■ **I-spy pages**   Build your own I-spy drawings within which children can search for and find specific objects.

■ **Cut-and-paste activity pages**   Create educationally themed drawings that children can print out and use to cut and paste certain objects onto the page where they belong.

■ **Paper lanterns**   Design your own paper lantern printouts for children to color, cut, and assemble.

Scrapbooking Design

If you've ever wondered what all the scrapbooking fuss was about, think of the words *story*, *share*, *love*, *laugh*, and *inspire* and then imagine looking through a really fun photo album. That's it. Though, generally, scrapbooking is a hobby for moms and grandmothers, anyone with the desire to tell a story creatively through imagery can do it.

Illustrator is a wonderful tool for designing scrapbook layouts, embellishments, and stylized lettering. Popular scrapbooking themes include baby's first year, weddings, family vacations, birthdays, holidays, special events, and school days, though other themes are perfectly acceptable if you have the photos and creativity to fulfill them.

Use Illustrator to design fun shapes (stars, flowers, polka dots, circles), borders (checked, striped), text blocks (poetry, memories, funny jokes), and other design embellishments (arrows, symbols, illustrations) that can be easily cut out and adhered to your layouts. If you have a decent printer, you can print your scrapbook designs on a variety of plain, patterned, and printed papers and cardstocks. Otherwise, try to use heavy printing paper (28–32 lb), which is slightly thicker and more durable than regular 20-lb copier paper.

If you like the idea of visual storytelling but aren't crazy about sitting down with glue and ribbon, consider digital scrapbooking, where your photos, thoughts, and designs can be stored and shared electronically.

 For a giant scoop of scrapbooking inspiration, check out www.twopeasinabucket.com.

22

Taking Illustrations to the Web

How to…

- Design web layouts
- Slice images
- Create buttons and image maps
- Optimize web graphics
- Create mobile content

Many web designers today who work in HTML use bitmap applications like Photoshop or Fireworks to mock up their web layouts and optimize graphics for the Web. Flash users, on the other hand, tend to prefer creating graphics in Illustrator because both Illustrator and Flash use vector art, which creates smaller file sizes, and Illustrator artwork can be directly imported into Flash. So, though technically Illustrator is not a web graphics program, you can use it to design and optimize graphics for the Web. In fact, Illustrator uses the same optimization engine as Photoshop, which is fairly intuitive and easy to use.

In this chapter, you'll discover how to use Illustrator to create web layouts, buttons, and other web graphics for web sites, blogs, and MySpace and Facebook pages, as well as learn to use the Attributes, Flash Text, Actions, and SVG Interactivity panels, use Device Central to help with the development of mobile content, and slice and optimize graphics for the Web.

Designing Web Layouts

In setting up your work environment, the first thing you'll want to do is choose the Web workspace (Window | Workspace | Web) so the panels in the panel dock are arranged to support the creation of web graphics. The next step is to create a new, blank file in the right format. When the New Document dialog box opens (File | New) be sure to select the Web option under the New Document Profile menu. The default size for a web file here is 800×600, though you

Ideal Web Layout Sizes

Even though most new computer monitors come factory preset with resolutions of 1024×768 or higher, web sites still tend to be designed for the 800×600 or 1024×768 monitor resolution sizes. To ensure your designs fit snugly inside a browser window without scrolling horizontally, use 760×420 as the custom pixel dimensions for your web layout instead of 800×600, and use 955×600 as the custom pixel dimensions for your web layout instead of 1024×768.

can use any of the other presets in the Size menu or create a custom size by entering pixel dimensions in the Width and Height fields (see the sidebar for recommended sizes). Leave the orientation set to Landscape and ignore the Bleed area. In the Advanced section of the dialog box, leave the color mode set to RGB, the Raster Effects set to Screen (72 ppi), and the Preview Mode set to Default. Click OK.

With your new document open, turn on your rulers (View | Show Rulers), which should already be set to display in pixels, and begin to assemble all the pieces of the web site's home page onto the artboard in a visually pleasing way. If desired, use the guides and grid to assist you in the orderly placement of your content.

Most home pages include a logo, company tagline or slogan, navigation bar, general information about the web site, and a footer with text-only navigation links, copyright, and sometimes contact information. Other items that could go onto the page might include a site search bar, the date, shopping cart, account and help links, user sign in / log in / sign up links, photographs, graphics, newsletter signup, testimonials, links to other pages, specials, advertisements, navigational breadcrumbs, and information about contests and sweepstakes. Figure 22-1 shows a sample layout with rulers and guides.

If the web content for your layout exceeds the height of your document, select the Artboard tool on the Tools panel and adjust the height of your artboard in the Height field on the Control panel. To exit the Artboard mode, select another tool on the Tools panel.

Figure 22-1 Create your web layout using rulers and guides to help with the placement of text, graphics, and photographs

Having some knowledge of web site production can be very helpful during the design process. If you don't have any personal experience with this, consider consulting with a web designer or programmer to ensure that your visual ideas can be easily translated onto the Web.

 Adobe Dreamweaver is the number one web development program used by web designers and programmers. If you want to learn how to use this exciting software program, get the Telly Award–winning *Dreamweaver for Designers* training DVD with Sue Jenkins (ClassOnDemand.com), *Dreamweaver CS4 For Dummies All-in-One Desk Reference* by Sue Jenkins (Wiley), and *Web Design For Dummies All-in-One Desk Reference* by Sue Jenkins (Wiley).

Pixel Preview

Illustrator creates vector shapes, which by their nature are high resolution. This means that what you see on your monitor isn't necessarily what you'll see on the Web when you optimize

Regular Preview Mode   Pixel Preview Mode

FIGURE 22-2 Use Pixel Preview mode to preview your work in a simulated web environment

the graphics. That's because browsers display images at only 72 pixels per inch (ppi) in the RGB color space. To simulate a web environment, switch over to the Pixel Preview mode by choosing View | Pixel Preview or by pressing the keyboard shortcut, ALT+CTRL+Y (Win) or OPT+CMD+Y (Mac).

Once in Pixel Preview mode, zoom into an area of your work with text or fine lines to preview how the optimization process may alter your graphics. What you'll see, essentially, is how the Pixel Preview mode makes your work look as if it's raster (built with pixels) rather than vector, as shown in the example in Figure 22-2. If desired, leave the workspace in Pixel Preview mode or switch back into the regular preview mode by selecting Pixel Preview again to toggle it off.

Slicing Images

On the Web, the larger the image, the bigger it is in file size, and the longer it takes to download and display in a browser window. With slices, you can cut up a larger graphic into smaller pieces that are high in quality but low in file size. In addition, since most web layouts include graphics and photos, being able to isolate each piece and optimize them separately as GIFs, PNGs, and

JPGs can improve quality and save additional file size. Then, using HTML and CSS code, you can reassemble the pieces together on your web pages.

Slicing images in Illustrator is a bit less intuitive than it is in Fireworks and Photoshop, but it generally works in the same way. Though you can create slices by cutting freehand, it's much faster and more precise when you create slices with the aid of horizontal and vertical guides. Add guides along the left, right, top, and bottom margins of your layout, put guides on all four sides of your navigation area, and anywhere else you think you need them.

Creating Slices

Illustrator uses a table concept when creating slices so every rectangular slice is like a piece in a rectangular grid puzzle. Use the slicing tools to carve up the spaces until the entire layout is sliced. The two slicing tools in Illustrator are the Slice tool and the Slice Selection tool, both of which look like X-Acto knives and are located near the bottom of the Tools panel.

To slice your layout with the Slice tool, select the Slice tool and drag a marquee shape around the first area you'd like to turn into a slice. Upon releasing your mouse, Illustrator will add a slice border and number to the slice area, while the remaining parts of your layout will appear grayed out with a second *auto slice*. The second slice isn't actually made yet, but Illustrator anticipates this move in an effort to create slices for each part of the layout. Illustrator numbers slices from top to bottom, left to right. Continue to slice the rest of your artwork, like the example in Figure 22-3. The slices you make (not the auto slices) are independent from the artwork and will appear as objects in the Layers panel, allowing you to select, resize, move, and delete them as needed.

Tip To toggle on and off the visibility of slices on the artboard, select View | Hide Slices or View | Show Slices.

You can also slice your image by selecting one or more objects in your layout and choosing Object | Slice | Create From Selection or Object | Slice | Make. Or, to have Illustrator create slices based on the document guides, choose Object | Slice | Create From Guides.

FIGURE 22-3 Use the Slice tool and slice commands to cut a web layout into smaller pieces

Each image slice can be set to one of three types: Image, No Image, or HTML Text. To set the type, select the slice with the Slice Selection tool, and choose Object | Slice | Slice Options to set and specify the desired options in the Slice Options dialog box:

- **Image Slice**   Creates a slice that will be optimized as a web graphic. Set a name or ID for the slice, specify the URL of the HTML page the graphic will link to when clicked, set the Target for the URL to _self (which only becomes active when you input a URL) so that the link page opens in the same browser window, enter a message that will appear in the browser's status bar when a cursor is positioned over the graphic, and type in any desired Alt text, which will identify the slice with words that can be read by a screen reader for visually impaired web visitors. To set the background color of the table cell, choose an option from the Background dropdown menu at the bottom of the dialog box.

- **No Image Slice** Sets the background color of the table cell to the color of the graphic in the slice but does not create a graphic when optimized. To add placeholder text inside the table cell, click the Text Is HTML checkbox and type your text into the Text Displayed In The Cell field though be sure not to enter more text than can be displayed within the slice area. If desired, adjust the horizontal and vertical alignment of the cell and choose a background color from the Background dropdown menu.

- **HTML Text Slice** This option is active only when text is turned into a slice using the Object | Slice | Make command. Illustrator will convert the text and any of its basic formatting into HTML code when the slice is optimized. For example, if the text converted to a slice says SHOP SALE ITEMS, the slice will generate old formatting HTML that will specify the font color, size, and style, as in the following line of HTML code: <font size=5 color=#ffffff>SHOP SALE ITEMS </font>. Enable the Text Is HTML option to interpret HTML or display HTML tags as text. Other options for this setting include setting the cell alignment and background color.

Adjusting Slices

To adjust the slice boundaries, choose the Slice Selection tool and click inside the first slice that needs to be adjusted, then press SHIFT+click to add additional slices to the selection. When two or more slices are selected, placing your cursor above the slice borders will temporarily turn the cursor into a double-sided adjustment arrow so you can click and drag the boundaries to a new position. Repeat this select-and-drag process until all the boundaries in your layout are in the desired locations.

To duplicate, combine, divide, move, resize, align or distribute, resize, release, delete, or lock slices, do any of the following:

- Create a duplicate of any slice by selecting an existing slice with the Slice Selection tool and choosing Object | Slice | Duplicate Slice.

- Combine two or more slices into a single slice by selecting those slices with the Slice Selection tool and choosing Object | Slice | Combine Slices.

- Divide one or more slices into more slices, either vertically or horizontally, by selecting the slices with the Slice Selection tool and choosing Object | Slice | Divide Slices. When the Divide Slice dialog box appears, specify whether you'd like to divide the slice(s) horizontally, vertically, or both, enter the number of slices to be created, and if desired, the number of pixels per slice.

- To move a slice, drag the slice with the Slice Selection tool into the new position.

- To resize a slice, select the slice with the Slice Selection tool and drag any of the sides or corners of the slice.

- To align or distribute slices, use the Align panel.

- To resize all the slices so they fit to the edges of the artboard, choose Object | Slice | Clip To Artboard. Slices that extend beyond are truncated to fit to the edge of the artboard, all artwork remains the same, and autoslices within the artboard are extended to the artboard boundaries.

- To release a selected slice from the artwork but not delete it from the document, choose Object | Slice | Release.

- To delete and completely remove all slices from the layout, choose Object | Slice | Delete All. To delete a single slice, select it with the Slice Selection tool and press DELETE.

- To lock all the slices into place so you don't accidentally move or adjust them, choose View | Lock Slices. Or, to lock individual slices, click the Lock (Edit) column in the Layers panel next to the slice(s) you want to lock down.

Creating Buttons and Rollover Images

Many buttons on the Web are now created without graphics using list-style HTML type and Cascading Style Sheets (CSS), which makes the pages load much faster. The only drawback to HTML buttons is that the text must be rendered in one of the handful of "web safe" fonts (such as Verdana, Arial, Georgia, and Times New Roman), which can be very limiting. To use a different font, you'll need to create web button graphics. Also, if you want your buttons to have a rollover effect—in other words, when a visitor moves his or her cursor over the button it changes in some way and then changes back when the cursor moves off the button—then you'll need to create and optimize two same-sized versions of each button graphic, one for the *normal state* and one for the *over state*. Figure 22-4 shows an example of normal and over state button graphics. The JavaScript for the rollover function can be quickly assigned in a web development program like Dreamweaver.

Normal state

SHOP SALE ITEMS

SHOP SALE ITEMS

Over state

FIGURE 22-4 Create two same-sized graphics for each rollover button

Creating Image Maps

An image map refers to when an area of a web graphic is turned into a *hotspot* that, when clicked, will load another web page in the browser window. The hotspot attributes of the image map will be translated into HTML when the graphic gets optimized.

To create an image map, select the object on your artboard that will become the image map hotspot. Next, open the Attributes panel (Window | Attributes) and select a hotspot shape from the Image Map menu (see Figure 22-5). Hotspots can be rectangular or polygonal, depending on the area of the graphic you need to be active. To set the HTML of the hotspot, enter the URL of the file you want the hotspot to link to. The URL can be relative (such as contact.html) or absolute (such as www.adobe.com). To have message text appear as a browser screen tip when the visitor's cursor hovers over the hotspot, enter your message text in the text field below the URL field.

FIGURE 22-5 Create image maps with the Attributes panel

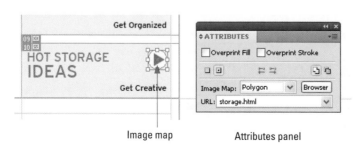

Image map   Attributes panel

Creating SVG Files

All of the image formats normally used for the Web (GIF, PNG, JPG) are bitmap. However, you can save your web content in vector format using the SVG export options found when using the Save, Save As, Save a Copy, and Save for Web & Devices commands. The SVG format is XML-based, which allows for high-quality feature-rich web content when you combine Illustrator objects and SVG Effects (see Chapter 18) with JavaScript.

To add interactivity to your objects on a web page, you need to know how to work with JavaScript so you can enter JavaScript commands into the SVG Interactivity panel. If you're already familiar with JavaScript, use Illustrator for interactivity to your Illustrator file. Otherwise, you're better off leaving the coding to a professional.

To add interactivity, begin by opening the SVG Interactivity panel by choosing Window | SVG Interactivity. Then, select the object on your artboard you'd like to add JavaScript to. Back in the SVG panel, choose an event handler from the panel's Event menu that will trigger the JavaScript. For example, the *onMouseOver* event triggers the JavaScript action to begin when the pointer is moved on top of the associated object on the web page. Next, type or paste in the desired JavaScript code, such as *"window.status='Close window'; return true"*, into the JavaScript field and press ENTER (Win) or RETURN (Mac). The full script will then appear in the preview panel so you can verify the code before optimizing the graphics for the Web. To link a JavaScript file to the Illustrator file, click the Link JavaScript Files button at the bottom of the panel. In the JavaScript Files dialog box, click the Add button to link files to the document, the Remove button to remove a selected entry from the file, the Clear button to delete all events from the file, and the Done button to close the dialog box.

 To learn more about working with JavaScript, read *How to Do Everything with JavaScript*, by Scott Duffy (McGraw-Hill).

Optimizing Web Graphics

Before adding your graphics to a web page, they must be compressed, or *optimized*, to reduce the file size so they'll load faster in the browser window. You can choose from three web compression formats, depending on the type of image:

- **GIF** (Graphics Interchange Format)   Best for images with large flat areas of color. Supports up to 256 colors, as well as animation and background transparency.

- **JPEG** (Joint Photographic Experts Group)   Best for photos and graphics with gradient blends. Supports millions of colors, but not transparency or animation.

- **PNG** (Portable Network Graphic)   Best for images with large flat areas of color, and PNG-8 is the recommended replacement for GIF images for the newest web browsers. PNG-8 supports up to 256 colors, while PNG-24 supports millions of colors and background transparency. (PNG-24 is not yet supported by most browsers.)

Save For Web & Devices

Use the Save For Web & Devices dialog box to optimize all of your web graphics. The dialog box supports the optimization of GIF, JPG, PNG-8, PNG-24, SWF, SVG, and WBMP file formats. You can also choose to save a single graphic, all slices, selected slices, just the HTML, or both the graphics and the HTML.

To optimize the graphics in your layout, choose File | Save For Web & Devices. The dialog box that opens has four tabs along the top to assist you in selecting the best optimization settings. Click the 4-Up tab to preview your original artwork and three different optimization settings, as illustrated in Figure 22-6.

Use the tools in the Toolbox along the left side of the dialog box to navigate around the preview windows, and use the settings in the Optimize panel to adjust the optimization settings for each selected pane in the 4-Up preview area. At the bottom of each preview pane is a display of optimization information, such as the file name, file size, number of colors, and estimated download time at the default 28.8K modem, to assist you in choosing the best setting for optimization. To preview download times at different Internet connection speeds, select an option (for example, DSL, Cable, T-1) from the Preview menu above the top right preview pane.

Toolbox   Display tabs   Original artwork   Optimized artwork and optimization details   Preview menu   Optimize panel

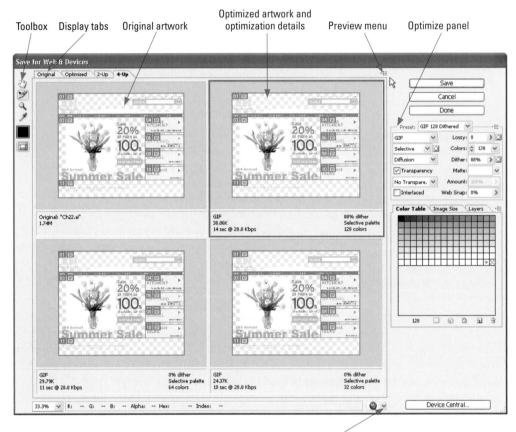

Preview in Default Browser

To test different optimization settings, click a preview pane to select it and choose a graphic format from the Preset menu or a file type from the Optimized file format menu. For example, you may want to compare three different GIF or JPG presets to see which one produces the best quality at the lowest file size. Use the rest of the settings below the Preset menu to fine-tune the presets or create your own custom optimization settings. You can learn about what each of the settings does by hovering your cursor over the different input fields in the Optimize panel. To preview any of the optimization settings in a selected pane, click the Preview In Default Browser button at the bottom of the dialog box.

The following offers a general overview of each of the Optimization panel settings.

FIGURE 22-6 The Save For Web & Devices dialog box

GIF and PNG settings:

- **Optimized File Format**   Choose GIF, JPG, PNG-8, PNG-24, SWF, SVG, or WBMP.

- **Lossy**   Increases the compression to produce smaller file sizes. Higher lossy numbers result in lower-quality images with smaller file sizes.

- **Color Reduction Algorithm**   Choose from Perceptual, Selective, Adaptive, Restrictive (Web), Custom, Black and White, Grayscale, Mac OS, and Windows. For best results, leave this option set to Selective.

- **Colors in Color Table**   Select the number of colors in your image; from 2 to 256.

- **Dither**   This setting controls how colors that are not in the color table will be approximated using colors in the color table. When enabled, select a Diffusion, Pattern, or Noise dither and adjust the amount of dithering from 0% to 100% with the Dither menu.

- **Transparency**   Pick a transparency setting of either None, Diffusion, Pattern, or Noise. If desired, adjust the amount of transparency dithering in the Amount menu.

- **Matte**   Choose a matte (background) color for a graphic to match the color of the page the graphic will be placed upon.

- **Interlaced**   (GIFs and PNG-8 only) Creates an image that will load in multiple passes in the browser window.

- **Web Snap**   Adjusts the colors in the Color table to match the nearest Web-safe color based on the percentage entered in the menu from 0% to 100%.

- **Color Table**   Displays all the colors detected in the image, up to 256 colors. Web-safe color swatches have a tiny diamond in their centers.

- **Image Size**   Displays the dimensions of the original image along with width, height, and percent fields to adjust the image size.

- **Layers**   Select the Export As CSS Layers option to have Illustrator export each layer in the Layers panel as HTML Layers using the *<div>* tag. Slices will still be marked up with Table HTML code; however, the entire table will be sitting inside of the layer.

JPEG settings:

- **Compression Quality**   Controls the loss of image quality during compression. Choose from Low, Medium, High, Very High, and Maximum.

- **Quality**   Controls the loss of image quality during compression numerically. Higher numbers produce better quality images with larger file sizes.

- **Progressive Browser Display**   Creates an image that will load in multiple passes in the browser window.

- **Blur**   Adds a blur to all the hard edges in the graphic to reduce file size.

- **ICC Profile**   Adds an ICC profile to the graphic, which is read by some browsers to improve the quality of colors in the image.

- **Matte**   Choose a matte (background) color for the graphic so as to match the color of the page the graphic will be placed upon.

- **Image Size**   Displays the dimensions of the original image along with width, height, and percent fields to adjust the image size.

- **Layers**   Check the Export As CSS Layers option to have Illustrator export each layer in the file as an HTML layer using the *<div>* tag.

To optimize a web graphic using the optimization settings in any one of the panes, select the desired preview pane and click the Save button. When working with sliced images, you can either select all the slices with the Slice Selection tool before clicking the Save button, or click the Save button and then choose the preferred option (All Slices, All User Slices, or Selected Slices) from the Slices dropdown list at the bottom of the Save Optimized As dialog box.

When the Save Optimized As dialog box appears, the soon-to-be optimized file will automatically be named after the original Illustrator file along with the selected file format extension, such as *colorlids.gif*. Use the dialog box to specify a location to save the file into, choose a Save As Type And Slices option, leave the Settings option set to Default Settings, and click the Save button. The file can be saved as image only,

HTML Output Uses Table-Based Formatting

By default, Illustrator's HTML output uses table-based formatting to reassemble the optimized graphics onto the web page. Tables, however, are no longer the standard method of web page production. Instead, designers use more standards-compliant Layers, which can be relatively or absolutely positioned on a web page as well as styled using CSS. You can still output HTML and graphics, but be prepared to rewrite the HTML and CSS.

HTML only, or HTML and images, which outputs an HTML file and a folder full of images, complete with any customized settings like JavaScript, URL links, and image maps.

The Actions Panel

Web graphics can also be optimized quickly using Illustrator's Actions panel (Window | Actions). Actions are prerecorded scripts that can be played back on a file at any time. To use the Action commands to save a web graphic in the Web GIF 64 Dithered, JPG Medium, or PNG-24 formats (the latter of which isn't supported by web browsers yet), follow these steps:

1. Select the objects on your artboard that you want to optimize.

2. Select the desired Save For Web action layer in the Actions panel.

3. Click the Play Current Selection button at the bottom of the Actions panel. This opens the selection inside the Save For Web & Devices dialog box with the format in the action preselected. If needed, make adjustments to the optimization settings.

4. Click the Save button to save the graphic onto your computer.

5. In the Save Optimized As dialog box, specify a location to save the file into, enter a file name, select a Save As Type And Slices option, leave the Settings option set to Default Settings, and click the Save button.

Saving Illustrator Files for Flash and Mobile Content

In Chapter 13, you learned a few things about integrating Illustrator artwork into Flash by exporting a SWF file both with and without animation using the File | Export command and choosing the Flash (*.SWF) option from the Save As Type. You can also (since CS3) optimize your art as a SWF file through the Save For Web & Devices dialog box or save your Illustrator files with the .ai file extension and import them into Flash. This method preserves your text, symbols, flash text, layers, clipping masks, effects, and more.

 Tip When saving SWF files through the Save For Web & Devices dialog box, change the Preserve setting from Editability to Appearance to further reduce the output file size.

The Flash Text Panel

Illustrator point text, area text, and text on a path can all be exported to Flash by either exporting Illustrator text as area type into the SWF format, or by copying and pasting text directly from Illustrator into Flash. Before exporting text, you must first set the Flash type through the Flash Text panel.

Open the Flash Text panel by choosing Window | Type | Flash Text or by selecting a text object and clicking the Flash Text button on the Control panel. When the panel opens, select one of the three text types: Choose Static Text to export the text as an object that cannot be edited in Flash; select Dynamic Text to export the text as editable, dynamically updatable text that can be programmed with Action script commands and tags for things like stock quotes and news headlines; or choose Input Text to export the text as editable, dynamically updatable text that also lets web users edit text inside the Flash Player for web items like forms and polls. After that, be sure to enter an instance name for the text object, choose a rendering type from the Rendering Type menu, and select any of the other optional settings as desired.

 Tip To learn even more about setting Illustrator text for Flash movies, see the video at www.adobe.com/go/vid0199.

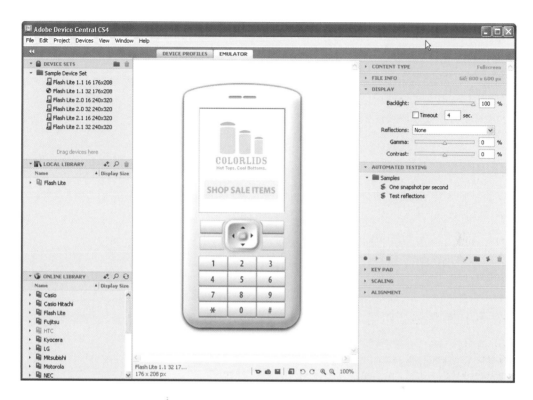

FIGURE 22-7 Preview your mobile content in Device Central

Saving Mobile Content

With Illustrator art designed for mobile content, you can either create designs and import or export them to Flash, where you can create animations and other effects, or if the design is to be used as simple wallpaper, static advertising, or web graphics, you can preview your work in Adobe's Device Central software, which is part of the standard Illustrator software installation, before exporting through the Save For Web & Devices dialog box.

To preview your design on a simulated handheld mobile device, select the unsliced objects on your artboard, choose File | Save For Web & Devices, and click the Device Central button at the bottom of the dialog box to launch the Adobe Device Central CS4 application window. Figure 22-7 shows an example of Illustrator artwork on the Flash Lite handheld device. When you're ready to save your work, export your designs in the Save For Web & Devices dialog box.

To watch a video about creating Illustrator graphics for mobile devices, see www.adobe.com/go/vid0207.

23

Printing Your Work

How to…

- Understand printing basics
- Set up your document
- Use the Print dialog box
- Print composites and color separations
- Trap images
- Use color management
- Create custom print presets

When it comes to printing, there's more you can do to improve the quality of your output than simply choosing the number of pages and clicking the Print button. In this chapter, you'll discover new ways to make the best quality print. You'll learn some basic principles of printing, understand how to best set up your documents for print, get an overview of the entire Print dialog box, and find out how to print composites and color separations. You'll also find information about color management, trapping, and how to create your own sharable custom print presets for future printing projects.

Printing Basics

Illustrator functions in a high-resolution 300-dpi (dots per inch) world where vector shapes and paths are drawn using mathematical equations. Onscreen, you see a visual representation of those objects. However, to print them, the objects must be translated into a PostScript programming language that tells your printer how to convert each of the document's objects into the roughly 8.5 million dpi that make up a standard 8.5×11-inch page. That's a lot of dots! The good news is you don't have to understand any of this as long as you find a printer that is capable of printing your beautiful vector work in the size you need it, whether it's a simple logo on the side of a pen, or a fully designed banner advertisement that will hang vertically from the façade of a museum.

Two kinds of prints can be made in Illustrator. The first is called a *composite*, which is a single flat file that includes all the shapes, paths, effects, colors, and tints used to build the file. The other kind is called a *color separation*, which prints separate printouts or plates for each process (CMYK) and spot color used. These separate plates are needed to professionally process your images on a high-quality printing press.

Document Setup

Before you send your document to your printer or send your artwork to a professional, make sure the file is set up properly in the Document Setup dialog box. Choose File | Document Setup to open the dialog box or press the keyboard shortcut CTRL+ALT+P (Win) or CMD+OPT+P (Mac). There you can check the orientation and size of the printable area of your artboard options, as well as the bleed and view options, transparency settings, and type options. Any object that sits on or outside the edges of the artboard(s) will be cut off and not print. You can also control which objects will print by toggling off the visibility of certain layers in your work—only visible printable layers will print, while layers in the Layers panel that are hidden or have their printing option disabled will be ignored.

Printing Composites

Printing a composite is like getting a quick version of what you see on your monitor. On a color printer, you'll get a color printout that closely matches the original onscreen version, and on a black and white printer, all the colors are reproduced in grayscale.

Print Dialog Box Options

To select a printer and set the number of copies to be printed, as well as specify which of the pages will print when working with multiple artboards, choose File | Print to open the Print dialog box, as seen in Figure 23-1. In addition, you can use the different categories along the left side of the dialog box to control other print features:

General:

- **Copies**   Sets the number of copies that will be printed for each artboard in the file.

- **Pages**   Select All to print all pages in your file, or choose Range to specify which pages of the document should print, as in 1-4, 6-9.

- **Media**   Sets the size, width and height, and orientation of your file.

- **Options**   Sets placement, scale, and layer print options. The placement sets the printing origin relative to the paper's edges. If the file is too large for the printer, adjust the scale or use the Tile Pages setting. If desired, change the layer visibility settings through the Print Layers menu.

FIGURE 23-1 The Print dialog box

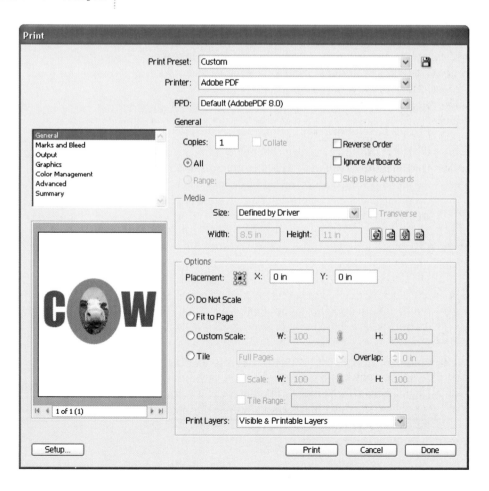

Marks and Bleed:

- **Marks**   Turn on all printer's marks or only selected marks. Leave the Mark Type set to Roman, and if needed, adjust the mark weight and offset from the artwork.
- **Bleed**   Disable the Use Document Bleed Settings to override the document's bleed settings with new measurements that control how artwork bleeds off the paper's edge.

Output:

- **Mode**   Determines if the print will be a Composite or Separation, or depending on your printer, an In-Rip Separation for raster image processors.
- **Emulsion**   Sets the position of the emulsion (plate) layer. Up (Right Reading) is the default and means the layer is facing you so you can read the text, whereas Down (Right Reading) means the layer is facing away from you, like a mirror image.
- **Image**   Sets the image to print as a positive or negative.
- **Printer Resolution**   This setting adjusts the printer resolution (dpi) and screen frequency (lpi).
- **Document Ink Options**   This area controls how the inks are printed, and whether black inks will be overprinted and spot colors will be converted to process colors.

Graphics:

- **Paths**   The Flatness slider adjusts the quality of lines in your artwork.
- **Fonts**   When using PostScript fonts, this setting determines how those fonts get downloaded to the printer.
- **Options**   Control the PostScript language and Data Format for PostScript fonts. Enable the Compatible Gradient and Gradient Mesh Printing options to convert those objects into a JPEG format based on the Document Raster Effects Resolution displayed.

Color Management:

▪ **Print Method**   By default, most printers use the U.S. Web Coated (SWOP) v2 Document Profile. To adjust this preset, select different options from the Color Handling, Printer Profile, and Rendering Intent menus.

Advanced:

▪ **Print as Bitmap**   Enable this option to convert your vector image into bitmap.

▪ **Overprint and Transparency Flattener Options**   Specify overprint and transparency settings.

Summary:

▪ The **Options** area lists a summary of all the options specified in each category for your file. Potential printing problems are listed in the **Warnings** area.

Printing Color Separations

Color separations are needed whenever your color artwork will be printed on a professional printing press. In a separated file, a printing plate for each color is created and then colors are applied to the paper in the press one at a time on single drum printers or all at once on multidrum printers. Separations come in two flavors: one for process colors and another for spot colors. The Process separations use four inks (CMYK) to reproduce millions of colors, whereas Spot separations use custom mixed inks (like Pantone) to print objects, like logos and business cards, with more precise color accuracy.

Process Color Separations

Process color (four-color) separations are needed to reproduce any artwork that includes color photos and/or objects using three or more colors. Process color uses four color plates to create millions of colors by combining cyan, magenta, yellow, and black inks (CMYK). It's important to keep in mind, however, that our monitors show us color in RGB mode and printers print colors in CMYK—two separate color gamuts with different benefits and restrictions. The biggest restriction when it comes to printing color on laser printers and imagesetters is that these printers can only produce about 256 shades of each color, which limits the colors you can safely use in your CMYK print projects. Sadly, some colors, like certain greens and reds, simply cannot be reproduced in print.

Nonetheless, process color separations do create beautiful realistic color images by ensuring that each plate is printed with different sized and angled line screens. When the ink from each plate is combined, the resulting image appears in rich seamless full color.

Sometimes you may need to combine process and spot colors in a single document, and sometimes you may need to use the same color as a process and a spot color, which isn't possible if you're using the same swatch. As a workaround, create two swatches of the same color and make one of them process and the other one spot. Then, apply the colors as needed to your artwork.

Spot Color Separations

Spot colors tend to be more expensive than their process color counterparts. They are often used in two- and three-color print jobs to achieve precise smooth colors that would otherwise need to be created by combining two process colors. You do have to create a plate for each spot color, and the more plates there are, the more expensive the job. Still, spot colors are also perfect for adding unusual inks to a project, like metallic or fluorescent colors, as well as applying a finishing varnish coating for a glossy look.

Printing Your Color Separations

Before you print your color separations, be sure to calibrate your monitor, ensure that your file is in CMYK mode (File | Document Color Mode | CMYK), and check that your Document Raster Effects settings are at 300 dpi or higher.

To print color separations, follow these steps:

1. Choose File | Print.

2. Select a printer (or an Adobe PostScript or Adobe PDF file) and PPD (PostScript Printer Description) file from the General category of the Print dialog box.

3. In the Output category, choose Separations or In-Rip Separations from the Mode menu, and if desired, adjust the Emulsion, Image, and Printer Resolution settings.

4. In the Document Ink Options area, choose the color plates to be separated. To prevent a plate from printing, click the printer icon next to the color. To convert a spot color into a process color, click the spot color icon next to the ink. Check the Convert All Spot Colors To Process option to make all the spot colors print as part of the process color plates. Check the Overprint Black option to overprint all the black ink (this produces rich blacks). If your work has two or more spot colors, adjust the screen frequency, angle, or shape of the halftone dots for best results.

5. Select any other options as needed in the other categories of the Print dialog box.

6. Click the Print button.

Tip To make an object print on all plates, convert it to a Registration color in the Swatches panel. The Registration color swatch icon is at the top of the panel, second from the left between the None and White swatches. The color will appear black on the screen, so to change it use the Color panel to specify the color you need. That color will then be used for your object and all registration objects.

Trapping

Trapping is a special technique that can help fix plate alignment problems during the printing process, to ensure that color separations print more accurately without making any white space gaps between the inks for areas surrounding two adjacent colors. To fix any potential problems in advance, you can create a trap to *spread* or *choke* colors that touch in your artwork. To spread a color, make the color of the foreground object bleed or spread outward past its boundaries into the surrounding background. To choke a color, make the background color overlap or spread inward towards the edges of your foreground object (thus the concept of choking or restricting the foreground object).

Trapping is hard, and if done badly can ruin your Illustrator document. Therefore, either only attempt trapping on a copy of your original file, or hire a professional to do the trapping for you. Even better, lots of service bureaus have special equipment that can automatically create the traps for you, and the extra cost will be well worth it.

Nonetheless, to trap images yourself, first select all the objects in your document that touch or overlap. With the Pathfinder panel (Window | Pathfinder) open, choose the Trap command from the panel's options menu. In the resulting dialog box, adjust the thickness, height/width, tint reduction, and other options as needed. When finished, click OK.

Printing Files with Gradients, Meshes, and Color Blends

Files that include lots of gradients, meshes, and color blends can sometimes take a long time to print smoothly or at all. To help prevent printing problems, try to keep gradients, meshes, and color blends to a minimum. If your printer is really sluggish, consider rasterizing the gradients and meshes during the printing process by selecting the Compatible Gradient And Gradient Mesh Printing option in the Graphics category of the Print dialog box.

Color Management

When it comes to printing, you have two options for dealing with color management: either Illustrator can handle managing the colors to be printed, or you can set your printer to manage the colors it gets from Illustrator. By default, Illustrator is set to manage colors so you can disable the printer's color management and let the application convert colors appropriate for the selected printer. To have your PostScript printer handle the color management instead, select a PostScript printer from the Printer menu in the Print dialog box and set the Color Handling in the Color Management area to Let PostScript Printer Determine Colors.

Creating Custom Print Presets

Setting up the Print dialog box takes time and care, especially when outputting files for different printers and print jobs. To keep from having to set up the dialog box each time you print your file, create a custom profile that you can use again and again at any time.

To create a custom print preset, choose File | Print and use the dialog box to apply your custom settings. When finished, click the Save Preset button (the disk icon button in the upper right corner), give your preset a name, and click OK. Custom presets are saved in a preferences file. You can also create new existing presets through the Print Presets dialog box (Edit | Print Presets), as well as edit or delete them.

To use a custom print preset, select it by name from the Print Preset menu at the top of the Print dialog box before printing.

Custom presets can be shared with other computers and service bureaus through a simple import and export process in the Print Presets dialog box (Edit | Print Presets). To export presets, select one or more presets from the listing, click the Export button, select a location to save the file into, and click the Save button. To import presets, click the Import button, navigate to and select the presets file to be loaded, and click the Open button.

Appendix

Real World Illustrators

In this section, you'll meet five professional working artists who use Illustrator as part of their everyday professional workflow. As you'll see, each designer uses the software in a unique and interesting way. By looking at samples of their work and learning more about their individual backgrounds, it is my hope you'll be inspired to reach new heights with your own work in Illustrator.

Barbara Zuckerman

Artist and designer, Barbara Zuckerman, has been using Illustrator in her work for over 15 years. She holds a BFA in Communications Design from Syracuse University and an MFA in Book Arts and Printmaking from The University of the Arts in Philadelphia. She is the Creative Director of BZ Designstuff (www.bzdesignstuff.com) and participates in the Illustration/art blog www.invisibleman.com.

Barbara LOVES using Illustrator because it gives her the flexibility to be both extremely precise and loose in her work, both for her design and illustration clients as well as for her own fine art, printmaking, and bookbinding projects. Figures A-1 and A-2 demonstrate Barbara's eclectic illustrative style. Barbara works exclusively with a graphics-tablet stylus—even carries one around with her when she's working on-the-go—when she creates her print projects, logos, brochures,

FIGURE A-1 Identity Crisis, miniature book/exquisite corpse

cards, illustrations, and books. Three of Barbara's favorite
Illustrator features are the Align panel, the Live Trace tool, and
the Distort and Transform effects. She also regularly creates
her own color libraries to save time and work consistently with
color.

FIGURE A-2 Topaz, a gemstone
calendar project

Janet Allinger

Janet Allinger is an award-winning illustrator and graphic
designer who specializes in illustration, packaging, logos, book
covers, and custom print and web graphics. She began using
Illustrator back in 1989 while working for a small automotive
design company that wanted to move away from the drafting

table to computers. Since then, this self-taught designer and fine artist has been running her own design studio (www.janetallinger.com) and showing her work at galleries up and down the West Coast. She was a featured artist in Roger G. Taylor's *Marilyn in Art* book (Pop Art Books, London), her work has been published in *Sunset* and *D&G* magazines, and been featured on design packaging for Trader Joe's and Pelican Ranch Winery.

Janet considers Illustrator the best graphic program out there, and combined with her Wacom Cintiq graphics-tablet stylus (of which she said, "It has changed my life!"), she believes this technology has made being a designer so much easier than it used to be. Though she favors the Pen tool for making basic and unique shapes, like the line work in Figures A-3 and A-4, her favorite tool, by far, is the Pencil tool. "It's just like drawing on paper without the eraser crumbs," she said. Other preferred tools include the Magic Wand for quick color selections, the Pathfinder to combine shapes, and the Live Trace tool for converting photos and scanned sketches into vector art.

FIGURE A-3 I was Googled and I didn't feel a thing!

FIGURE A-4 BookGroup Betty

Chris Reed

Chris Reed is an illustrator and designer with 25 years of freelance illustration experience working with magazines, newspapers, educational publishing, design studios, and corporations. He holds a BFA from the School of Visual Arts and has been using Illustrator professionally for about seven years. Before that, Chris used to work with markers on watercolor paper. After making the switch to Illustrator, Chris finds that he works much more quickly and has extra time to play around with color and composition at the same time.

Chris begins his projects by scanning line work he has drawn by hand and then bringing it into Illustrator to convert it into vector art. Most of his projects, such as Figures A-5 and A-6, are for print and T-shirt design, though his studio (www.chrisreedstudio.com) does take on projects that range from conceptual and humorous editorial work to fun and whimsical surface design. He also frequently licenses his work for greeting cards, gift bags and tags, wrapping paper, fabric banners, and children's clothing. The Pen tool and Type tool

FIGURE A-6 Germ Man

FIGURE A-5 Robots

are Chris' two favorites. He uses the Pen tool for both personal and design-oriented projects quite a bit, and having started his career with press type, he's overjoyed that Illustrator gives him access to unlimited type options. He's also very fond of the Undo command—CTRL+Z (Win) or CMD+Z (Mac)—and using the SHIFT key to select multiple objects.

Heidi Udvardy

With over 16 years in surface design and product development, Heidi Udvardy's textile designs (www.udvardydesign.com) can be seen on a variety of home furnishing products including pillows for Crate & Barrel, bedding for Waterford, and sample textiles for Nordstrom. Heidi combines her knowledge of traditional painting with digital production to create sophisticated designs. In addition, Heidi creates designs for the fashion industry, as well as the infants/children's, bedding, tabletop, and stationery markets.

Heidi has been using Illustrator for about ten years, both with and without a graphics-tablet stylus. She loves the clean lines and precision Illustrator affords her, especially its ability to create the illusion of a stitched line. As a textile designer, she uses Illustrator to create designs and patterns that need to be repeated, like the examples shown in Figures A-7 and A-8, which she then takes into Photoshop to create the repeat. To generate her designs, Heidi often begins with an existing illustration from

FIGURE A-7 British Home Shops Promo

Figure A-8 Primark, designs for textiles

a design studio and uses those elements to create coordinates, repeats, and layout changes per her client's request. She also produces original designs by sketching freehand, scanning her work, placing it into Illustrator, and then tracing it by hand using the Pen tool. Colors and patterns are applied in Illustrator, or line work is taken into Photoshop for further refinement and repeating. Heidi uses the Pencil tool to get her ideas down quickly, and the Pen tool to trace her scanned artwork and refine her lines. She's also a big fan of the resizing tools, the Group/Ungroup command, and the Zoom In/Out keyboard shortcuts, CTRL++ and CTRL+− (Win) and CMD++ and CMD+− (Mac).

Susan Hunt Yule

Susan Hunt Yule is a freelance illustrator (www.susanhuntyule.com) who works in both print and interactive media including advertising, editorial, and book work. She holds a BA (Hons) from St. Martins School of Art in London and has worked as an illustrator for print and interactive media for many years, before and since going digital. Susan has been painting watercolors for a long while and more recently has begun designing jewelry for Zarah, developing illustrative maps and plans, as shown in Figures A-9 and A-10, and designing interactive multimedia projects. Most notably, Susan's illustrations have appeared in The Society of Illustrators 49th and 50th Annual Shows, and as

FIGURE A-9 Treasure map

spots in various magazines and publications such as *Consumer Reports*, *Parents* magazine, and the *Chicago Tribune*.

Until recently, Susan was mostly using Illustrator as a tool for creating certain things that she'd bring into Photoshop or InDesign; however, over the past few years she's started doing

FIGURE A-10 Airplane

work directly in Illustrator for print and Flash projects. Susan uses a Wacom graphics-tablet stylus and thinks working with a mouse is like dancing with one foot tied behind your back! She favors the Pen tool and transformation tools, like rotate, scale, and shear; frequently arranges her objects using the shortcuts, CTRL+] and CTRL+[(Win) or CMD+] and CMD+[(Mac); and likes to lock and unlock her selections with the shortcuts, CTRL+2 and CTRL+ALT+2 (Win) or CMD+2 and CMD+OPT+2 (Mac).

Index